Happiness
and Discontent

The Great Books Foundation

A nonprofit educational organization

Published and distributed by

 The Great Books Foundation
A nonprofit educational organization

35 East Wacker Drive, Suite 2300
Chicago, IL 60601-2298

First Printing
9 8 7 6 5 4 3 2 1

Library of Congress Cataloging-in-Publication Data
Happiness and discontent.
         p.   cm. — (50th anniversary series)
      Contents: The highest good / Aristotle — A river sutra (selection) / Gita
Mehta — The three lives of Lucie Cabrol / John Berger — Happiness /
Mary Lavin — Endless mountains / Reynolds Price — As you like it / William
Shakespeare — Poetry / Emily Dickinson — Questions for Middlemarch
(George Eliot) — Questions for An imaginary life (David Malouf)
      ISBN 1-880323-82-6
      1. Literature — Collections.   2. Group reading.   3. Reader-response
criticism.   I. Great Books Foundation (U.S.)   II. Series: Great Books Foundation
50th anniversary series.
PN6014.H3115 1998
808.8—DC21   98-24335

CONTENTS

No

*"So that's why Aristotle thinks that animals and children
should not be called happy!" "Is happiness the ultimate good?"
"Does one have a right to be happy?"*

Anyone who has been in a book discussion group has experienced the joy of new insight. Sometimes an idea or question occurs to us during the group meeting. Often, it is afterward—sometimes much later—that an idea we had overlooked unexpectedly strikes us with new force. A good group becomes a community of minds. We share perspectives, questions, insights, and surprises. Our fellow readers challenge and broaden our thinking as we probe deeply into characters and ideas. They help us resolve questions, and raise new ones, in a creative process that connects literature with life.

It is this kind of experience that makes book discussion groups worthwhile, and that the Great Books Foundation fosters for thousands of readers around the world.

The Great Books Foundation is a pioneer of book discussion groups that bring together dedicated readers who wish to continue to learn throughout their lives. The literature anthologies published by the Foundation have been the focus of many enlightening discussions among people of all educational backgrounds and walks of life. And the *shared inquiry* method practiced by Great Books groups has proven to be a powerful approach to literature that solves many practical concerns of new discussion groups: How can we maintain a flow of ideas? What kinds of questions should we discuss? How can we keep the discussion focused on the reading so that we use our time together to really get at the heart of a work—to learn from it and each other?

With the publication of its 50th Anniversary Series, the Great Books Foundation continues and expands upon its tradition of helping all readers engage in a meaningful exchange of ideas about outstanding works of literature.

ABOUT HAPPINESS AND DISCONTENT

The reading selections in *Happiness and Discontent* have been chosen to stimulate lively shared inquiry discussions. This collection brings together works from around the world that speak to each other on a theme of universal human significance. In this volume you will find Aristotle's classic exploration of the nature of happiness; contemporary fiction by Mary Lavin, Reynolds Price, Gita Mehta, and John Berger; drama by William Shakespeare; and poetry by Emily Dickinson.

These are carefully crafted works that readers will interpret in different ways. They portray characters whose lives and motivations are complex, embody concepts that go beyond simple analysis, and raise many questions to inspire extended reflection.

As an aid to reading and discussion, open-ended *interpretive questions* are included with each selection in the volume, and also for the recommended novels *Middlemarch* by George Eliot and *An Imaginary Life* by the Australian novelist David Malouf. A fundamental or *basic* interpretive question about the meaning of the selection is printed in boldface, followed by a list of related questions that will help you fully discuss the issue raised by the basic question. Passages for *textual analysis* that you may want to look at closely during discussion are suggested for each set of questions. Questions under the heading "For Further Reflection" can be used at the end of discussion to help your group consider the reading selection in a broader context.

About Shared Inquiry

The success of Great Books discussions depends not only on thought-provoking literature, but also on the shared inquiry method of discussion. A shared inquiry discussion begins with a basic interpretive question—a genuine question about the meaning of the selection that continues to be puzzling even after careful reading. As participants offer different possible answers to this question, the discussion leader or members of the group follow up on the ideas that are voiced, asking questions about how responses relate to the original question or to new ideas, and probing what specifically in the text prompted the response.

In shared inquiry discussion, readers think for themselves about the selection, and do not rely on critical or biographical sources outside the text for ideas about its meaning. Discussion remains focused on the text. Evidence for opinions is found in the selection. Because interpretive questions have no single "correct answer," participants are encouraged to entertain a range of ideas. The exchange of ideas is open and spontaneous, a common search for understanding that leads to closer, more illuminating reading.

Shared inquiry fosters a habit of critical questioning and thinking. It encourages patience in the face of complexity, and a respect for the opinions of others. As participants explore the work in depth, they try out ideas, reconsider simple answers, and synthesize interpretations. Over time, shared inquiry engenders a profound experience of intellectual intimacy as your group searches together for meaning in literature.

Improving Your Discussions

The selections in *Happiness and Discontent* will support seven meetings of your discussion group, with each selection and the three poems being the focus of a single meeting. Discussions usually last about two hours, and are guided by a member of the group who acts as leader. Since the leader has no special knowledge or qualification beyond a genuine curiosity about the text, any member of the group may lead discussion. The leader carefully prepares the interpretive questions that he or she wants to explore with the group, and is primarily responsible for continuing the process of questioning that maintains the flow of ideas.

To ensure a successful discussion, we encourage you to make it a policy to read the selection twice. A first reading will familiarize you with the plot and ideas of a selection; on a second reading you will read more reflectively and discover many aspects of the work that deepen your thinking about it. Allowing a few days to pass between your readings will also help you approach a second reading with greater insight.

Read the selection actively. Make marginal comments that you might want to refer to in discussion. While our interpretive questions can help you think about different aspects of the work, jotting down your own questions as you read is the best way to engage with the selection and bring a wealth of ideas and meaningful questions to discussion.

During discussion, expect a variety of answers to the basic question. Follow up carefully on these different ideas. Refer to and read from the text often—by way of explaining your answer, and to see if the rest of the group understands the author's words the same way you do. (You will often be surprised!) As your group looks closely at the text, many new ideas will arise.

While leaders in shared inquiry discussion strive to keep comments focused on the text and on the basic interpretive question the group is discussing, the entire group can share responsibility for politely refocusing comments that wander from the text into personal anecdotes or issues that begin to sidetrack discussion.

Remember that during shared inquiry discussion you are investigating differing perspectives on the reading. Talk should focus foremost on characters in the story or play, or on the statements of the author, not on participants' daily lives and concerns or current social topics. By maintaining this focus, each discussion will be new and interesting, with each participant bringing a different perspective to bear on the text. After the work has been explored thoroughly on its own terms, your thinking about important issues of the day or in your own life will be enhanced. We have found that it is best to formally set aside a time—perhaps the last half-hour of discussion or over coffee afterward—for members of the group to share personal experiences and opinions that go beyond a discussion of the selection.

DISCUSSING THE POETRY SELECTIONS

Many book groups shy away from the challenge of discussing poetry, but the shared inquiry method will enable you to make poetry a very satisfying part of your discussion group. Poetry, by its very nature, communicates ideas through suggestion, allusion, and resonance. Because meaning in poetry resides in the interaction between author and reader, and is brought to light through the pooling of different perspectives and readers' responses, poems are ideal for shared inquiry discussion.

We suggest that you discuss the three poems in *Happiness and Discontent* in turn, rather than all together as a group. The accompanying interpretive questions will help you focus on each poem individually, and the questions marked "For Further Reflection" will help you consider common and differing elements of the poems.

It will be helpful to read each poem aloud before beginning discussion. Because poetry is usually more densely constructed than prose and highly selective in detail, it often lends itself to what we call *textual analysis*—looking closely at particular lines, words, and images as an entryway to discussing the whole work. Having readers share their different associations with a word or image can often help broaden interpretations.

DISCUSSING THE NOVELS

Many novels might come to mind that relate to the theme of happiness and discontent. We have recommended *Middlemarch* and *An Imaginary Life* as particularly enriching novels on this theme, and have provided interpretive questions that can be a significant aid to the reader. Even readers familiar with these novels will find a shared inquiry discussion of them a fresh and rewarding experience.

Most shared inquiry groups discuss a novel at a single discussion; some prefer to spread the discussion over more than one session, especially for longer novels. Since it is usually not realistic to expect participants to read a novel twice in full before discussion, we recommend that you at least reread parts of the novel that seemed especially important to you or that raised a number of questions in your mind. Our passages for textual analysis suggest parts of the novel where reading twice might be most valuable. You might even begin your discussion, after posing a basic question, by looking closely at one or two short passages to get people talking about central ideas and offering a variety of opinions that can be probed and expanded into a discussion of the whole work.

HOW THE GREAT BOOKS FOUNDATION CAN HELP YOU

The Great Books Foundation can be a significant resource for you and your discussion group. Our staff conducts shared inquiry workshops throughout the country that will help you or your entire group conduct better discussions. Thousands of people—from elementary school teachers and college professors to those who just love books and ideas—have found our workshops to be an enjoyable experience that changes forever how they approach literature.

The Foundation publishes a variety of reading series that might interest you. We invite you to call us at 1-800-222-5870 or visit our Web site at http://www.greatbooks.org. We can help you start a book group, put you in touch with established Great Books groups in your area, or give you information about many special events—such as poetry weekends or week-long discussion institutes—sponsored by Great Books groups around the country.

Finally, we invite you to inquire about Junior Great Books for students in kindergarten through high school, to learn how you can help develop the next generation of book lovers and shared inquiry participants.

We hope you enjoy *Happiness and Discontent* and that it inaugurates many years of exciting discussions for your group. Great Books programs—for children as well as adults—are founded on the idea that readers discussing together can achieve insight and great pleasure from literature. We look forward, with you, to cultivating this idea through the next century.

*Footnotes by the author are not bracketed; footnotes by
the Great Books Foundation, an editor,
or a translator are [bracketed].*

THE HIGHEST GOOD

Aristotle

ARISTOTLE (384–322 B.C.) was born in
Stagirus, a Greek colony in Macedonia.
His father was physician to the Macedonian
court, and Aristotle probably studied biology
and medicine as a boy. At seventeen, he
entered Plato's Academy in Athens, where
he studied and lectured for twenty years.
When Plato died, Aristotle left Athens and
lived with a circle of philosophical friends
in what is now Turkey and on the island
of Lesbos. In 343, he accepted an invitation
to serve as a tutor to thirteen-year-old
Alexander, future king of Macedonia.
Aristotle returned to Athens in 335, where
in 323 his friendships with Macedonians
made him a target of anti-Macedonian
feeling then current in Athens. Accused,
like Socrates, of the capital crime of impiety,
and certain of condemnation, Aristotle left
Athens but died the following year in Chalcis,
Greece, of a stomach ailment. Like Plato,
Aristotle wrote popular works in the form
of dialogues, but these are lost. His surviving
writings, which probably represent his more
mature thinking, were most likely presented
first as lectures or reading assignments for
his students, and were assembled by his
followers after his death.

The Good as the Aim of Action

EVERY ART or applied science and every systematic investigation, and similarly every action and choice, seem to aim at some good; the good, therefore, has been well defined as that at which all things aim. But it is clear that there is a difference in the ends at which they aim: in some cases the activity is the end, in others the end is some product beyond the activity. In cases where the end lies beyond the action, the product is naturally superior to the activity.

Since there are many activities, arts, and sciences, the number of ends is correspondingly large: of medicine the end is health; of shipbuilding, a vessel; of strategy, victory; and of household management, wealth. In many instances several such pursuits are grouped together under a single capacity: the art of bridle-making, for example, and everything else pertaining to the equipment of a horse are grouped together under horsemanship; horsemanship in turn, along with every other military action, is grouped together under strategy; and other pursuits are grouped together under other capacities. In all these cases the ends of the master sciences are preferable to the ends of the subordinate sciences, since the latter are pursued for the sake of the former. This is true whether the ends of the actions lie in the activities themselves or, as is the case in the disciplines just mentioned, in something beyond the activities.

POLITICS AS THE MASTER SCIENCE OF THE GOOD

Now, if there exists an end in the realm of action which we desire for its own sake, an end which determines all our other desires; if, in other words, we do not make all our choices for the sake of something else—for in this way the process will go on infinitely so that our desire would be futile and pointless—then obviously this end will be the good, that is, the highest good. Will not the knowledge of this good, consequently, be very important to our lives? Would it not better equip us, like archers who have a target to aim at, to hit the proper mark? If so, we must try to comprehend in outline at least what this good is and to which branch of knowledge or to which capacity it belongs.

This good, one should think, belongs to the most sovereign and most comprehensive master science, and politics[1] clearly fits this description. For it determines which sciences ought to exist in states, what kind of sciences each group of citizens must learn, and what degree of proficiency each must attain. We observe further that the most honored capacities, such as strategy, household management, and oratory, are contained in politics. Since this science uses the rest of the sciences, and since, moreover, it legislates what people are to do and what they are not to do, its end seems to embrace the ends of the other sciences. Thus it follows that the end of politics is the good for

---

1. [*Politikē* is the science of the city-state, the *polis*, and its members, not merely in our narrow "political" sense of the word but also in the sense that a civilized human existence is, according to Plato and Aristotle, only possible in the *polis*. Thus *politikē* involves not only the science of the state, "politics," but of our concept of "society" as well. —TRANS.]

man. For even if the good is the same for the individual and the state, the good of the state clearly is the greater and more perfect thing to attain and to safeguard. The attainment of the good for one man alone is, to be sure, a source of satisfaction; yet to secure it for a nation and for states is nobler and more divine. In short, these are the aims of our investigation, which is in a sense an investigation of social and political matters.

THE LIMITATIONS OF ETHICS AND POLITICS

Our discussion will be adequate if it achieves clarity within the limits of the subject matter. For precision cannot be expected in the treatment of all subjects alike, any more than it can be expected in all manufactured articles. Problems of what is noble and just, which politics examines, present so much variety and irregularity that some people believe that they exist only by convention and not by nature. The problem of the good, too, presents a similar kind of irregularity, because in many cases good things bring harmful results. There are instances of men ruined by wealth, and others by courage. Therefore, in a discussion of such subjects, which has to start from a basis of this kind, we must be satisfied to indicate the truth with a rough and general sketch: when the subject and the basis of a discussion consist of matters that hold good only as a general rule, but not always, the conclusions reached must be of the same order. The various points that are made must be received in the same spirit. For a well-schooled man is one who searches for that degree of precision in each kind of study which the nature of the subject at hand admits: it is obviously just as foolish to accept arguments of probability from a mathematician as to demand strict demonstrations from an orator.

Each man can judge competently the things he knows, and of these he is a good judge. Accordingly, a good judge in each particular field is one who has been trained in it, and a good judge in general, a man who has received an all-round schooling. For that reason, a young man is not equipped to be a student of politics; for he has no experience in the actions which life demands of him, and these actions form the basis and subject matter of the discussion. Moreover, since he follows his emotions, his study will be pointless and unprofitable, for the end of this kind of study is not knowledge but action. Whether he is young in years or immature in character makes no difference; for his deficiency is not a matter of time but of living and of pursuing all his interests under the influence of his emotions. Knowledge brings no benefit to this kind of person, just as it brings none to the morally weak. But those who regulate their desires and actions by a rational principle will greatly benefit from a knowledge of this subject. So much by way of a preface about the student, the limitations which have to be accepted, and the objective before us.

HAPPINESS IS THE GOOD, BUT MANY VIEWS ARE HELD ABOUT IT

To resume the discussion: since all knowledge and every choice is directed toward some good, let us discuss what is in our view the aim of politics, i.e., the highest good attainable by action. As far as its name is concerned, most people would probably agree: for both the common run of people and cultivated men call it happiness, and understand by "being happy" the same as "living well" and "doing well." But when it comes to defining what happiness is, they disagree, and the account given by the common run differs from that of the philosophers. The former say it is some clear and obvious good, such as pleasure, wealth, or honor; some say it is one thing and others another, and often the very same person identifies it with different things at different times: when he is sick he thinks it is health, and when he is poor he says it is wealth; and when people are conscious of their own ignorance, they admire those who talk above their heads in accents of greatness. Some thinkers[2] used to believe that there

---

2. [The Platonic school.]

exists over and above these many goods another good, good in itself and by itself, which also is the cause of good in all these things. An examination of all the different opinions would perhaps be a little pointless, and it is sufficient to concentrate on those which are most in evidence or which seem to make some sort of sense. . . .

VARIOUS VIEWS ON THE HIGHEST GOOD

. . . It is not unreasonable that men should derive their concept of the good and of happiness from the lives which they lead. The common run of people and the most vulgar identify it with pleasure, and for that reason are satisfied with a life of enjoyment. For the most notable kinds of life are three: the life just mentioned, the political life, and the contemplative life.

The common run of people, as we saw, betray their utter slavishness in their preference for a life suitable to cattle; but their views seem plausible because many people in high places share the feelings of Sardanapallus.[3] Cultivated and active men, on the other hand, believe the good to be honor, for honor, one might say, is the end of the political life. But this is clearly too superficial an answer: for honor seems to depend on those who confer it rather than on him who receives it, whereas our guess is that the good is a man's own possession which cannot easily be taken away from him. Furthermore, men seem to pursue honor to assure themselves of their own worth; at any rate, they seek to be honored by sensible men and by those who know them, and they want to be honored on the basis of their virtue or excellence. Obviously, then, excellence, as far as they are concerned, is better than honor. One might perhaps even go so far as to consider excellence rather than honor as the end of political life. However, even excellence proves to be imperfect as an end: for a man might possibly possess it while asleep or while

---

3. [Sardanapallus is the Hellenized name of the Assyrian king Ashurbanipal (669–626 B.C.). Many stories about his sensual excesses were current in antiquity. —TRANS.]

being inactive all his life, and while, in addition, undergoing the greatest suffering and misfortune. Nobody would call the life of such a man happy, except for the sake of maintaining an argument. . . .[4] In the third place, there is the contemplative life, which we shall examine later on. As for the money-maker, his life is led under some kind of constraint: clearly, wealth is not the good which we are trying to find, for it is only useful, i.e., it is a means to something else. Hence one might rather regard the aforementioned objects as ends, since they are valued for their own sake. But even they prove not to be the good, though many words have been wasted to show that they are. Accordingly, we may dismiss them.

The Good Is Final and Self-Sufficient; Happiness Is Defined

Let us return again to our investigation into the nature of the good which we are seeking. It is evidently something different in different actions and in each art: it is one thing in medicine, another in strategy, and another again in each of the other arts. What, then, is the good of each? Is it not that for the sake of which everything else is done? That means it is health in the case of medicine, victory in the case of strategy, a house in the case of building, a different thing in the case of different arts, and in all actions and choices it is the end. For it is for the sake of the end that all else is done. Thus, if there is some one end for all that we do, this would be the good attainable by action; if there are several ends, they will be the goods attainable by action.

Our argument has gradually progressed to the same point at which we were before, and we must try to clarify it still further. Since there are evidently several ends, and since we choose some of these—e.g., wealth, flutes, and instruments generally—as a

---

4. [Here Aristotle makes reference to a lost work.]

means to something else, it is obvious that not all ends are final. The highest good, on the other hand, must be something final. Thus, if there is only one final end, this will be the good we are seeking; if there are several, it will be the most final and perfect of them. We call that which is pursued as an end in itself more final than an end which is pursued for the sake of something else; and what is never chosen as a means to something else we call more final than that which is chosen both as an end in itself and as a means to something else. What is always chosen as an end in itself and never as a means to something else is called final in an unqualified sense. This description seems to apply to happiness above all else: for we always choose happiness as an end in itself and never for the sake of something else. Honor, pleasure, intelligence, and all virtue we choose partly for themselves—for we would choose each of them even if no further advantage would accrue from them—but we also choose them partly for the sake of happiness, because we assume that it is through them that we will be happy. On the other hand, no one chooses happiness for the sake of honor, pleasure, and the like, nor as a means to anything at all.

We arrive at the same conclusion if we approach the question from the standpoint of self-sufficiency. For the final and perfect good seems to be self-sufficient. However, we define something as self-sufficient not by reference to the "self" alone. We do not mean a man who lives his life in isolation, but a man who also lives with parents, children, a wife, and friends and fellow citizens generally, since man is by nature a social and political being. But some limit must be set to these relationships; for if they are extended to include ancestors, descendants, and friends of friends, they will go on to infinity. However, this point must be reserved for investigation later. For the present we define as "self-sufficient" that which taken by itself makes life something desirable and deficient in nothing. It is happiness, in our opinion, which fits this description. Moreover, happiness is of all things the one most desirable, and it is not counted as one good thing among many others. But if it were counted as one among many others, it is obvious that the addition of even the least of the goods would make it more desirable; for the addition would produce an extra amount of good, and the greater amount of good is always more desirable than the lesser. We see then that happiness is something final and self-sufficient and the end of our actions.

To call happiness the highest good is perhaps a little trite, and a clearer account of what it is, is still required. Perhaps this is best done by first ascertaining the proper function of man. For just as the goodness and performance of a flute player, a sculptor, or any kind of expert, and generally of anyone who fulfills some function or performs some action, are thought to reside in his proper function, so the goodness and performance of man would seem to reside in whatever is his proper function. Is it then possible that while a carpenter and a shoemaker have their own proper functions and spheres of action, man as man has none, but was left by nature a good-for-nothing without a function? Should we not assume that just as the eye, the hand, the foot, and in general each part of the body clearly has its own proper function, so man too has some function over and above the functions of his parts? What can this function possibly be? Simply living? He shares that even with plants, but we are now looking for something peculiar to man. Accordingly, the life of nutrition and growth must be excluded. Next in line there is a life of sense perception. But this, too, man has in common with the horse, the ox, and every animal. There remains then an active life of the rational element. The rational element has two parts: one is rational in that it obeys the rule of reason, the other in that it possesses and conceives rational rules. Since the expression "life of the rational element" also can be used in two senses, we must make it clear that we mean a life determined by the activity, as opposed to the mere possession, of the rational element. For the activity, it seems, has a greater claim to be the function of man.

The proper function of man, then, consists in an activity of the soul in conformity with a rational principle or, at least, not without it. In speaking of the proper function of a given individual we mean that it is the same in kind as the function of an individual who sets high standards for himself: the proper function of a harpist, for example, is the same as the function of a harpist who has set high standards for himself. The same applies to any and every group of individuals: the full attainment of excellence must be added to the mere function. In other words, the function of the harpist is to play the harp; the function of the harpist who has high standards is to play it well. On these assumptions, if we take the proper function of man to be a certain kind of life, and if this kind of life is an activity of the soul and consists in actions performed in conjunction with the rational element, and if a man of high standards is he who performs these actions well and properly, and if a function is well performed when it is performed in accordance with the excellence appropriate to it; we reach the conclusion that the good of man is an activity of the soul in conformity with excellence or virtue, and if there are several virtues, in conformity with the best and most complete.

But we must add "in a complete life." For one swallow does not make a spring, nor does one sunny day; similarly, one day or a short time does not make a man blessed and happy. . . .

POPULAR VIEWS ABOUT HAPPINESS CONFIRM OUR POSITION

We must examine the fundamental principle with which we are concerned, [happiness], not only on the basis of the logical conclusion we have reached and on the basis of the elements which make up its definition, but also on the basis of the views commonly expressed about it. For in a true statement, all the facts are in harmony; in a false statement, truth soon introduces a discordant note.

Good things are commonly divided into three classes: (1) external goods, (2) goods of the soul, and (3) goods of the body. Of these, we call the goods pertaining to the soul goods in the highest and fullest sense. But in speaking of "soul," we refer to our soul's actions and activities. Thus, our definition tallies with this opinion which has been current for a long time and to which philosophers subscribe. We are also right in defining the end as consisting of actions and activities; for in this way the end is included among the goods of the soul and not among external goods.

Also the view that a happy man lives well and fares well fits in with our definition: for we have all but defined happiness as a kind of good life and well-being.

Moreover, the characteristics which one looks for in happiness are all included in our definition. For some people think that happiness is virtue, others that it is practical wisdom, others that it is some kind of theoretical wisdom; others again believe it to be all or some of these accompanied by, or not devoid of, pleasure; and some people also include external prosperity in its definition. Some of these views are expressed by many people and have come down from antiquity, some by a few men of high prestige, and it is not reasonable to assume that both groups are altogether wrong; the presumption is rather that they are right in at least one or even in most respects.

Now, in our definition we are in agreement with those who describe happiness as virtue or as some particular virtue, for our term "activity in conformity with virtue" implies virtue. But it does doubtless make a considerable difference whether we think of the highest good as consisting in the possession or in the practice of virtue, viz., as being a characteristic or an activity. For a characteristic may exist without producing any good result, as for example, in a man who is asleep or incapacitated in some other respect. An activity, on the other hand, must produce a result: [an active person] will necessarily act and act well. Just as the crown at the Olympic Games is not awarded to the most beautiful and the strongest but to the participants in the contests—for it is among them that the victors are found—so the good and noble things in life are won by those who act rightly.

The life of men active in this sense is also pleasant in itself. For the sensation of pleasure belongs to the soul, and each man derives pleasure from what he is said to love: a lover of horses from horses, a lover of the theater from plays, and in the same way a lover of justice from just acts, and a lover of virtue in general from virtuous acts. In most men, pleasant acts conflict with one another because they are not pleasant by nature, but men who love what is noble derive pleasure from what is naturally pleasant. Actions which conform to virtue are naturally pleasant, and, as a result, such actions are not only pleasant for those who love the noble but also pleasant in themselves. The life of such men has no further need of pleasure as an added attraction, but it contains pleasure within itself. We may even go so far as to state that the man who does not enjoy performing noble actions is not a good man at all. Nobody would call a man just who does not enjoy acting justly, nor generous who does not enjoy generous actions, and so on. If this is true, actions performed in conformity with virtue are in themselves pleasant.

Of course it goes without saying that such actions are good as well as noble, and they are both in the highest degree, if the man of high moral standards displays any right judgment about them at all; and his judgment corresponds to our description. So we see that happiness is at once the best, noblest, and most pleasant thing, and these qualities are not separate, as the inscription at Delos makes out:

> *The most just is most noble, but health is the best,*
> *and to win what one loves is pleasantest.*

For the best activities encompass all these attributes, and it is in these, or in the best one of them, that we maintain happiness consists.

Still, happiness, as we have said, needs external goods as well. For it is impossible, or at least not easy, to perform noble actions if one lacks the wherewithal. Many actions can only be performed with the help of instruments, as it were: friends, wealth, and political power. And there are some external goods the absence of which spoils supreme happiness, e.g., good birth, good children, and beauty: for a man who is very ugly in appearance or ill-born or who lives all by himself and has no children cannot be classified as altogether happy; even less happy perhaps is a man whose children and friends are worthless, or one who has lost good children and friends through death. Thus, as we have said, happiness also requires well-being of this kind, and that is the reason why some classify good fortune with happiness, while others link it to virtue.

HOW HAPPINESS IS ACQUIRED

This also explains why there is a problem whether happiness is acquired by learning, by discipline, or by some other kind of training, or whether we attain it by reason of some divine dispensation or even by chance. Now, if there is anything at all which comes to men as a gift from the gods, it is reasonable to suppose that happiness above all else is god-given; and of all things human it is the most likely to be god-given, inasmuch as it is the best. But although this subject is perhaps more appropriate to a different field of study, it is clear that happiness is one of the most divine things, even if it is not god-sent but attained through virtue and some kind of learning or training. For the prize and end of excellence and virtue is the best thing of all, and it is something divine and blessed. Moreover, if happiness depends on excellence, it will be shared by many people; for study and effort will make it accessible to anyone whose capacity for virtue is unimpaired. And if it is better that happiness is acquired in this way rather than by chance, it is reasonable to assume that this is the way in which it is acquired. For, in the realm of nature, things are naturally arranged in the best way possible—and the same is also true of the products of art and of any kind of causation, especially the highest. To leave the greatest and noblest of things to chance would hardly be right.

A solution of this question is also suggested by our earlier definition, according to which the good of man, happiness, is some kind of activity of the soul in conformity with virtue. All the other goods are either necessary prerequisites for happiness, or are by nature co-workers with it and useful instruments for attaining it. Our results also tally with what we said at the outset: for we stated that the end of politics is the best of ends; and the main concern of politics is to engender a certain character in the citizens and to make them good and disposed to perform noble actions.

We are right, then, when we call neither a horse nor an ox nor any other animal happy, for none of them is capable of participating in an activity of this kind. For the same reason, a child is not happy, either; for, because of his age, he cannot yet perform such actions. When we do call a child happy, we do so by reason of the hopes we have for his future. Happiness, as we have said, requires completeness in virtue as well as a complete lifetime. Many changes and all kinds of contingencies befall a man in the course of his life, and it is possible that the most prosperous man will encounter great misfortune in his old age, as the Trojan legends tell about Priam. When a man has met a fate such as his and has come to a wretched end, no one calls him happy.

CAN A MAN BE CALLED "HAPPY" DURING HIS LIFETIME?

Must we, then, apply the term "happy" to no man at all as long as he is alive? Must we, as Solon would have us do, wait to see his end?[5] And, on this assumption, is it also true that a man is actually happy after he is dead? Is this not simply absurd, especially for us who define happiness as a kind of activity? Suppose we do not call a dead man happy, and interpret Solon's words to mean that only when a man is dead can we safely say that he has been happy, since he is now beyond the reach of evil and misfortune—this view, too, is open to objection. For it seems

---

5. [This is one of the main points made by Solon, Athenian statesman and poet of the early sixth century B.C., in his conversation with the Lydian king, Croesus, in Herodotus I. 32. —TRANS.]

that to some extent good and evil really exist for a dead man, just as they may exist for a man who lives without being conscious of them, for example, honors and disgraces, and generally the successes and failures of his children and descendants. This presents a further problem. A man who has lived happily to his old age and has died as happily as he lived may have many vicissitudes befall his descendants: some of them may be good and may be granted the kind of life which they deserve, and others may not. It is, further, obvious that the descendants may conceivably be removed from their ancestors by various degrees. Under such circumstances, it would be odd if the dead man would share in the vicissitudes of his descendants and be happy at one time and wretched at another. But it would also be odd if the fortunes of their descendants did not affect the ancestors at all, not even for a short time.

But we must return to the problem raised earlier, for through it our present problem perhaps may be solved. If one must look to the end and praise a man not as being happy but as having been happy in the past, is it not paradoxical that at a time when a man actually is happy this attribute, though true, cannot be applied to him? We are unwilling to call the living happy because changes may befall them and because we believe that happiness has permanence and is not amenable to changes under any circumstances, whereas fortunes revolve many times in one person's lifetime. For obviously, if we are to keep pace with a man's fortune, we shall frequently have to call the same man happy at one time and wretched at another and demonstrate that the happy man is a kind of chameleon, and that the foundations [of his life] are unsure. Or is it quite wrong to make our judgment depend on fortune? Yes, it is wrong, for fortune does not determine whether we fare well or ill, but is, as we said, merely an accessory to human life; activities in conformity with virtue constitute happiness, and the opposite activities constitute its opposite.

The question which we have just discussed further confirms our definition. For no function of man possesses as much stability as do activities in conformity with virtue: these seem to be even more durable than scientific knowledge. And the higher the virtuous activities, the more durable they are, because men who are supremely happy spend their lives in these activities most intensely and most continuously, and this seems to be the reason why such activities cannot be forgotten.

The happy man will have the attribute of permanence which we are discussing, and he will remain happy throughout his life. For he will always or to the highest degree both do and contemplate what is in conformity with virtue; he will bear the vicissitudes of fortune most nobly and with perfect decorum under all circumstances, inasmuch as he is truly good and "four-square beyond reproach."

But fortune brings many things to pass, some great and some small. Minor instances of good and likewise of bad luck obviously do not decisively tip the scales of life, but a number of major successes will make life more perfectly happy; for, in the first place, by their very nature they help to make life attractive, and secondly, they afford the opportunity for noble and good actions. On the other hand, frequent reverses can crush and mar supreme happiness in that they inflict pain and thwart many activities. Still, nobility shines through even in such circumstances, when a man bears many great misfortunes with good grace not because he is insensitive to pain but because he is noble and high-minded.

If, as we said, the activities determine a man's life, no supremely happy man can ever become miserable, for he will never do what is hateful and base. For in our opinion, the man who is truly good and wise will bear with dignity whatever fortune may bring, and will always act as nobly as circumstances permit, just as a good general makes the most strategic use of the troops at his disposal, and a good shoemaker makes the best shoe he can from the leather available, and so on with experts in all other fields. If this is true, a happy man will never become miserable; but even so, supreme happiness will not be his if a fate such as Priam's befalls him. And yet, he will not be fickle and changeable; he will not be dislodged from his happiness easily by any misfortune that comes along, but only by great and numerous disasters such as will make it impossible for him to become happy again in a short time; if he recovers his happiness at all, it will be only after a long period of time, in which he has won great distinctions.

Is there anything to prevent us, then, from defining the happy man as one whose activities are an expression of complete virtue, and who is sufficiently equipped with external goods, not simply at a given moment but to the end of his life? Or should we add that he must die as well as live in the manner which we have defined? For we cannot foresee the future, and happiness, we maintain, is an end which is absolutely final and complete in every respect. If this be granted, we shall define as "supremely happy" those living men who fulfill and continue to fulfill these requirements, but blissful only as human beings. So much for this question.

Do the Fortunes of the Living Affect the Dead?

That the fortunes of his descendants and of all those near and dear to him do not affect the happiness of a dead man at all seems too unfeeling a view and contrary to the prevailing opinions. Many and different in kind are the accidents that can befall us, and some hit home more closely than others. It would, therefore, seem to be a long and endless task to make detailed distinctions, and perhaps a general outline will be sufficient. Just as one's own misfortunes are sometimes momentous and decisive for one's life and sometimes seem comparatively less important, so the misfortunes of our various friends affect us to varying degrees. In each case it makes a considerable difference whether those who are affected by an event are living or dead; much more so than it matters in a tragedy whether the crimes and horrors have been perpetrated before the opening of the play or are part of the plot. This difference, too, must be taken into account and perhaps still more the problem whether the dead participate in any good or evil. These considerations suggest that even if any good or evil reaches them at all, it must be something weak and negligible (either intrinsically or in relation to them), or at least something too small and insignificant to make the unhappy happy or to deprive the happy of their bliss. The good as well as the bad fortunes of their friends seem, then, to have some effect upon the dead, but the nature and magnitude of the effect is such as not to make the happy unhappy or to produce any similar changes.

The Psychological Foundations of the Virtues

Since happiness is a certain activity of the soul in conformity with perfect virtue, we must now examine what virtue or excellence is. For such an inquiry will perhaps better enable us to discover the nature of happiness. Moreover, the man who is truly concerned about politics seems to devote special attention to excellence, since it is his aim to make the citizens good and law-abiding. We have an example of this in the lawgivers of Crete and Sparta and in other great legislators. If an examination of virtue is part of politics, this question clearly fits into the pattern of our original plan.

There can be no doubt that the virtue which we have to study is human virtue. For the good which we have been seeking is a human good and the happiness a human happiness. By human virtue we do not mean the excellence of the body, but that of the soul, and we define happiness as an activity of the soul. If this is true, the student of politics must obviously have some knowledge of the workings of the soul, just as the man who is to heal eyes must know something about the whole body. In fact, knowledge is all the more important for the former, inasmuch as politics is better and more valuable than medicine, and cultivated physicians devote much time and trouble to gain knowledge about the body. Thus, the student of politics must study the soul, but he must do so with his own aim in view, and only to the extent that the objects of his inquiry demand: to go into it in greater detail would perhaps be more laborious than his purposes require.

Some things that are said about the soul in our less technical discussions are adequate enough to be used here, for instance, that the soul consists of two elements, one irrational and one rational. Whether these two elements are separate, like the parts of the body or any other divisible thing, or whether they are only logically separable though in reality indivisible, as convex and concave are in the circumference of a circle, is irrelevant for our present purposes.

Of the irrational element, again, one part seems to be common to all living things and vegetative in nature: I mean that part which is responsible for nurture and growth. We must assume that some such capacity of the soul exists in everything that takes nourishment, in the embryonic stage as well as when the organism is fully developed; for this makes more sense than to assume the existence of some different capacity at the latter stage. The excellence of this part of the soul is, therefore, shown to be common to all living things and is not exclusively human. This very part and this capacity seem to be most active in sleep. For in sleep the difference between a good man and a bad is least apparent—whence the saying that for half their lives the happy are no better off than the wretched. This is just what we would expect, for sleep is an inactivity of the soul in that it ceases to do things which cause it to be called good or bad. However, to a small extent some bodily movements do penetrate to the soul in sleep, and in this sense the dreams of honest men are better than those of average people. But enough of this subject: we may pass by the nutritive part, since it has no natural share in human excellence or virtue.

In addition to this, there seems to be another integral element of the soul which, though irrational, still does partake of reason in some way. In morally strong and morally weak men we praise the reason that guides them and the rational element of the soul, because it exhorts them to follow the right path and to do what is best. Yet we see in them also another natural strain different from the rational, which fights and resists the guidance of reason. The soul behaves in precisely the same manner as do the paralyzed limbs of the body. When we intend to move the limbs to the right, they turn to the left, and similarly, the impulses of morally weak persons turn in the direction opposite to that in which reason leads them. However, while the aberration of the body is visible, that of the soul is not. But perhaps we must accept it as a fact, nevertheless, that there is something in the soul besides the rational element, which opposes and reacts against it. In what way the two are distinct need not concern us here. But, as we have stated, it too seems to partake of reason; at any rate, in a morally strong man it accepts the leadership of reason, and is perhaps more obedient still in a self-controlled and courageous man, since in him everything is in harmony with the voice of reason.

Thus we see that the irrational element of the soul has two parts: the one is vegetative and has no share in reason at all, the other is the seat of the appetites and of desire in general and partakes of reason insofar as it complies with reason and accepts its leadership; it possesses reason in the sense that we say it is "reasonable" to accept the advice of a father and of friends, not in the sense that we have a "rational" understanding of mathematical propositions. That the irrational element can be persuaded by the rational is shown by the fact that admonition and all manner of rebuke and exhortation are possible. If it is correct to say that the appetitive part, too, has reason, it follows that the rational element of the soul has two subdivisions: the one possesses reason in the strict sense, contained within itself, and the other possesses reason in the sense that it listens to reason as one would listen to a father.

Virtue, too, is differentiated in line with this division of the soul. We call some virtues "intellectual" and others "moral": theoretical wisdom, understanding, and practical wisdom are intellectual virtues, generosity and self-control moral virtues. In speaking of a man's character, we do not describe him as wise or understanding, but as gentle or self-controlled; but we praise the wise man, too, for his characteristic, and praiseworthy characteristics are what we call virtues.

Happiness, Intelligence, and the Contemplative Life

Now, if happiness is activity in conformity with virtue, it is to be expected that is should conform with the highest virtue, and that is the virtue of the best part of us. Whether this is intelligence or something else which, it is thought, by its very nature rules and guides us and which gives us our notions of what is noble and divine; whether it is itself divine or the most divine thing in us; it is the activity of this part [when operating] in conformity with the excellence or virtue proper to it that will be complete happiness. That it is an activity concerned with theoretical knowledge or contemplation has already been stated.

This would seem to be consistent with our earlier statements as well as the truth. For this activity is not only the highest—for intelligence is the highest possession we have in us, and the objects which are the concern of intelligence are the highest objects of knowledge—but also the most continuous: we are able to study continuously more easily than to perform any kind of action. Furthermore, we think of pleasure as a necessary ingredient in happiness. Now everyone agrees that of all the activities that conform with virtue, activity in conformity with theoretical wisdom is the most pleasant. At any rate, it seems that [the pursuit of wisdom or] philosophy holds pleasures marvelous in purity and certainty, and it is not surprising that time spent in knowledge is more pleasant than time spent in research. Moreover, what is usually called "self-sufficiency" will be found in the highest degree in the activity which is concerned with theoretical knowledge. Like a just man and any other virtuous man, a wise man requires the necessities of life; once these have been adequately provided, a just man still needs people toward whom and in company with whom to act justly, and the same is true of a self-controlled man, a courageous man, and all the rest. But a wise man is able to study even by himself, and the wiser he is the more is he able to do it. Perhaps he could do it better if he had colleagues to work with him, but he still is the most self-sufficient of all. Again, study seems to be the only activity which is loved for its own sake. For while we derive a greater or a smaller advantage from practical pursuits beyond the action itself, from study we derive nothing beyond the activity of studying. Also, we regard happiness as depending on leisure; for our purpose in being busy is to have leisure, and we wage war in order to have peace. Now, the practical virtues are activated in political and military pursuits, but the actions involved in these pursuits seem to be unleisurely. This is completely true of military pursuits, since no one chooses to wage war or foments war for the sake of war; he would have to be utterly blood-thirsty if he were to make enemies of his friends simply in order to have battle and slaughter. But the activity of the statesman, too, has no leisure. It attempts to gain advantages beyond political action, advantages such as political power, prestige, or at least happiness for the statesman himself and his fellow citizens, and that is something other than political activity: after all, the very fact that we investigate politics shows that it is not the same [as happiness]. Therefore, if we take as established (1) that political and military actions surpass all other actions that conform with virtue in nobility and grandeur; (2) that they are unleisurely, aim at an end, and are not chosen for their own sake; (3) that the activity of our intelligence, inasmuch as it is an activity concerned with theoretical knowledge, is thought to be of greater value than the others, aims at no end beyond itself, and has a pleasure proper to itself—and pleasure increases activity; and (4) that the qualities of this activity evidently are self-sufficiency, leisure, as much freedom from fatigue as a human being can have, and whatever else falls to the lot of a supremely happy man; it follows that the activity of our intelligence constitutes the complete happiness of man, provided that it encompasses a complete span of life; for nothing connected with happiness must be incomplete.

However, such a life would be more than human. A man who would live it would do so not insofar as he is human, but because there is a divine element within him. This divine element is as far above our composite nature[6] as its activity is above the active exercise of the other, [i.e., practical], kind of virtue. So if it is true that intelligence is divine in comparison with man, then a life guided by intelligence is divine in comparison with human life. We must not follow those who advise us to have human thoughts, since we are [only] men, and mortal thoughts, as mortals should; on the contrary, we should try to become immortal as far as that is possible and do our utmost to live in accordance with what is highest in us. For though this is a small portion [of our nature], it far surpasses everything else in power and value. One might even regard it as each man's true self, since it is the controlling and better part. It would, therefore, be strange if a man chose not to live his own life but someone else's.

Moreover, . . . what is by nature proper to each thing will be at once the best and the most pleasant for it. In other words, a life guided by intelligence is the best and most pleasant for man, inasmuch as intelligence, above all else, is man. Consequently, this kind of life is the happiest. ∽

---

6. [Man, consisting of soul and body, i.e., of form and matter, is a composite being, whereas the divine, being all intelligence, is not.—TRANS.]

INTERPRETIVE QUESTIONS
FOR DISCUSSION

Why does Aristotle believe that one must pursue "the good" in order to be happy?

1. Does Aristotle think that there is one "good . . . at which all things aim," or that there are many goods that are the objects of our actions? (3)

2. Do people naturally desire what is good, according to Aristotle? (3–6)

3. Does Aristotle believe that wicked people also aim at the good, or only that they should do so if they wish to be happy?

4. Does Aristotle maintain that the good "is the same for the individual and the state"? (4–5)

5. If all aim at the good and at happiness, why is there disagreement about what happiness is? (6–8)

6. Does Aristotle believe that some people choose unhappiness?

7. Is a good person automatically happy, according to Aristotle?

8. Would Aristotle consider a person who has not attained happiness to be bad or merely unfortunate?

Suggested textual analysis
Pages 3–5: beginning, "Every art or applied science," and ending, "an investigation of social and political matters."

Why does Aristotle maintain that "happiness has permanence and is not amenable to changes under any circumstances"?

1. Why does Aristotle define happiness, the "highest good," as "an activity of the soul in conformity with excellence or virtue"? (10–11)

2. Why does Aristotle begin his discussion of happiness by describing the science of politics? (4–6)

3. What does Aristotle mean when he states, "And there are some external goods the absence of which spoils supreme happiness"? (13)

4. Who is the best judge of politics and the good, according to Aristotle? (5–6)

5. Why is the happy life most immune from the force of passion? (6)

6. Why would a person fail to fulfill his or her "proper function" if that is the path to happiness, and happiness is everyone's aim? (10–11)

7. Does Aristotle think that luck determines one's happiness, or that a person can control whether or not he or she is happy?

8. Why does Aristotle insist that happiness can only be attained "in a complete life"? (11)

Suggested textual analyses

Pages 10–11: beginning, "To call happiness the highest good," and ending, "a short time does not make a man blessed and happy. . . ."

Pages 15–18: beginning, "Must we, then," and ending, "So much for this question."

Does Aristotle believe that the "common run of people" can be happy?

1. Why does Aristotle believe that happiness requires a person to have "high standards"? (11)

2. Can happiness mean different things to different people, according to Aristotle?

3. Does Aristotle believe it is possible for one person to make another person happy? Can a person ruin another's happiness?

4. Why does Aristotle think that we must understand the "proper function" of human beings if we are to understand happiness? (10–11)

5. Do all people have the same "proper function," according to Aristotle? (10–11)

6. Does Aristotle believe that a statesman is more likely to find happiness than a bridle maker?

7. Why does Aristotle insist that neither children nor animals can be happy? (15)

8. Since "man is by nature a social and political being," why is his greatest happiness found in the solitary life of contemplation? (22–24)

Suggested textual analysis
Pages 22–24: from "Now, if happiness is activity," to the end of the selection.

FOR FURTHER REFLECTION

1. Is it possible to define happiness? Would defining happiness help one to achieve happiness?

2. Can evil people be happy, or should their pleasure be called something other than happiness?

3. Are people who challenge themselves to meet high standards happier than those who do not?

4. Contrary to the grandiose ideas of philosophers, is true happiness to be found in the small things of life—including pursuits that one enjoys although they could not be justified as important?

5. Does one need to engage in intellectual activity to be fully human and have a "true self"?

6. Do human beings have a "proper function"?

7. Has there been a net gain of happiness with the advance of civilization?

8. Will one be increasingly happy the more one aims at the good?

9. Can the person who views money-making as the good be happy?

A RIVER SUTRA

(selection)

Gita Mehta

GITA MEHTA (1943–) was born in Delhi, India, into a well-known political family. Her parents were active in India's struggle for liberation from British rule, and at the age of three Mehta was sent to boarding school, "because my mother was racing around trying to get my father out of jail." Mehta was educated in India and at Cambridge. Besides being the author of the novel *Raj* and a collection of essays, *Snakes and Ladders: Glimpses of Modern India,* Mehta has written, produced, and directed documentaries for American, British, and European television. She divides her time between New York, London, and India. *A River Sutra*—a collection of interlocking stories—is her second novel.

T HE GOVERNMENT still pays my wages but I no longer think of myself as a bureaucrat. Bureaucrats belong too much to the world, and I have fulfilled my worldly obligations. I am now a *vanaprasthi*, someone who has retired to the forest to reflect.

Of course, I was forced to modify tradition, having spent my childhood in Bombay and my career as a civil servant working only in cities. Although my desire to withdraw from the world grew more urgent as I aged, I knew I was simply not equipped to wander into the jungle and become a forest hermit, surviving on fruit and roots.

Then shortly after my wife passed away I learned of a vacant post at a Government rest house situated on the Narmada River. I had often stayed in such rest houses while touring the country-side on official business. Over time I had even developed an affection for these lonely sanctuaries built by the Moghul emperors across the great expanse of India to shelter the traveler and the pilgrim, a practice wisely maintained by subsequent administrations.

But the bungalow's proximity to the Narmada River was its particular attraction. The river is among our holiest pilgrimage sites, worshipped as the daughter of the god Shiva.[1] During a tour of the area I had been further intrigued to discover the criminal offense of attempted suicide is often ignored if the offender is trying to kill himself in the waters of the Narmada.

To the great surprise of my colleagues, I applied for the humble position of manager of the Narmada rest house. At first they tried to dissuade me, convinced that grief over my wife's death had led to my aberrant request. Senior bureaucrats, they argued, should apply for higher office. Finding me adamant, they finally recommended me for the post and then forgot me.

For several years now, thanks to the recommendations of my former colleagues, this rest house situated halfway up a hill of the Vindhya Range has been my forest retreat.

It is a double-storied building constructed from copper-colored local stone, the upper floor comprising three spacious and self-contained suites which overlook the gardens, the ground floor occupied by a dining room and drawing room opening onto a wide veranda. Happily, the interiors retain their original mosaic tiles, having escaped the attentions of a British administrator who plastered the outside walls at the turn of the century, giving the exterior of the bungalow with its pillared portico and balustraded steps an air more Victorian than Moghul.

To one side of the gardens, hidden by mango trees, is a small cottage in which I live. On the other side, the gardens lead to a stone terrace overlooking the Narmada, which flows seven hundred feet below.

Spanning a mile from bank to bank, the river has become the object of my reflections.

A great aid to my meditations is the beauty of our location. Across the sweep of water, I can see fertile fields stretching for

---

1. Shiva is one of the three gods of the Hindu triad—Brahma, Vishnu, and Shiva. He is the supreme god to his votaries. Shiva is also thought to date from the pre-Hindu period. When worshipped as the God of Death, he is the oldest god in India.

miles and miles into the southern horizon until they meet the gray shadows of the Satpura Hills. On this riverbank, towering bamboo thickets and trees overgrown with wild jasmine and lantana creepers cover the hillsides, suspending the bungalow in jungle so dense I cannot see the town of Rudra, only nineteen kilometers away, where my clerk, Mr. Chagla, lives.

Poor Mr. Chagla must bicycle for over an hour to reach us, but as we are without a telephone his daily return to town is vital for organizing our supplies and attending to other business. Rudra has the nearest post office, as well as a doctor who presides over a small hospital and a branch police station with four constables.

Below Rudra, visible from our terrace at the bend of the river, sprawls the temple complex of Mahadeo. At sunset I often sit on the terrace with our bungalow guests to watch the distant figures of the pilgrims silhouetted against the brilliant crimsons of the evening sky descending the stone steps that lead from Mahadeo's many temples to the river's edge. With twilight, the water at Mahadeo starts flickering with tiny flames as if catching fire from the hundreds of clay lamps being floated downstream for the evening devotions.

My day usually begins on this terrace. I have formed the habit of rising before dawn to sit here in the dark with my face turned toward the river's source, an underground spring that surfaces four hundred kilometers to the east.

In the silence of the ebbing night I sometimes think I can hear the river's heartbeat pulsing under the ground before she reveals herself at last to the anchorites of Shiva deep in meditation around the holy tank at Amarkantak. I imagine the ascetics sitting in the darkness like myself, their naked bodies smeared in ash, their matted hair wound on top of their heads in imitation of their Ascetic god, witnessing the river's birth as they chant:

Shiva-o-ham, Shiva-o-ham,
I that am Shiva, Shiva am I.

Then streaks of pale light send clouds of noisy birds into the sky, evoking crowds of pilgrims swarming through Amarkantak's temples for the morning worship.

By the time the red ball of the sun appears over the hills, the activity I have been imagining at the river's source becomes the reality of the rest house with the appearance of our gardeners, our sweepers, and the milkman.

After issuing instructions to the early staff, I leave the bungalow by the northern gate for my morning walk. Almost immediately I enter the jungle. Under the great trees glistening with dew—teak, peepul, silk cotton, mango, banyan—the mud path is still deserted, crossed only by bounding monkeys, leaping black buck, meandering wild boar as if the animals are glorying in their brief possession of the jungle. On my return in two hours I will be greeted on this path by sturdy tribal women from the nearby village of Vano collecting fuel for their cooking fires.

Our bungalow guards are hired from Vano village and enjoy a reputation for fierceness as descendants of the tribal races that held the Aryan invasion of India at bay for centuries in these hills. Indeed, the Vano village deity is a stone image of a half-woman with the full breasts of a fertility symbol but the torso of a coiled snake, because the tribals believe they once ruled a great snake kingdom until they were defeated by the gods of the Aryans. Saved from annihilation only by a divine personification of the Narmada River, the grateful tribals conferred on the river the gift of annulling the effects of snakebite, and I have often heard pilgrims who have never met a tribal reciting the invocation

Salutation in the morning and at night to thee, O Narmada! Defend me from the serpent's poison.

The Vano villagers also believe their goddess cures madness, liberating those who are possessed.

Beyond the valley on the next range of hills is a Muslim village with a small mosque adjoining the tomb of Amir Rumi, a Sufi saint of the sixteenth century. My friend Tariq Mia is mullah of the village mosque, and most mornings I walk all the way to the village in order to chat with Tariq Mia, for the old man is the wisest of all my friends.

On my way to Tariq Mia I sometimes pause at the summit of our hill to enjoy the view. Between the eastern hills I can see foaming waterfalls where the river plummets through marble canyons into the valley below the rest house, and if I turn west I can watch the river broadening as it races toward the Arabian Sea to become seventeen kilometers wide at its delta.

A day seldom passes when I do not see white-robed pilgrims walking on the riverbanks far below me. Many are like myself, quite elderly persons who have completed the first stages of life prescribed by our Hindu scriptures—the infant, the student, the householder—and who have now entered the stage of the *vanaprasthi,* to seek personal enlightenment.

I am always astonished at their endurance, since I know the Narmada pilgrimage to be an arduous affair that takes nearly two years to complete. At the mouth of the river on the Arabian Sea, the pilgrims must don white clothing out of respect for Shiva's asceticism before walking eight hundred kilometers to the river's source at Amarkantak. There they must cross to the opposite bank of the river and walk all the way back to the ocean, pausing only during the monsoon rains in some small temple town like Mahadeo, which has accommodated the legions of devout who have walked this route millennium upon millennium.

Then I remind myself that the purpose of the pilgrimage is endurance. Through their endurance the pilgrims hope to generate the heat, the tapas, that links men to the energy of the universe, as the Narmada River is thought to link mankind to the energy of Shiva.

It is said that Shiva, Creator and Destroyer of Worlds, was in an ascetic trance so strenuous that rivulets of perspiration began flowing from his body down the hills. The stream took on the form of a woman—the most dangerous of her kind: a beautiful virgin innocently tempting even ascetics to pursue her, inflaming their lust by appearing at one moment as a lightly dancing girl, at another as a romantic dreamer, at yet another as a seductress loose-limbed with the lassitude of desire. Her inventive variations so amused Shiva that he named her Narmada, the Delightful One, blessing her with the words "You shall be forever holy, forever inexhaustible." Then he gave her in marriage to the ocean, Lord of Rivers, most lustrous of all her suitors.

Standing here on the escarpment of the hill, a light wind cooling my body after its exertions, I can see the river flowing to meet her bridegroom in all those variations that delighted the Ascetic, while on her banks the pilgrims move slowly toward their destination. From this distance the white-robed men and women seem the spume of the river's waves, and as I watch them I wait to hear the sound of Tariq Mia's voice calling the faithful to prayer.

[*During the narrator's visit, Tariq Mia tells him about a music teacher who lived with the mullah for several months after his pupil, a blind boy uniquely gifted as a religious singer, was murdered by a rich and powerful man. Although finally convinced by Tariq Mia that he was not responsible for the boy's death, the music teacher threw himself under the train that was taking him back to Calcutta. When the narrator asks Tariq Mia why the music teacher committed suicide, the mullah replies, "Perhaps he could not exist without loving someone as he had loved the blind child. I don't know the answer, little brother. It is only a story about the human heart."*]

Loud laughter pierced the morning silence as I walked through the jungle back to the bungalow. The Vano village women were collecting fuel by the sides of the mud path.

Through the undergrowth I could see their slender brown arms reaching for the dry branches fallen on the mud. As I approached them I saw the saris sliding from their shoulders, baring their waists and the curve of their full breasts to my view as they stacked bundles of wood onto the small donkeys grazing under the trees.

The sturdy bodies of the village women, their catlike faces with the triangular tattoo marks high on each cheekbone, were such a relief after Tariq Mia's story that I returned their greetings with uncharacteristic warmth.

They nudged each other in surprise. "The sahib finds your face pretty today, Rano."

"It must be the season. Spring rouses even old tigers from their rest."

"It's true. Don't you see a prowl to the sahib's walk this morning?"

Their provocative laughter followed me down the gentle incline of the path. "Be careful not to walk alone, sisters. The mango trees are in bloom."

"Kama[2] must be sharpening his arrows of blossoms and stringing his bow with bees, sisters. Take care the sahib does not lure us to a seduction."

I could not help smiling at the women's references to Kama, God of Love, with his sugarcane bow strung with honeybees and his five flowered arrows of desire. There was indeed a mood of longing in the jungle. Small flowers foamed over the leaves of the mango trees, the wind carried the scent of lemon blossoms and sandalwood to my nostrils.

The call of the koil bird, that strange imitation of a woman's cry at the moment of sexual fulfillment, hung suspended in the air, and I felt mythology might at any moment become reality. That Kama might suddenly draw his sugarcane bow, known as the Exciter of Madness, and unleash one of his five arrows on a hapless wanderer who would then crave some unsuspecting woman as an incarnation of Delight, the Goddess of

---

2. Kama, God of Love, was incinerated by a glance from Shiva's third eye when he disturbed the meditating god. He then became known as Ananga, the bodiless one.

Involuntary Allure. And to make sure of victory Kama might call on his friends—Spring with his ruthless hands and his beautiful body clothed only in lotus buds, or the Malayan Wind carrying the aromatic perfumes of the South, or most dangerous of all, Amorous Mood.

Grateful to the laughing women for lifting my gloom, I turned to wave at them but they had disappeared and only the green canopy of the jungle rustled over the hill.

Mr. Chagla leaned from the window of his office as I opened the small wooden gate at the back entrance to the bungalow. "Sir! Sir! One minute, sir."

He hurried into the garden, the slight roll to his gait emphasizing the endearing roundness of his whole appearance. Although Mr. Chagla bicycles a good two hours every day, from the town of Rudra to the bungalow and back again, his exertions seem to make little impression on his plump body or interfere with the genial innocence of his open nature, which finds delight in the smallest incident.

"The sugarcane men came while you were on your walk, sir."

"I'm sorry, Chagla. I was unavoidably detained at the mosque."

"Mention not, sir. I purchased three bundles. At this very time they are stacked against the kitchen wall. We will have lots of juice for the visitors."

He handed me a letter with the indulgence of a parent handing a child a toy and I felt his expectant gaze on my face as I read.

The letter was from an old colleague. "My nephew, Nitin Bose, will be coming to your bungalow for a few weeks' leave. He is interested in tribal customs. He is a very brilliant young man and has recently been made a director of a big tea company. Please keep an eye on him. I count on your understanding and discretion."

"Well, sir? Which suite shall I prepare?" Mr. Chagla's smile tightened the shining skin of his round face.

"The letter doesn't say when the visitor is arriving."

"We must prepare for all eventualities, sir. Shall I move in extra beds at least?"

"We are only expecting one young man. No mention is made of a wife or children." The brown eyes lost their bright anticipation and I added hurriedly, "But send me a glass of sugarcane juice while I read the post. If it is sweet enough, we'll buy some more to make cane sugar."

Cheered by an opportunity to give pleasure, Mr. Chagla moved toward the kitchen with his rolling walk.

My house had already been swept and dusted. The green-painted wooden shutters were open and the papers on my table rustled in the breeze. I sat down to work but found I could not concentrate on the list of accounts Mr. Chagla had prepared for my approval.

The teasing of the women had left me restless. Behind me I could hear the rushing of the waterfalls. I pushed the papers away and walked to the end of my small lawn to look down at the Narmada River.

At noon the sun is so strong its harsh light gives the river the appearance of beaten metal, but at this hour the morning light catches every nuance of the water's movement. Below me the wind was tossing the rippling waves up so that they sparkled in the light before disappearing into the shadows below. I watched the water sparkling and disappearing, sparkling and disappearing, like the anklets encircling a woman's foot, and thought of the Ascetic watching the dancing woman formed by the rivulets from his own penance.

A flock of parakeets, messengers of Kama, God of Love, settled in a green cloud on the mango tree shading my head. I smiled, remembering how the Ascetic had sneered at Kama's power, even though the gods had warned the Ascetic that he too must feel Desire for without Desire the play of the worlds would cease.

But still the Ascetic had sneered as he was pierced by the five flower-tipped arrows unleashed by Kama from his sugarcane bow—the Enchanter, the Inflamer, the Parcher, the Paroxysm of Desire, the Carrier of Death.

Then Maya, the Illusion of the Worlds, had appeared—the only woman capable of arousing the lust of the Destroyer of Worlds. Enraged at the destruction of his meditation, the Ascetic had opened his third eye, the Lotus of Command, and reduced Kama to ashes, even as he himself was being consumed by Desire.

Suddenly I was alarmed by the prospect of our new visitor. My colleague's letter had said his nephew was interested in tribal customs, but what did the young man really know about the beliefs of the tribals?

Did he know the goddess who had incinerated even the Great Ascetic in the fires of longing, the goddess whose power had been acknowledged by the ancient sages with such fearful names as the Terrible One, the Implacable Mother, the Dark Lady, the Destroyer of Time, the Everlasting Dream—did he know the goddess had been worshipped by the tribal inhabitants of these jungles for thousands of years?

Now the teasing of the Vano women seemed more threatening than Tariq Mia's tale of murder and suicide. Would a brilliant mind be enough to protect the young man from the dark forces of the jungles, from the tribal worship of that Desire which even their conquerors had acknowledged to be invincible, describing it as the firstborn seed of the mind?

"Sir, taste this." Mr. Chagla was standing at my side with a glass of sugarcane juice. "You will definitely find it up to the mark, sir."

His eager face smiled encouragingly at me, pulling me back into the day.

∞

A full month passed before I heard from my colleague again. By then the clusters of mango blossoms had hardened into fruit and I had long forgotten my brief moment of anxiety.

Those varieties of mangoes not sweet enough to eat were already sliced and pickled, marinating in lemon juice in large glass jars on the ledge outside the pantry. Mr. Chagla had arranged for the delivery of bundles of sugarcane and I had myself stirred the boiling cane juice. Now there were enough hard rounds of brown cane sugar sitting in the dark, net-covered larder to last us through the monsoons.

Mr. Chagla laughed when I passed him the telegram from my old colleague, informing me that Nitin Bose was arriving by train the next day.

"We will have no juice for him, sahib. But don't worry. The cook will some way revive Mr. Bose from his dusty journey."

"Prepare the north suite, Chagla. Apparently our visitor is interested in the tribals. From his balcony he will be able to see Vano village. And when you return to Rudra make arrangements to meet the train."

The noise of a motorcycle roaring down the path behind the bungalow interrupted my instructions, and Mr. Chagla followed me across the garden.

"But this is Shashi, my school friend from so many years," Mr. Chagla announced in surprise as a constable from Rudra police station parked his motorcycle at the gate. "What can he want?"

"You will have to accompany me at once, sahib!" the constable shouted at me. "There has been some trouble with one of your visitors."

"But, Shashi, we have no visitors at all!" Mr. Chagla cried. "Who is creating such a mistake?"

"What can I do, Chagla? Your address was in his pocket. 'Care of the Narmada rest house.'"

"Shashi, you are not telling sense to my sahib. Who is this he? Where is this he?"

"In a cell at the police station in Rudra."

"A prisoner?" I asked.

"Well, that's the problem, sahib. We think he was trying to kill himself. We found him standing on the very edge of a cliff, staring down into the Narmada."

"Oof-oh. What a terrible thing!" Mr. Chagla shook his round head in dismay. "Was he going to jump in?"

"We are not sure of his real actual intentions. When we asked what he was doing there on the cliff he only said, 'Bring me my oil and my collyrium. Sister, bring the mirror and my vermilion.'"

Mr. Chagla stared at him dumbstruck. The constable looked away in embarrassment, and for a moment we all stood there in silence. Then Mr. Chagla recovered himself sufficiently to demand, "And his good name, Shashi. What is the poor fellow's good name?"

The constable turned to me, opening his hands in a gesture of helplessness. "That is another problem, sahib. He gives only a woman's name but he is most certainly a man."

I couldn't control my curiosity. "What name does he give?"

"Rima, sahib. We have confined him, but we have not charged him. How can we charge a man under the name of Miss Rima Bose?"

The telegram had informed us of the imminent arrival of Nitin Bose. I remembered my old friend had ended his letter by saying he depended on my discretion. I wondered if the constable's prisoner was my colleague's nephew, and why my colleague hadn't warned me that his nephew was mad.

"Has your prisoner been seen by the doctor?"

The constable was affronted. "Of course, sahib. Very first thing. The doctor sent me to bring you. He says he can do nothing."

"But what is wrong with him?"

The constable lowered his voice and Mr. Chagla inclined his plump torso forward to listen more closely. "The prisoner told to the doctor that he is possessed."

Remounting his motorcycle, the constable waited for me to climb onto the pillion seat behind him. "Now, sahib, please hurry. My sergeant must be waiting so anxiously for your arrival."

Mr. Chagla unlocked the chain of his bicycle. "Don't be alarmed whatsoever, sir. Shashi is a capital driver, safe as anything. And I will be following close behind, to solve this mystery."

The wind whipped past my face, making my eyes water as we raced through the jungle toward Rudra. By the time the motorcycle bumped onto the tarmac road, my eyes were watering so badly the small painted houses were only a blur of lime-greens and blues connected by bougainvillea bushes and rows of black crows perched on electric wires.

The constable slowed down as we neared a square building with iron-barred windows. I recognized Dr. Mitra's spare frame leaning down to talk to a policeman at the entrance of the police station.

"My dear fellow, what a business." Dr. Mitra helped me off the motorcycle and led me up the concrete stairs. "I have just come back from the station with the poor chap's luggage. It was addressed to your bungalow. Were you expecting someone by the name of Nitin Bose?"

When he saw my expression he placed a lean arm around my shoulder. "Don't worry. It will soon be sorted out. In any case, the young man is not at all menacing. Come, see for yourself."

We passed the police desk and entered a corridor that led to a solitary cell at the back of the building. The police sergeant was sitting on an iron cot talking to a young man who was pacing silently up and down the cell.

The distinction of the young man surprised me. There was an air of authority to his carriage, and his well-cut cotton suit still flattered his body even though the cloth was creased. As he retraced his steps, through the stubble covering his dark skin I saw he had an aristocratic face with strong features.

The police sergeant got up wearily. "The prisoner won't talk to me, sahib. I can't even get him to admit his name is Nitin Bose."

Dr. Mitra gently pushed me into the cell. "You try talking to him. Perhaps you will have better luck than us. Say you were expecting him."

The sergeant followed Dr. Mitra down the corridor, leaving me alone with the young man.

"Your uncle and I were deputy secretaries at the same time," I began awkwardly. "In the Ministry of Agriculture. In fact, he sent me a telegram, saying I should expect you tomorrow. But you are already here."

I laughed nervously, unnerved by Nitin Bose's silence. "For two years our offices were adjacent. Right next to each other. Perhaps that is why he suggested you stay in our bungalow. . . ."

The young man suddenly gripped my shoulders. I was not frightened by the pressure of his fingers when I saw the fear deep in his eyes.

"You must help me," he whispered. "Read my diary. You will understand why I must find the shrine."

His voice broke and he sat down on the iron cot.

"What shrine?" I asked, moved by his desperation.

He struggled to control himself. When he was able to speak he answered, "They say there is a shrine to a goddess in these jungles. A tribal goddess, who cures the madness of those who are possessed. Can you help me find it?"

His request was so simple I almost started laughing again from sheer relief. The bitterness in his eyes stopped me and I said soberly, "Our bungalow guards worship at that shrine. They can take you there any time you wish."

"Then I must come with you."

I shook my head in alarm, unprepared to take responsibility for a man in his state. To my horror he knelt on the floor and seized my feet. "I will cause no trouble, I swear it. If I cannot visit the shrine I will have to kill myself. I can't go on like this."

I backed out of the cell. "Let me consult the doctor. We must abide by the doctor's advice."

A policeman came to lock the cell door as I hurried into the police sergeant's office, where Mr. Chagla was helping Dr. Mitra go through the young man's suitcase.

The police sergeant was describing each item to the constable, Shashi, who was carefully recording it in a lined ledger.

"Have you found a diary?" I asked. "He says it explains everything. And he wants to return to the rest house with me."

Mr. Chagla triumphantly handed me a leatherbound volume.

"Congratulations, my dear fellow." Dr. Mitra took my other hand between his bony fingers.

"For what?"

"You have brought the boy back to his senses. I knew it was a temporary aberration. He has probably been undergoing some severe emotional strain—overwork, an unhappy love affair, that sort of thing—and was suffering from momentary amnesia. I believe it happened to Agatha Christie once."

Hardly able to contain his glee at such a happy ending, Mr. Chagla threw his arm around his constable friend.

Dr. Mitra turned to the sergeant. "You haven't charged the prisoner with any crime. Release him into the capable hands of our friend and I will drive them all back to the rest house."

"No, no. Something might happen to him. We are too isolated." I looked to Mr. Chagla for support, but his plump face was stretched in a smile.

"What harm can come to him in our lovely bungalow, sir? We have guards. I am there. Shashi will arrive like a flash if we are in need of help."

"At least let me read the diary. We can collect him tomorrow."

Dr. Mitra objected. "If he stays overnight the police will have to charge him."

Seeing the dismay on Mr. Chagla's face, I accepted defeat and went to Dr. Mitra's car.

The police constables loaded the young man's luggage into the boot. Nitin Bose climbed in beside me, and Dr. Mitra steered the car onto the road.

All the way to the rest house Mr. Chagla chatted happily with Dr. Mitra. His good humor was so much stronger than the silent despair of the young man sitting at my side that I felt almost equal to the situation by the time we reached our gates.

To my relief, Mr. Chagla took immediate charge of our new resident. He bustled about organizing Nitin Bose's luggage and issuing instructions to the cook and to the bearers. Leaving him to show Bose to his rooms, Dr. Mitra and I went to sit on the terrace.

The lights of Mahadeo's temples sparkled reassuringly at the river's bend, and above us Mr. Chagla's round shadow was visible against Nitin Bose's windows as he gesticulated to the bearer serving Bose his dinner.

"Do you think a man can be possessed, Dr. Mitra?" I asked.

"If a man believes strongly enough that he is possessed, then I suppose you could say he is possessed."

"Bose wants to visit a shrine that he thinks can cure him. The local villagers worship there. Will it be all right if he goes with them?"

"Certainly. In fact, I advise it. The young man has imagined his sickness. Let him imagine his cure."

He stood up, seeing Mr. Chagla walking down the garden. "Anyway, let me know what you discover in his diary. It may tell us more about this unfortunate situation."

"Our visitor is tucked up neat and tidy for the night," Mr. Chagla announced with satisfaction as I accompanied him and Dr. Mitra back to the car. "But I have left a guard outside his room, in case he becomes silly again."

As the car's headlights sliced into the darkness of the jungle, I returned to my house to read the young man's diary.

THE EXECUTIVE'S STORY

I suppose in a way my life really began when I came to live on this tea estate. Or perhaps it is ending here.

In any case I know something strange is happening to me, and I must keep a written record of the events leading to my present situation before I am no longer able to relate them.

First I should describe the world I inhabited before I came here. I was a young executive in Calcutta's oldest tea company. Like myself, all my young colleagues had been educated at exclusive boarding schools and obtained their jobs through family connections.

Outside our office Calcutta crumbled under the weight of neglect, exploitation, poisonous humidity, traffic jams, power failures, and roads plowed up like rice fields to make an underground railway, while a whole generation stoically waited for the city to return to what it once had been as more trainloads of refugees arrived to sleep on railway platforms already overcrowded with refugees from the partition of India fifty years earlier, the war in Bangladesh twenty years earlier, the devastations of nature that daily drew the desperate to a great metropolis itself desperately surviving as if a war had just ended.

But we experienced only claustrophobia as we stared through the darkened windows of our air-conditioned cars at the crowds teeming across the broken pavements.

It was not that we were unfeeling. But we were young and we believed success lay in imitating the anglicized aloofness of our superiors who assured us the city had passed the point of no return.

They counseled us to make the best of a bad job. So we played golf at the Tolleygunge Club. Drank at the Saturday Club. Ate Chinese meals at the Calcutta Club. Raced at the Turf Club.

The drinking helped. And the meaningless adulteries. Also, we read avidly. On our bedside tables the novels of the moment were stacked on top of *Time, Newsweek,* the *Economist,* for those nights when there wasn't a woman in the bed. Or for dawn, when we returned from driving our women to their own homes and saw the sheets crumpled with humidity and sweat, saw the long black hairs lying like accusations on the pillow, and knew our lives were leaking away.

Occasionally the sluggish indolence of our lives was disrupted by the arrival of the boys from the tea estates. They were not prematurely aged by their life in the lonely tea gardens like the English tea estate managers described in eighteenth-century diaries, men without teeth or hair who came to Calcutta only to bid for wives when the ships from London discharged their cargoes of desperate Englishwomen trying to escape lives of penury back home.

Our tea garden colleagues were young, good-looking Indians, bursting with alien energy. We listened to their boasts of rogue elephants tracked, man-eating tigers shot, hot-blooded women tamed, and envied the cowboy quality to their headlong pursuit of pleasure during the weeks they spent in the city.

Vying with each other to buy them drinks, we waved at the barman behind the long wooden bar at the Saturday Club. "A patiala peg for the sahib, Moses."

"Come on, yaar,[3] this one's on me."

The tea estate boys obliged us by consuming whole bottles of whisky while we watched, fascinated by their careless self-destruction.

"Yaar, I don't know how your liver can take such punishment."

"Practice, yaar. What do you think I do three hundred and thirty days in the year, up on the estate?"

"What, yaar?"

"Drink, shoot, and fuck."

"Come off it, yaar. Who can you fuck in the wilderness?"

"Armies of women. Real women who will do anything to please a man."

"For instance? No, let me sign for this one."

"Cheers. And what sexual appetites! It's all they think about."

"No wonder you tea estate chaps become such elbow-benders. I couldn't touch those hideous creatures unless I was stinking drunk."

"Come on, yaar, admit it. I bet they smell like hell, your real women."

"I might admit this much. Mrs. Sushila Ghosh smells better than them." The tea estate boy would empty his glass. "And now, yaar, I mustn't keep such a fragrant lady waiting."

---

3. Slang for friend, pal.

Sometimes when I was stuck in a traffic jam behind a bus listing under the weight of passengers clinging to its step rails, I marveled that the clerks squeezed against each other could laugh and joke with each other as they did, and I wondered if the fight for survival could opiate them as luxury had opiated me, or whether they also dreamed of glorious adventures.

And when those freewheeling tea estate boys came into the office after a night of suicidal drinking followed by love-making in air-conditioned bedrooms scented with tuber roses bought fresh every morning from the New Market, I felt a spasm of envious admiration. Life on the tea estates seemed a real man's life.

The nearest we got to danger was gambling. Ashok, who had spent most of his time in the betting shops of London while working toward his accountancy degree, offered odds on the movement of two clouds in the sky outside our office windows. The exact time a peon would take to bring us tea. Whose bored wife's eye would next begin to wander.

Everything was an occasion for a wager. When I was offered the choice between managing a tea estate or going on an executive training course, the betting began again.

"Avoid the estate, yaar. You'll be an alcoholic in a year."

"Six months."

"Nine."

Despite the dire predictions of my companions, I opted for the tea estate.

"Okay, what odds are you giving me? I say it will take him a year."

"Now, Ashok. Don't do all that seven-to-two shit. Just keep it simple. Three to one."

"Done. Three to one says he will be an alcoholic within a year."

"Don't be an ass, yaar Nitin. You will have no one to talk to. Those tea estate buggers are all mad. Driven crazy by loneliness."

To me, suffocated by the sheer weight of Calcutta's inescapable humanity, the solitude of the tea estate was its most attractive prospect.

Still, I found it hard to believe such solitude existed as the jeep wound its way through the deserted Himalayan foothills toward my tea estate.

During the eight-hour drive from the small airport to the tea garden, I stared in awe at the green emptiness stretching in circles below the hill road. Each shepherd beating his animals off the road, each coolie laboring under the bundles tied to his head, required an individual greeting, so rare was human encounter. Overhead the small clouds rose like foam above the distant Himalayas before breaking in a white wave as the wind swept them toward the plains, and I felt like a pebble thrown into a wooded ocean, expanding the empty horizon as an alien object moves the water outward.

Long before I reached my tea estate I had gone from disbelief, to tranquility, to that possessiveness by which one is oneself possessed.

Occasionally the jeep passed a village of thatched cottages that looked more Shakespearean than Indian with their plastered walls and weathered timber beams, isolated in miles of tea bushes just coming into leaf.

As dusk fell we could no longer see the fields of tea bushes. Only the dim lanterns from the tea pickers' colonies broke the darkness. Then night enclosed us in a velvet embrace, and the lights from the tea pickers' huts were no less gentle than the stars in that tranquil sky.

The sweep of our headlights lit the deodar tree spreading its branches above the walls of my new residence. A guard saluted as the jeep rounded a drive outlined by painted bricks, and in the portico five turbanned and cummerbunded servants bowed to me.

It was all so ridiculously English I started laughing. Even when the driver braked and the servants came forward to open my door I could not stop laughing at the thought that I had entered a British fantasy of India, untouched by the chaos of the last forty years.

To reassure the servants that I was as pukka⁴ as any other sahib, I began issuing orders in an unnaturally military way. They lost the looks of insecurity brought on by my display of levity, as I supervised the unloading of my luggage. My barked orders, my courtesy underlined by firmness, my eye for detail, drew a portrait of my persona for them to circulate on the estate.

The head bearer ushered me into my bedroom, and I wanted to laugh again when I saw the massive ebony bed with serpents carved on the headboard enclosed in the billowing mosquito net suspended from an iron hoop in the high ceiling, standing there like an altar built for the worship of the senses.

But I controlled myself as the other servants brought in the large cabin trunk my grandfather had taken with him to Cambridge University three years before the Great War. Although he had been a physicist, my grandfather had been an avid reader of Indian philosophy and mythology, and on the day my transfer to the tea gardens had been confirmed my grandmother had sent me his cabin trunk filled with books. I could not imagine why my grandmother thought someone of my generation would have the faintest interest in all those Puranas and Vedas and Upanishads and God knows what. But I had brought them with me in case I ran out of reading material.

Now I ordered the servants to remove the books wedged into the trunk. They looked embarrassed as the volumes piled up on the floor around them. Facing the magnificent bed shrouded in its veils of fine netting was the house's sole bookcase, a plywood construction obviously used by previous inhabitants for pornographic paperbacks or detective stories. A copy of Goren's *Contract Bridge* lay mournfully on the warping middle shelf.

I instructed the servants to stack the books against the wall until new bookshelves could be made. From the glances they

---

4. Slang for "the real thing."

threw in my direction I knew I had succeeded in establishing myself as a scholar, and they would tell the estate workers that I was a just man, capable of controlling my disappointment that my library could not be housed immediately instead of abusing them.

Satisfied by my own performance, I sat alone in the wood-beamed dining room reveling in my good fortune, the only noise the sound of crickets outside and the creaking of the pantry door each time the head bearer brought me another dish.

The extraordinary thing about inventing a persona is that one is loathe to give it up, especially if the fiction sits comfortably.

I found I enjoyed being the young paterfamilias of my realm, enjoyed being treated with undisguised respect by the gentle tribal women picking leaves as I walked through the rows of tea bushes with my overseer, Mr. Sen.

A fussy, pedantic man, always looking for the small fault to assert his power, Mr. Sen continually provided me with opportunities to exhibit my tolerant good sense. I took care to do so with a delicacy that could not offend his authority until, over the months, both the tea pickers and the clerical staff under Mr. Sen became dependent on my judgment.

Nature conspired in my fiction that first year. The rains came at exactly the right time to produce the tenderest leaves, and the crop from my estate was the best received by Head Office. The Chairman telegrammed his personal congratulations and the workers responded to their bonus with small presents for me, as if I were a family elder.

I suppose I had begun to exhibit the mannerisms of an elder. Certainly, my old self of the Calcutta days was less and less present, my new self increasingly so, like a shortening shadow merges with its subject. I hardly drank, and I never thought about women. If women showed themselves in my dreams as I lay asleep in the ebony bed, they did so with such subtlety that I awoke with no memory of them.

The dreams I remembered were linked to my grandfather's library.

To my surprise I had become fascinated by the endless legends contained in the Puranas. After a day spent walking through tea gardens laid out with mathematical precision or studying columns of figures at my office desk while the long blades of the wooden fan stirred the air, I found it a delight to sit on the veranda in the evenings reading the labyrinthine tales of demons, sages, gods, lovers, cosmologies.

I even discovered mythological tales dealing with the very area in which my tea estate was situated, legends of a vast underground civilization stretching from these hills all the way to the Arabian Sea, peopled by a mysterious race half human, half serpent. Naturally I viewed the legends through the prism of anthropology, assuming the nomadic Aryan scribes who had recorded the legends had been overwhelmed by the sophistication of the people they had conquered.

But I enjoyed their poetic descriptions of palaces and universities constructed from many-colored marbles. Of gardens more beautiful than those of the gods themselves with ponds of crystalline water alive with leaping fish, silver among the water lilies, and trees bending under the weight of flowering vines. A world devoted to pleasure and learning, its serenity guarded by hooded serpents with great gems flashing from their hoods.

Apparently its inhabitants had even had a particular love of magic, spending happy hours entertaining each other with magic tricks.

After dinner I would sit on the veranda in my wicker armchair, staring into the velvet night, the stars so low in the sky I felt I had only to reach up and pull one down to shed more light on my open book, imagining that the gentle tribals I had seen bending over the tea bushes were in fact descendants of this civilization, still able to do the great Indian rope trick, and when I fell asleep in my ebony bed under the sails of mosquito netting, I dreamed of legendary kingdoms guarded by hooded cobras.

The second year the rains were again kind to us. Our tea crop was so outstanding the Chairman sent a member of the board to invite me to return to Calcutta as a director of the company. To my delight this exalted person turned out to be my friend, Ashok.

"So, yaar, tell me the truth. How long did it take?"

"Did what take?" I asked.

"Be serious, yaar. To become an alcoholic."

He would not believe I was not a drunk until we passed evening after evening on my veranda, I pouring a single drink for myself but many for him. My abstemiousness exasperated him. When I said I did not want to leave the tea estate, Ashok told me I was losing my mind.

Raising his voice above the singing of the crickets and the deep-throated belches of the garden frogs, he said, "You are definitely going mad, yaar. You hardly drink. You want to stay in this godforsaken wilderness when you could be a director of the company. You mastermind these perfect crops all day but at night you do nothing but read."

He leaned over and stared at me. "Admit it, yaar. It is downright sinister for a man your age not to have had a woman for two solid years!"

He went on and on trying to convince me to return to Calcutta in that soft blackness which had never ceased to affect me as it had from the first night, but which obviously upset him with its emptiness.

Not wishing to offend an old friend, I made excuses. "Which woman would live with me without marriage? And you've seen the tea pickers. Could you take them to bed?"

"Then come back to Calcutta, yaar, before it drops off or withers away like some unwatered tea bush."

Too much drink made him insensitive to my silence, and I was glad the next morning to wave Ashok good-bye.

But his words left a mark on my mind as if he had dropped a bottle of ink across a favorite book. Like some small night animal, sexual restlessness began to gnaw at the edges of my content. After dinner I sat on the veranda, unable to relax in the wicker armchair as insects and moths flung themselves ceaselessly against the glass domes covering the lightbulbs. The darkness that had always seemed so serene now mirrored my restless mind. For the first time I was lonely, and when I entered my bedroom I felt the massive bed sneering at my unused manhood.

Whatever I saw mocked my efforts to recover my composure. The women laughing at each other across the tea bushes now seemed knowingly voluptuous, revealing their breasts, their rounded bellies, their bared calves too much to my view. Even when I went shooting in the jungle I heard only the mating call of animals and I was disgusted with the gun in my hands.

My grandfather's books offered no escape. Once I pulled the Rig-Veda from the bookshelf, hoping to find some philosophical consolation in it, but the passage I read shocked me, so accurately did it describe my loneliness.

At first was Death.
That which did mean an utter emptiness.
And emptiness, mark thou, is Hunger's Self.

Determined to recover my tranquility, I plunged into my work with redoubled intensity. It did no good. Everything about my work annoyed me. The stupidity of the workers with their constant demands for advances against their salaries. The stubbornness of the union leaders. The inefficiency of the clerical staff in the office.

I frequently found myself shouting in irritation when something small had been overlooked, as if I had become Mr. Sen. The workers responded by withdrawing their affection, leaving me frozen in that isolation which had led so many of my colleagues to become alcoholics.

Now I followed the example of my predecessors, putting aside my books to sit in the darkness, a bottle of whisky at my elbow, while the head bearer waited in the garden, drawing on his bidi as I drank myself into oblivion. Then, my body a dead weight across his shoulders, he dragged me into the bedroom and somehow undressed me and pushed me through the mosquito net where I lay in a stupor of stale whisky fumes never sure if I was awake or asleep.

Perhaps my loneliness caused my mind to create its own enslavement. Or perhaps I had already become the victim of my grandfather's books. In any case, one night I was lying in my bed when I was awakened by a perfume that subsumed the smell of whisky that had become the companion to my sleep.

As that musky fragrance enveloped me, calming me and exciting me at the same time, I felt a softness press against my shoulder. Stretching out my hand, I grasped the swelling firmness of a woman's breast. But the petals of a flower garland intruded between my lips and her flesh, a girdle chain between my thigh and her smooth hip, an anklet between my hand and her slender foot. Maddened by the fragile barrier of her ornaments, I crushed her in my embrace. Her body encircled mine like a flowering creeper grips a tree. She made a sound between a sigh and a laugh, her breath moist against my ear. Then a low voice asked, "Why did you not send for me earlier?"

Was I bewitched that night by the moon throwing its feverish light across the bed, gilding her supple body silver as she rode mine? Or was it the long eyes sliding like fish above her slanting Mongol cheekbones? The slender shoulders pulled forward by the weight of her breasts? The perspiration shining on her narrow waist above the mango curve of her hip?

Was it the perfect oval cast by our shadow on the sheets as she pressed her feet against my chest when I enclosed her in my embrace? The sight of her limbs turning the dark blue of a lotus calyx as the clouds obscured the moon? Or was it the heavy plait coiling and uncoiling against our bodies until it unraveled under the billowing curtain of the mosquito net to cocoon us in a second curtain, blacker than the night outside?

I did not know whether I had fashioned her from the night and my own hunger, even though her small teeth pierced my skin again and again like the sudden striking of a snake, and I heard the hissing of her pleasure against my throat. But when she left my bed I was already asleep, dreaming I still held a creature half serpent in my arms, my sated senses pulling me into the underground world of my grandfather's legends.

If in the morning the mirror had not reflected the vermilion marks of her painted feet on my chest or the streaks of her black collyrium on my skin I would not have believed she existed. Seeing them, I was sick with love as if I had been pierced by all five arrows of desire.

The next night I lay in my bed, my limbs trembling in anticipation as I waited for her. Yet I was asleep again when her low voice in my ear awoke me, and I was again asleep before she left me.

Knowing the urgency of my desire, I could not understand my inability to stay awake. After the first few nights I realized I was enchanted.

What can I tell you of the months that followed? I was intoxicated by a pleasure that left me both satisfied and delicately unsatisfied. I never saw her by daylight, and if I had I would not have recognized her. At some point in our lovemaking she had revealed her name was Rima, yet I did not search for her among the tribal women bending over the tea bushes, fearful that the brilliant sun might rob me of my enchantment.

My body knew the contours of her body, my hands the features of her face, but to my eyes she was an endless play of shadows, entering my bed in darkness when I was no longer capable of waiting for her so that always she surprised my senses.

She even knew when our passion was in danger of becoming repetition. Then she seduced me with tribal songs in a language I could not understand so that I heard only the sweetness of the melodies. She told me tales of a great serpent kingdom lying inches beneath the soil. She spoke to me of charms that gave men the strength of elephants in rut and of magic performed during the eclipse of the moon when a man's soul could be captured inside the two halves of a coconut.

She swore she had seen an old woman raise flames from the palms of her hands, and a tribal priest cover a mango seedling with his shawl, then pull it away to reveal a dwarf tree bending under the weight of ripe mangoes. Swarming like clusters of black bees in the whiteness of her eyes, her pupils mesmerized me as her low voice gave substance to the worlds I had dreamed of when reading my grandfather's books.

Once again I took pleasure in my work as manager of the garden, and the tea pickers again treated me with the esteem they had withdrawn. Maybe they laughed at me when I sometimes did not answer their questions, but often the only sound I heard were her songs floating in my mind.

For a long time I believed these melodic fragments surfaced from my unconscious. When I finally realized they were actually being sung by the women as they picked leaves, I asked Mr. Sen to translate the words.

Poor Mr. Sen looked embarrassed but at my insistence he mournfully translated,

Which god is notorious
In the neighborhood?

Look! It is the god of fucking
Who is notorious in the neighborhood.

The women noticed what we were doing and shouted with laughter as they changed their song.

On the hill
See the peacock's feathers sway
As I am swaying on your lap,
Sighing on your lap,
Smiling on your lap.
O, my handsome friend.

Then to my delight the women began singing the song Rima often sang to awaken me, and I wrote the words down as Mr. Sen translated.

Bring me my oil and my collyrium.
Sister, bring my mirror and the vermilion.
Make haste with my flower garland.
My lover waits impatient in the bed.

For a year Rima came to me every night, sliding into my ebony bed to coil her limbs around me. Like a magician she drew me into a subterranean world of dream, her body teaching mine the passing of the seasons, the secret rhythms of nature, until I understood why my grandfather's books called these hills Kamarupa, the Kingdom of the God of Love.

The Chairman's telegram ended my delirium. "Head Office reorganizing Company. Proceed to Calcutta immediately to study innovations."

I tore the telegram in a rage, certain that Ashok had forced the Chairman's decision, but there was nothing I could do. The telegram was not a suggestion. It was a command.

Rima wept as if her heart were breaking when I told her I was leaving. Gratified by her tears, I made love to her with an ardor that surprised me, so exhausted by my exertions I almost didn't hear her ask, "Should I return to my husband? He works as a coolie at the railway depot in Agartala. Should I join him while you are gone?"

Such was my enchantment with Rima's strangeness that I did not find it odd that she was married. And I could tolerate the thought that another man might embrace her. After all, who had I slept with all those years in Calcutta but other men's wives?

But that he should be a coolie. That I should love a coolie's wife. Waves of disgust engulfed me and I wanted to vomit with shame. At that moment the spell in which Rima held me was broken. For the first time I remained awake when she climbed out of the bed to wrap herself in her sarong. Her limbs were squat and ugly in the light of dawn.

How glad I was to return to Calcutta and the insouciance of my old life of clubs, friends, and betting.

The very superficiality of my colleagues dulled my shame. How hard I laughed at their jokes as they bought drinks for me at the bars of the Saturday Club, the Tolleygunge Club, the Calcutta Club, the Turf Club.

How lightheartedly I flirted with the sophisticated, husky-voiced women whose boredom I briefly diverted by the novelty of my presence. And when they took me to their bedrooms, I kept the lights on as I kissed their large eyes that did not slant upward like Rima's, until I buried the memory of Rima's body in their warm brown flesh.

I could no longer resist the excitement of Head Office. The international shipping arrangements and insurance problems, the constant deadlines presented by bids taken in London or Hong Kong, made my life in the tea garden seem primitive, governed as it was by the grinding slowness of the changing seasons. I did not want to go back to that isolated house or the demands of the bovine tea pickers. I did not want to return to Rima.

Encouraged by Ashok, the Chairman invited me again to become a director. This time I accepted eagerly and it was agreed that I would return to the tea garden to organize things for my successor, then take a few weeks' leave before assuming my new appointment.

I felt a certain trepidation at returning to the tea estate for the last time. Rima had wept so much at my departure for Calcutta that I dreaded her reaction when she learned I would be leaving her permanently.

I could no longer remember any desire for Rima but I could not overlook her poverty, and I decided it was only fair that she should earn something from our association. Hoping to avoid recriminations, I left money with the head bearer, instructing him to deliver it to Rima.

To my surprise she did not try to see me. I knew she was in the tea garden because at night I heard a voice singing in the darkness outside,

Bring me my oil and my collyrium.
Sister, bring my mirror and the vermilion.

I pretended not to hear and continued reading, but even in my cowardice I appreciated Rima's discretion in leaving me alone, which seemed so elegant in someone of her origins.

Her subtlety was greater than I understood. By standing outside my bedroom every night, she succeeded in turning my cowardice into guilt. Night after night I lay in the ebony bed unable to concentrate on my book as I listened to the voice outside my window singing,

Make haste with my flower garland.
My lover waits impatient in the bed.

Unable to tolerate my guilt, one night I opened the door leading into the garden. I could still hear her singing but there was no one there. Then I heard her call, "Nitin. Nitin Bose."

"Rima, come inside. I want to talk to you." There was no answer so I repeated my request. Again she did not respond. For several minutes I stood there calling her to come inside, but no one replied.

Instead of returning to my room, I waited in the shadows. After a while I heard a rustling in the undergrowth, then the sound of breaking twigs as footsteps retreated into the woods that ringed my house. I ran to the wall. As I flung my leg over it I heard her call again, "Nitin. Nitin Bose."

"Rima, wait! I must talk to you!" I shouted.

"Nitin Bose!" The voice grew fainter as she ran into the trees. The darkness was so dense I wished I had taken a torch from the guard so I could see my way. Then I remembered the moon was in eclipse that night, and the superstitious guard would not venture out of doors on a night so full of ill omen.

Heedless of the low branches whipping against my body, I ran after her through the jungle, calling her name, my voice loud in the night.

Suddenly, almost in front of me, she shouted, "Nitin. Nitin Bose."

"Yes," I answered in surprise. There was the noise of something being clapped over something else, like two books slapped together. As I heard that sound I felt the air being sucked out of my lungs.

Nothing touched me but I felt as if a pump had been forcibly placed over my lips and nose. I gasped for air, unable to breathe. Over the noise of my own suffocation I heard laughter, then the striking of a match. A lantern flared in the darkness, lighting a woman's face from below as she adjusted the flame.

Rima placed the lantern at her feet and retrieved something from the ground.

"You will never leave me now, no matter how far you go," she said triumphantly, waving her trophy in front of me. It was a coconut, the split halves covering each other. I clutched at her, feeling myself begin to fall, but she eluded me and I hit the ground. Picking up her lantern, she disappeared into the jungle.

I lay under the trees, the stench of decomposing vegetation filling my nostrils as I tried to suck air into my bursting lungs. Over my harsh breathing I could hear her vengeful song growing fainter and fainter in the darkness:

Bring me my oil and my collyrium.
Sister, bring my mirror and the vermilion.
Make haste with my flower garland.
My lover waits impatient in the bed.

It is the last clear memory I have.

The passage that follows was dictated by the head bearer at my request.

"At dawn the guard made a round of the house before he went to his quarters. The door of your bedroom was open and your bed had not been slept in. Finding you nowhere on the grounds, the guard went to search for you in the woods.

"He found you lying in the mud. He asked if you were all right but you talked only nonsense, calling the name Rima again and again and singing a song our tribal women sing at the time of marriage.

"The guard ran to my room and woke me up. Together we managed to carry you from the woods to your bed. We could see you were not physically ill and we were frightened. We realized you had gone out during the eclipse. Perhaps you did not know that a man can become fatally ill or mad if he walks outside during the eclipse of the moon. We sent for the priest of the tribal village to ask his advice before we informed Mr. Sen.

"The priest tried to talk to you, asking why you had been walking in the jungle on such an inauspicious night. Who had you gone to meet. But you just sang and called this Rima's name, your eyes so strange, like a madman's. The priest told us to let no one see you and he went away.

"He returned an hour later with a covered basket. He asked me to heat some milk while he went to your bedside. I brought the warm milk, thinking he had some medicine for you. When I reached your bed I screamed with fear and dropped it. The priest was holding a snake only inches from your face and reciting some spell. I could see the snake's tongue flicking out to touch the skin of your face. But you did not wince, or even blink. That frightened me even more.

"I heated fresh milk. The priest took the bowl and put it on the floor for the snake. While the snake was drinking the milk he prayed to it in a language I could not understand. Suddenly you said to him, 'What are you doing in my room?'

"The priest explained you had been singing and talking about a woman named Rima. He asked you to get up and write an account of everything you remembered about your association with her.

"All day you sat at your desk writing. The effort exhausted you and you were already asleep when the priest returned. He asked me to warm some milk and performed the same ceremony of the morning, praying to the snake while it drank the milk. At that point you woke up, but you were not strange-seeming anymore. You even told the priest, 'I don't know what made me behave this way.'

"The priest explained, 'Someone has taken possession of you. The magic you are under is stronger than my powers. It will start exerting its strength again. Your memory will be affected. You will believe yourself to be someone else.'

" 'What nonsense!' you shouted at the priest. 'I don't believe in magic. Someone must be trying to poison me. Was I bitten by that snake?'

" 'This serpent has helped you. But only a little. And not for very long.'

"You refused to believe the priest. For the next week you sent for the doctor every day. The doctor kept telling you there was nothing wrong with you. Then you began drinking whisky, but the more you drank the less control you had over your mind, singing that song about oil and vermilion or calling yourself Rima. Finally I sent for the priest again.

"He told me, 'If your sahib wants to recover his mind he must worship the goddess at any shrine that overlooks the Narmada River. Only that river has been given the power to cure him.' "

When I finally closed Nitin Bose's diary, it was too late to sleep. I was sorry for the young man, but his story made no sense to me. Exhausted by my own incomprehension, I went to the terrace.

As always, the darkness that precedes the dawn stilled my mind. I could not see the Narmada, but I sat with my face turned to the east where the river reveals herself to the holy men ringing the pool at Amarkantak, wondering what the ascetics thought about as they watched the water flowing from some secret stream, whispering in eddies below their crossed legs, mysterious and alluring in the dying night.

Did they brood on the Narmada as the proof of Shiva's great penance, or did they imagine her as a beautiful woman dancing toward the Arabian Sea, arousing the lust of ascetics like themselves while Shiva laughed at the madness of their infatuation?

Dawn lightened the sky and I was able to see the Narmada leaping headlong through the distant marble rocks, the spraying waterfalls refracting the first rays of sun into arcs of color as if the river were a woman adorning herself with jewels.

Below the terrace the water was still dark, appearing motionless in the shadows like a woman indolently stretching her limbs as she oiled herself with scented oils, her long black hair loosened, her eyes outlined in collyrium.

I watched the water slowly redden, catching reflections from the rose colors of dawn, and imagined the river as a woman painting her palms and the soles of her feet with vermilion as she prepared to meet her lover.

It was the first time I had entertained such thoughts about the river. Now the legends of the Narmada merged with Nitin Bose's story as I struggled to understand the power of the woman who had enchanted him.

If even the Great Ascetic could not withstand the weapons unleashed from Kama's sugarcane bow strung with honeybees, how could poor Nitin Bose survive as Kama's arrows found their mark, piercing him with enchantment, inflaming him with lust, parching him with desire, rendering him helpless with the paroxysms of his own longing, until he was wounded with that fifth and fatal arrow, the Carrier of Death?

The sun appeared above the Vindhya Hills, a fiery ball of light leeching the color from the water until it shone like glass, as hard as woman's pursuit of a lover. The bright light hurt my eyes. I turned from the terrace and saw the staff waiting for my instructions. I issued the first orders of the morning. Then I wrote a note to Mr. Chagla advising him to keep an eye on Nitin Bose because I was going to bed.

"Sir! Wake up, sir. You must get ready!"

I opened my eyes. Mr. Chagla's round face was peering down at me, moisture beading his fingerprints on an iced glass.

"Here, sir. Drink some juice."

"How is our visitor, Chagla?"

"Excellent, sir. You will see when he comes back from the shrine."

"You let him go to the shrine by himself?"

"As if, sir! The guards went with him. Also, their wives."

"They are illiterate villagers." I could hear my voice rising with fear. "Why didn't you accompany him? What if he harms himself?"

"I couldn't, sir. They will not let outsiders come to their shrine. But I have given stern instructions. Mr. Bose must be returned to us in A-one condition."

"How has Bose gone with them? He is not a tribal."

"They say he has been touched by the power of the goddess so he is not an outsider anymore. Anyway, don't perturb yourself, sir. I know everything what is going to happen. Their shrine is only a big banyan tree. Nothing harmful. There the villagers will have an assembly with Mr. Bose. Now hurry, sir. You must take refreshment. The cook is waiting in the dining room with your meal."

Mr. Chagla left my room and I washed hastily. As I was dressing I shouted to him through the closed door, "What happens in the assembly? Did the guards tell you?"

"The tribals will beg the goddess to forgive Mr. Bose for denying the power of desire."

"Power of desire?" I demanded as I came out, reassured by the brilliant afternoon sunlight and my starched clothes. "Chagla, have you been infected by this foolishness?"

Mr. Chagla looked at me with the anxiety of a parent watching a willful child. "But, sir, without desire there is no life. Everything will stand still. Become emptiness. In fact, sir, be dead."

I stared at him in astonishment, and Mr. Chagla's smooth face wrinkled with the effort of making me comprehend. "It is not a woman who has taken possession of Mr. Bose's soul, sir. How can such a thing ever happen?"

"Then what is all this goddess business?"

"Sir. Really, sir." Mr. Chagla sighed in frustration. "The goddess is just the principle of life. She is every illusion that is inspiring love. That is why she is greater than all the gods combined. Call her what you will, but she is what a mother is feeling for a child. A man for a woman. A starving man for food. Human beings for God. And Mr. Bose did not show her respect so he is being punished."

"By sitting under a tree?"

"No, sir. He will not be sitting. The villagers will be sitting. Mr. Bose will be making a mud image of the goddess."

"What for?"

"To carry to the river for immersing purposes. I have found a spot where we can observe the procession, hidden from the human eye. But you must eat first, sir. These tribals have no sense of time."

I could feel the situation sliding out of my control. "What is the point of the procession?"

"Ritual, ritual, and ritual, sir. Like repeating your two-times table."

"Chagla, you are not making sense."

"Certainly I am, sir. It is Mr. Bose who is making no sense, pretending desire is some kind of magic performed with black arts. But desire is the origin of life. For thousands of years our tribals have worshipped it as the goddess. You have heard the pilgrims praying 'Save us from the serpent's venom.' Well, sir, the meaning of the prayer is as follows. The serpent in question is desire. Its venom is the harm a man does when he is ignoring the power of desire."

Defeated by Mr. Chagla's good nature, I walked to the dining room, wondering if his open face and rotund body hid an understanding that I did not possess. As I ate, I tried to fathom what Mr. Chagla had been saying while my eyes wandered idly over the mosaics of flowers and birds inlaid into the dining-room walls.

The sound of drumbeats and singing voices brought Mr. Chagla running into the room. "Sir, hurry! The procession is coming through the jungle."

I ran up the stairs followed by the cook and other curious members of the bungalow staff. We crowded onto the terrace of Nitin Bose's suite, which overlooked the jungle.

Trees obscured the steep path leading down to the riverbank, but there was an open space where we could see a line of villagers following a garlanded idol carried on a platform supported by long bamboo poles. Four men held the poles to their shoulders. I recognized them as bungalow guards. Behind them I caught a brief glimpse of Nitin Bose's face. Then he disappeared down the curve of the path, and I could see only the idol above the bushes, rocking on its platform as the men descended the steep incline.

Mr. Chagla gently pulled at my elbow, whispering conspiratorially, "Sir, let us go to my hidey-hole to observe the ceremony."

I followed him down the stairs and into the garden. At a corner of the garden he opened a rusting iron gate that led to the water tanks below the terrace. The path was used once a year when the water tanks were inspected. Now Mr. Chagla walked in front of me crushing nettles and weeds underfoot to clear the way to a rock escarpment halfway down the hillside.

We crouched behind a boulder as the procession skidded down the steep path. Mr. Chagla had chosen a perfect vantage point. We had a clear view of the riverbank two hundred feet below us, and I could even see fish swimming in the clear water of the river slowly turning gray in the approaching dusk.

The procession stumbled down the slope, and the guards yelled to each other, struggling to keep the idol from sliding off the tilting platform as they lowered it to the ground.

The procession of villagers fell back to allow Nitin Bose to approach the idol. He looked dazed. For a long moment he stood in front of the mud image and nothing happened. Then, as if he had suddenly remembered an instruction, he put his arms around the idol, lifting it from the ground. Holding the idol, he walked into the water. The tribals waded in behind him, their hands raised, their faces turned to the west. The crimson sunset reddened their features as Nitin Bose immersed the idol in the river, chanting

Salutations in the morning and at night to thee, O Narmada. Defend me from the serpent's poison.

The mud idol began to disintegrate in the current, and we watched fragments of the image being swept downstream—a broken arm, a breast, torn garlands spinning in the water as they were carried toward the clay lamps floating in the darkness at the river's bend.

The temple bells from Mahadeo were ringing for the evening prayers. Mr. Chagla got to his feet and began stamping down the nettles. "It will be completely dark soon, sir. Let us return to the bungalow before we are eaten up by snakes."

I stood up. Below us I could barely see the shadowy figures of the Vano villagers still standing around Bose in the water. I followed Mr. Chagla up the pathway to the bungalow, the voices of the villagers growing fainter as they chanted after Nitin Bose,

Salutations in the morning and at night to thee, O Narmada. Defend me from the serpent's poison.

For three weeks Nitin Bose remained in the bungalow, a source of constant concern to me.

I could not concentrate on my dawn meditations listening to him sliding down the steep path that led to the river. I was always afraid he would fall or be bitten by a snake before he reached the riverbank to make his salutation.

In the evenings I no longer enjoyed watching the sunset from our terrace for fear some harm might come to him standing waist deep in the water below me, praying to the Narmada.

Never having been a parent, I found this unfamiliar burden of responsibility an irritant. I considered Nitin Bose a foolish young man who attracted misfortune, even though Mr. Chagla told me he appeared to be working on something because his desk was covered with papers.

I was greatly relieved when Nitin Bose finally left us and the bungalow returned to its routine serenity.

Shortly after his departure I received a letter from my old colleague thanking me for looking after his nephew.

"I knew I could rely on your discretion. Incidentally, Nitin showed me a most interesting essay he has written concerning the tribal practices in your area. I have asked him to submit it to the *Asia Review* for publication."

Mr. Chagla was pleased to hear about the essay. "And guess what, sir?"

"What, Chagla?"

"Only yesterday I heard some village children singing on the path to Vano. Do you know what they were singing?

Bring me my oil and my collyrium.
Sister, bring my mirror and the vermilion.

"Nothing is ever lost, sir. That is the beauty of a river view." ∾

INTERPRETIVE QUESTIONS
FOR DISCUSSION

Why does Nitin Bose go mad after ending his love affair with Rima?

1. During the long drive to the tea estate, why does Nitin Bose feel himself move "from disbelief, to tranquility, to that possessiveness by which one is oneself possessed"? (52)

2. Why does Nitin Bose so easily become a "pukka" sahib of the tea estate—a "British fantasy of India, untouched by the chaos of the last forty years"? (53) Why does he begin to "exhibit the mannerisms of an elder" and experience his "old self" as a shortening shadow merging with his "new self"? (54)

3. Why does Nitin Bose become fascinated by the Indian legends he reads in his grandfather's library? (55) Why, after being seized by sexual restlessness, does he think he has perhaps become the victim of his grandfather's books? (58)

4. Why does Ashok tell Nitin Bose that his contentment with his ascetic, isolated life means that he is going mad? (56)

5. Why is Nitin Bose content with his solitary life on the tea estate until Ashok's visit? What does Nitin Bose mean when he speculates that the loneliness triggered by Ashok's visit "caused my mind to create its own enslavement"? (58)

6. Why is Nitin Bose unable to recover his tranquility by plunging into his work with "redoubled intensity"? Why, feeling as if he had "become Mr. Sen," does Nitin Bose follow the example of his predecessors and begin drinking himself into oblivion? (57)

7. Why does Nitin Bose become "bewitched" by Rima? (58) Why, after Rima leaves his bed, does he dream that he still holds "a creature half serpent" in his arms, and that his sated senses have pulled him into the underground world of his grandfather's legends? (59; cf. 60)

8. When their passion is in danger of "becoming repetition," why does Rima seduce Nitin Bose with tribal songs, myths, and tales of magic? (59–60) Why does Rima's lovemaking teach Nitin Bose "the passing of the seasons, the secret rhythms of nature"? (61)

9. Why is Nitin Bose once again satisfied with managing the tea estate after Rima begins to come to him every night? (60)

10. Why is Nitin Bose's enchantment with Rima destroyed when he is recalled to Calcutta and learns that she is the wife of a coolie? (61)

11. Why does Nitin Bose interpret Rima's singing as a subtle device to induce guilt? Why does Nitin Bose become possessed by Rima when he chases her into the night, unable to tolerate his guilt and longing to talk to her? (63–64)

12. Why does Rima avenge herself on Nitin Bose by performing magic to capture his soul? (59, 64) Why is Rima's magic stronger than the tribal priest's? (66)

Suggested textual analyses

Pages 54–55: beginning, "I found I enjoyed," and ending, "guarded by hooded cobras."

Pages 61–64: beginning, "But that he should be a coolie," and ending, "she disappeared into the jungle."

Why do both the narrator and Nitin Bose attempt to deny the power of desire?

1. Why does Nitin Bose's story make no sense to the narrator? (66, 69)

2. Why does Nitin Bose feel claustrophobic and as if his life is "leaking away" when he is living carefree in Calcutta? (49) Why is he fascinated by the "careless self-destruction" of the tea estate boys and filled with "envious admiration"? (50–51)

3. Why is the narrator astonished by those who, unlike himself, seek to "generate the heat, the tapas, that links men to the energy of the universe" through the endurance of the Narmada pilgrimage? (37)

4. Why does recalling the myth of how Shiva, the Great Ascetic, incinerated Kama, the God of Love, cause the narrator to be alarmed by the prospect of a visit from a young man who is interested in tribal customs? (42)

5. Why does the narrator feel at first cheered but then threatened by the sexual teasing of the Vano women? (40, 42)

6. Why does the narrator fear that "mythology might at any moment become reality"? (39)

7. Are we meant to think that Nitin Bose is denying the power of desire when he tires of his adulterous liaisons in Calcutta?

8. Why does the simple and good-natured Mr. Chagla need to explain to the narrator that "the goddess is just the principle of life. She is every illusion that is inspiring love"? Why does it make sense to Mr. Chagla that Nitin Bose must be punished for not showing the goddess respect? (69)

9. Why does the narrator feel less sympathy for Nitin Bose than Mr. Chagla does? Why does the narrator consider Nitin Bose a "foolish young man"? (72)

10. Why does the narrator wonder whether the holy men meditating before the Narmada see the river as the proof of Shiva's great penance, or as a beautiful woman who arouses the lust of men like themselves? (66–67)

11. Are we meant to agree with the narrator when he claims to be a *vanaprasthi,* even though he continues to work for the government and enjoys the company of educated, worldly men? (33)

12. Why does Nitin Bose fail in his attempt to retire peacefully from life?

Suggested textual analyses

Pages 41–42: beginning, "A flock of parakeets," and ending, "pulling me back into the day."

Pages 68–70: beginning, "Sir! Wake up, sir," and ending, "the mosaics of flowers and birds inlaid into the dining-room walls."

Why can Nitin Bose resume his role as an urban executive after his sojourn to the Narmada River?

1. Why does Nitin Bose find the Head Office exciting after he leaves Rima and the tea estate, dismissing his three years of contentment in the tea garden as a "primitive" existence? (62)

2. Why does the superficiality of his friends in Calcutta dull the shame Nitin Bose feels when he discovers that he has loved a coolie's wife? (62)

3. Why does the sophisticated and educated Nitin Bose believe that if he cannot visit the Vano shrine he will have to kill himself? (45, 46)

4. Why does Nitin Bose's madness take the form of imagining that he is possessed and saying that he himself is Rima? (44, 66)

5. Why is the Narmada River "thought to link mankind to the energy of Shiva"? (37)

6. Why is the fertility goddess of the Vano villagers reputed to have the power to cure madness? (36) Why are we told that the Narmada River was created by the rivulets of perspiration flowing from Shiva when he was in a strenuous ascetic trance? (37–38)

7. Why does Mr. Chagla accept that Nitin Bose must go through the Vano ceremony because "ritual, ritual, and ritual" is as necessary as "repeating your two-times table"? (69)

8. Why does Nitin Bose's cure consist of making a mud image of the goddess that disintegrates in the river? (71)

9. Why are the Vano villagers able to help Nitin Bose recapture his soul? Why must Nitin Bose pray for three weeks to the Narmada River in order to be cured of his obsession? (71–72)

10. Why does Nitin Bose once again come to view Indian mythology "through the prism of anthropology" and write an article on Vano tribal practices, suitable for publication in the *Asia Review*? (55, 72)

11. Why does the tale of Nitin Bose end with Mr. Chagla's observing, "Nothing is ever lost, sir. That is the beauty of a river view"? (72)

12. Does Nitin Bose succeed or fail in his attempt to find spiritual peace and contentment?

Suggested textual analyses

Pages 35–38: beginning, "My day usually begins on this terrace," and ending, "calling the faithful to prayer."

Pages 70–72: from "We crouched behind a boulder," to the end of the story.

FOR FURTHER REFLECTION

1. Is all happiness, and all fulfillment of desire, only a passing, elusive state?

2. How do you interpret from a Western perspective the myth of Shiva—the Great Ascetic—creating from the sweat of his trance the most dangerous kind of seductive woman and blessing her as the Narmada River?

3. How can one know if one is denying the power of desire?

4. Do you agree that "without Desire the play of the worlds would cease"? Is desire the "origin of life"?

5. Should Westerners embrace the Hindu tradition of becoming a *vanaprasthi*?

6. Are we all in need of "ritual, ritual, and ritual" at some time in our lives?

THE THREE LIVES OF
LUCIE CABROL

John Berger

JOHN BERGER (1926–   ) was born in London. He began his career as a painter and drawing teacher. In addition to short stories and novels, Berger has written poetry, plays, and nonfiction works on topics ranging from literary and art criticism to history and sociology. When his novel *G* won the Booker Prize in 1972, Berger—an avowed Marxist—denounced the sponsors and proclaimed that he would donate half of the prize money to the Black Panthers. "The Three Lives of Lucie Cabrol" is the culminating story in *Pig Earth,* the first of three books in Berger's *Into Their Labours* trilogy, which chronicles the demise of European peasant life. Berger makes his home in a small village in the French Alps.

THE FIRST LIFE OF LUCIE CABROL

THE COCADRILLE WAS BORN in 1900 in the month of September. White cloud, like smoke, was blowing through the open door of the stable. Marius Cabrol was milking. His wife, Mélanie, was in bed, on the other side of the stable wall, attended by her sister and a neighbour. Their first child had been a boy, christened Emile. Marius, the father, hoped that the second would also be a son. He would be named Henri, after his grandfather.

The Cabrol farm is on a slope above the village which is called Brine. On the south side of the house the ground flattens out and there are plum trees and a quince. Beside the house is a stream which Henri, the grandfather, channelled to drive a saw. If a log started to roll from up there, it wouldn't stop till it reached the church. I like to think of the logs I have rolled from high up! If the log is not straight, it leaps like an animal. You watch it from above and it is like an animal galloping. Gradually as the slope levels out, it slows down. When you expect it to lie still, it leaps again. It takes a long time for the flat ground to kill a rolling log.

On the bed Mélanie gripped the headboard. The water was already boiling on the stove in the kitchen. The baby was born very quickly. When I think of her being born, my mind wanders and I see her fishing. She was fourteen and I was three years older. She walked upstream, watching both banks. When she prodded with a stick under a stone, two dark shadows slipped across the river to the other bank. From that moment onwards she never shifted her gaze. She tucked her skirt into its own waistband and without looking down for an instant she waded across. There she stood absolutely still. The water flowing round her thighs made the same noise as it does flowing round two small stationary rocks. One of the trout left the overhanging bank and darted under a boulder. Was it because she was so small that she was so quick? Or was it because, being blind to warnings, she could read signs which are lost on others? Frisking under the boulder, she trapped the fish and pressed upwards with all the force of her small hand against the stone. The fish was fixed there like a long tongue. And, like a tongue, it tried to retract itself, reaching back down the throat of the water. It tried to thrust forward out of the throat. It tried to turn on its side. Slowly, never letting up the pressure of her palm, she inserted a tiny finger between tongue and stone and two more fingers between tongue and palm. All this with one hand. The instant he went still, she had him out of the water wedged between her three fingers, two with their backs to him.

It's a girl! cried the neighbour.

La Mélanie looked tenderly, and with surprise, at the tiny body, the colour of a radish, held upside down.

Give her to me.

On the forehead of the baby's puckered face was a dark red mark.

Jésus! Forgive me! La Mélanie screamed. She is marked with the mark of the craving.

When a woman is pregnant, she sometimes craves for something special to eat or drink or touch. It is the right of the mother, by a kind of decree of nature, to have what she wants.

Yet often it is not possible, and it is then that she must be careful. For if one of her cravings is denied, the next time she touches her body, the touch may be printed in the same place on the embryo in her womb. And so it is better when one of her cravings has been unsatisfied, for her to touch deliberately her foot or her bottom: otherwise, without thinking, she may touch her cheek or her ear and this will be printed as a disfiguring mark on the child.

Jésus! cried La Mélanie again. I have marked her face with the mark of the craving.

Mélanie, be calm. It is not the mark of the craving. I've seen it often. It is where her face rubbed as she came out, said her sister.

The neighbour took the baby to press the top of her head so that it should be as round as possible.

It was when I wanted to eat freshwater fish! La Mélanie insisted.

Her sister was proved right, for in a few days the red mark disappeared, and only much later did La Mélanie ask herself whether her daughter had not, after all, been marked by the mark of another kind of craving. As a young child, two things were unusual about her. She remained very small. And as soon as she could crawl, and later walk, she had a habit of disappearing.

You lose her as easily as you lose a button, La Mélanie said.

I think of Lucie—for that is how she was christened—as a baby in her cradle. What is the difference between a baby and a small animal? An animal goes straight along its own path. A baby vacillates, rolling first to one side and then to the other. Either she's all smiles and gurgles, or a face all puckered up and bawling.

When she was six, Lucie was missing for a whole day. If I go out of the door now and take a few steps up the hillside to where the cows are grazing, I can see the track she took.

It leads to the skyline where the moon rises. In August when the cows are grazing up there, they are silhouetted as if against a great circular lantern. From there the path leads along the crest to a pass where there are some marmots, through a moraine of boulders the size of houses, along the edge of an escarpment, and finally down to the forest below.

In the evening Lucie came back with her hat full of mushrooms. Yet by that time, Marius à Brine had organised a search party. I remember the men filling their lamps with paraffin.

When there wasn't any work to be done at home, Lucie went to school. The village teacher was called Masson. He used to read from the *Life of Voltaire* and the curé preached against this book in church. One thing impressed me about the *Life of Voltaire*. When there was famine, he distributed sacks of grain among the peasants at Ferney. Otherwise, the *Life of Voltaire* belonged to that collection of books which we knew existed and which entailed a way of life we could not imagine. At what time of day did people read? we asked ourselves.

Masson was killed at Verdun. His name is on the war memorial. Each morning, before the first lesson began, he wrote on the blackboard the day of the week, the date of the month, and the year of the century. On the war memorial there is only the month and the year of his death: March 1916. After the date each morning, he wrote a saying on the blackboard which we children copied into our books:

Insults should be written on sand
Compliments should be inscribed on marble.

It was in her last year at school that Lucie was given the nickname of the Cocadrille. A *cocadrille* comes from a cock's egg hatched in a dung heap. As soon as it comes out of its egg, it makes its way to the most unlikely place. If it is seen by somebody it has not seen, it dies. Otherwise, it can defend itself and can kill anything it chooses, except the weasel. The poison, with which it kills, comes from its eyes and travels along its gaze.

Soon after Lucie was born, La Mélanie had another son, who was christened Henri. By the time he was two, he was larger than his sister, who could by then sit on the horse, fetch wood for the stove, and feed the chickens. It could be that her tiny size was a kind of provocation to jealousy. Small children normally accord rights according to size. Whatever the reason, Henri hated his sister. It was he who, forty years later, said to the Mayor: This sister has never brought anything but shame to our family.

One day Mélanie found three of her chickens dead. The killer was not a fox or a weasel, for the chickens were untouched.

Lucie killed them! shouted Henri, she looked at them and they died.

I never touched them!

She's a Cocadrille!

I'm not! I'm not!

The Cocadrille! The Cocadrille! shouted Henri.

Stop your bickering, the mother grumbled.

That time the nickname did not stick. The next time it did.

It was between Easter and Whitsun. Later, when I was in the Argentine, I used to tell myself that I could not die until I had seen another month of May, here in the mountains. The grass grows knee-high in the meadows and down the centre of the roads between the wheel ruts. If you are with a friend, you walk down the road with the grass between you. In the forest the late beech leaves come out, the greenest leaves in the world. The cows are let out of the stable for the first time. They leap, kick with their hind legs, turn in circles, jump like goats. The month itself is like a homecoming.

Her brother Emile had left in the autumn to work in Paris as a stoker for the central heating of the new department store of Samaritaine. La Mélanie could not read the postcard which had come, so she gave it to Lucie.

Emile's coming home!

When?

Sunday.

On the Friday Marius chose the largest of his black rabbits, and, holding it up by its ears, he felt its flesh through the fur.

Yes, you big crook, Emile is coming home!

He stroked it again and then knocked it unconscious with one blow. Delicately, he cut out its two eyes. Their lashes remained unhurt round the two holes through which the blood flowed when he hung it up by its hind legs to bleed. On Sunday morning Mélanie skinned it and cooked it in cider.

Emile's present for Lucie was a silver-painted model of the Eiffel Tower.

Did you see it? she asked in excitement.

You see it everywhere. It's three hundred metres high.

At the end of the meal La Mélanie collected up in her hands the neat piles of bones laid on the table beside each plate. The rabbit bones were so clean they looked as if they were made from horn or ivory on which there had never been meat. She was happy. Her son who had come home was already asleep in his room.

Each evening Henri and Lucie took the milk down to the dairy. Lucie's size never affected her strength. She was as tough as a mountain goat. The same as Henri, she carried twenty litres on her back, the can strapped on like a school satchel. That evening, after he had slept, Emile said he would go with them.

Give me the milk, Lucie.

She refused. Her head was scarcely higher than Emile's waist.

Could you find me a job in Paris? she asked.

You could work in a baker's.

Do you live in the same place as you work?

I catch the *métro*. The *métro* is a train, an electric train that goes underground . . .

What time do the trains start in the morning? asked Henri.

Early, but the Parisians can't get out of bed. So they're always in a hurry. You should see them running along the tunnels to catch the trains.

The trains don't stop? asked the Cocadrille.

The path down to the village followed a stream and near the bottom was a lilac tree. When the lilac was in flower, you could smell the tree thirty metres away.

Tell me more about Paris.

People sleep in the streets, said Emile.

Why?

If they asked for shelter, the Parisians would never let them come in.

Why don't they build sheds?

There is no wood to build with.

No trees?

It's forbidden.

Do you know what Grandfather Revuz did? Lucie asked. The Mayor told him he couldn't cut down an acacia. And he cut it down. After he cut it down, he said the leaves on that bush were too small for him to wipe his arse on! And if they were that small, he said, it couldn't have been an acacia.

Grandfather Revuz may think he's clever but he'd be lost in Paris, said Emile. Do you know how many horses there are there?

Fifty thousand! guessed Henri.

Two million, said Emile with pride.

Will you take me with you next time? Lucie asked.

They would lock you up! said Henri.

When they went into the dairy, the cheesemaker straightened his back, extended a hand, and shouted:

So 'Mile is back from Paris!

For the summer.

How old are you now?

Sixteen, Emile replied.

Never too young!

The cheesemaker, whose wife cuckolded him regularly, winked.

Henri and Lucie unstrapped their cans. In the middle of the dairy a cauldron hung from its wooden gallows. The dairy was well placed because it was cool even in summer. The cheesemaker's wife complained that her husband's feet were perpetually like ice.

Did you climb to the top? Lucie asked Emile.

What top?

The top of the Eiffel Tower!

You go up by a lift, Emile said.

Lift?

Yes, lift.

What's a lift? she asked.

The Cocadrille knows nothing, roared Henri, laughing. The proper place for her is her dung heap.

None of them was looking at her. She removed the lid of her milk can. She picked it up and, as you throw water out of a bucket, she hurled litres of milk into Henri's face. Whilst the milk was dripping from his hair, she screamed:

If you weren't a weasel I'd kill you!

The cheesemaker, swearing, tried to hit her, but she escaped, ran round the cauldron, and vanished out of the door.

The story soon reached the ears of Marius à Brine. He found his daughter by the washing trough and he started to beat her, shouting:

Milk is not water! Milk is not water!

After a few blows he stopped. She was staring at him with her bright blue eyes. She had eyes the colour of forget-me-nots. Her look forced him to gather her into his arms and to press her face against his stomach.

Ah! My Cocadrille. You came out like that, didn't you? You can't help it. You just came out like that.

She stepped with her small feet onto his boots and then he carried her on his feet across the yard, repeating and laughing: The Cocadrille! The Cocadrille!

And so the name Cocadrille, born of both hatred and love, replaced the name Lucie. When she was thirteen, a circus came to the village and put up its tent in the square. The circus consisted of one family, a goat which could stand on the smallest milking stool we ever saw, and two ponies. The father was ringmaster, the mother was acrobat, and their son was the clown. During the afternoon the son went round the cafés of the village and blew a trumpet to announce the evening performance. The men smiled at the trumpet but they did not invite him to drink, lest he make fun of them.

The circus also had an elephant. The elephant was a piece of grey cloth with a trunk sewn onto it. When the ringmaster turned to the benches where the kids were sitting and asked for volunteers, I rushed forward. I was the front of the elephant, and Joset, who was killed in an avalanche, was the back. Together we danced to an accordion which the clown was playing.

And now for a cow elephant! shouted the ringmaster, holding up a second piece of grey cloth. Two pretty girls please! The second piece of cloth had a pearl necklace painted on it, and from the huge folds of its ears hung a pair of earrings painted gold. The rings had been taken from a horse's bit.

The girls were all too shy. Not one put up her hand. I lifted up the cloth of the elephant's head and, facing the girls, cried out:

The Cocadrille! The Cocadrille! The Cocadrille!

And she came! Everyone in the tent clapped and laughed at the tiny figure who was going to be part of an elephant.

I heard the ringmaster whisper to his son:

She's a dwarf. Find out her age.

For a moment the Cocadrille stood there alone, eyes alight. Finally another girl climbed over the benches and joined her. Beside the Cocadrille, the other girl looked like a giant. The clown began to play music—a violin this time. The only way the Cocadrille could manage was to be the back of the elephant, and instead of bending forward at the waist, she stayed upright and pulled hard at the grey cloth so that it didn't sag in the middle of the animal's back. There we were, two elephants, a bull and a cow, with the violin playing.

There were pictures of elephants in our schoolbooks, because, from Hannibal to Napoleon, foreign generals had the idea of using elephants to cross the mountains. The four of us danced in the middle of the arena, and every time we stopped, the ringmaster cracked his whip over us, and the crowd shouted: Again! Again! Sometimes I caught sight of the Cocadrille's bare feet— she had kicked off her sabots—dancing jerkily at the back of the grey cow elephant.

Eventually they let us go. The clown son whispered something to the Cocadrille and then shook his head at his father, who shrugged his shoulders.

When I saw her next at school I asked her what she had thought of the circus. She didn't mention the dance of the elephants. What she liked, she said, was the clown on stilts. Could I make her a pair? I said I would.

I never made them. More than fifty years later she said to me—her eyes were stone-coloured by then—If I had a pair of stilts, I could cross the valley in ten strides. This was at the time when she was walking a hundred kilometres a week. Ten strides! she repeated.

The Cabrol farm at Brine is on the *advet,* the slope facing south. Opposite on the *ubac,* facing north, is a hamlet called Lapraz. There is a song about the cocks in each hamlet. The one at Lapraz, where there is less sun, calls out:

I sing when I can.

The cock at Brine crows:

I sing when I want!

To this the *ubac* cock replies:

Then be content!

It was on the slope facing Lapraz in August 1914 that the Cabrol family were scything their patch of oats when they heard the church bell ringing in the valley below.

The war has started, said Marius.

The massacre of the world has begun, said La Mélanie.

Women usually know better than men the extent of catastrophe. The Mayor delivered the mobilisation papers. Most of those called up were in high spirits. Never again, not once, were the cafés in the village to be so full as on the evening before the mobilised men left. Marius, older than most of the others—he was thirty-eight—was apprehensive. He avoided the cafés and spent the evening at home, giving instructions to Emile about what had to be done before the snow came, by which time he would be back, and the war would be over.

The band played as the men marched out of the village along the road which followed the river to the plain. The band was smaller than usual, for half its players were among the soldiers who were leaving. I had joined the band the previous autumn and I was the youngest drummer.

Marius did not come back before the snow came, nor before the New Year, nor before the spring. The endless time of war began. The seasons changed, the years passed, and all our lives, except those of the youngest children, who remembered nothing else, were in abeyance. Early in 1916 Emile and I were called up. Between young boys and old men there was nobody left. There were no full male voices to be heard. The horses became accustomed to the commands of women.

La Mélanie, the Cocadrille, and Henri ran the farm. There was so much to be done that the younger brother could not afford to quarrel openly with his sister. If Henri made the Cocadrille angry, she would disappear for the rest of the day, and he realised that they could not do without her labour even for a few hours.

Despite her size, she was tireless. She was like the small hummingbird who, when the time comes to migrate, can fly a thousand miles across the Bay of Mexico. She was not the second woman of the house, she was more like a hired hand—a man. A midget man with a difficult and unpredictable character. She drove the mare, she fetched wood, she led the horse when Henri ploughed, she fed the cows, she dug the garden, she made the cider, she preserved the fruit, she mended the harnesses. She never washed clothes nor sewed. In a *pailler* on top of her head she could carry eighty kilos of hay. If you saw her from behind, it looked like magic: the linen tent, full of hay, completely hid her and so it appeared to be moving down the slope, alone, on its lowermost corner. Both La Mélanie and Henri were somewhat frightened of her when she sat with them in the kitchen. They never knew how she could take what was said.

At the beginning of 1918 the family at Brine received a telegram informing them that Emile had been gravely wounded near Compiègne. Each evening the Cocadrille asked the milk, frothing in the wooden bucket, to keep her brother Emile alive.

He stayed alive and after months in hospital came home. When at last Marius too returned, Mélanie saw that her son now looked older than his father. Nobody in the village spoke of victory, they only spoke of the war being ended.

A year after his demobilisation Marius announced to Emile that La Mélanie was expecting another baby.

At her age! said Emile.

Marius nodded: It will be our last.

It will have to be!

The more scandalised the son's expression, the more the father smiled.

All the war I promised myself that.

And Mother?

I survived.

So we'll be four, concluded Emile.

He meant that the family inheritance would be divided into four.

Yes, if you count the Cocadrille.

Have you told the Cocadrille?

Not yet.

I wonder how she will take it.

It's for Mother to tell her.

It'll change the Cocadrille.

How is that?

It will change her. Me and the Cocadrille, we might be married now with our own children. Yet who is going to marry the Cocadrille? And I'm too sick to marry. It ought to be our turn and, instead, you've made another baby.

Call it an old man's last sin! Marius, however penitent, could not stop smiling.

In December 1919 La Mélanie's last baby was born and was christened Edmond. I stayed in the army an extra year to learn mechanics. I came back to the village at the beginning of 1920.

The following June, four men took the steep path, up to the *alpage*. They were young and they climbed quickly. With them they carried an accordion, eight loaves of bread, and a sack of coarse salt for the cattle. They had worked all day and it was beginning to become dusk.

At one point where the cumin grows profusely either side of the path, the one who was leading stopped and all four looked down at the village, seven hundred metres below.

You can see André's sheep, Robert said.

They could also see the road out of the village which followed the river and led to the plain.

He's slow, is André.

He slowed down ever since the death of Honorine.

He should marry again.

Who?

Philomène!

They laughed and looked down on the village, with the assurance of youth: an assurance which comes from the conviction that, because the young see clearly, they will avoid the mistakes of the old.

Philomène has driven stronger men than André out of the house!

Out of their minds!

When they arrived at the top, the pastures were full of small birds flying just above the grass. The flight of these birds is like a line of stitches, they beat their wings as fast as butterflies and with this they gain height; then they glide and lose height till they beat their wings again and begin another stitch. As they fly they chirp making a noise like castanets.

These birds, flying at the level of their hands, made the men think of the eyes and names of the girls they had come to visit. Very soon the birds would stop flying and night fall.

From time to time a visiting *archiprêtre* would preach a sermon against the immorality of leaving young women alone in the *alpage*. Our own curé knew that there was no alternative. It was the unmarried daughter, capable of looking after the cows and making the cheese, who had the pair of hands most easily spared from the work below. Old women still talk of their summers in the *alpage*.

Before making their visits that night, the four young men planned to sing. There is a place surrounded on three sides by a rock which resounds like the choir of a church. There they were going to sing to announce their arrival to the young women whom they had already, in imagination, chosen. Yet for their singing to be a surprise, they had to skirt the main group of chalets and reach the horseshoe of rocks unseen. This detour involved passing only one chalet, which was unimportant, because it was the Cocadrille's.

As the four approached, the Cocadrille came to her doorway. What emphasised her smallness was the fact that, although she wore the clothes of a woman, she had neither hips nor bust. She had the figure of the ideal servant, tiny but active, without age or sex. That summer she was twenty.

You have an accordion, she said.

Yes, we have.

I can dance, she replied.

Not in those sabots, you can't!

She kicked them off, just as she had kicked them off when she was dancing at the back of the elephant. Her feet were black with dirt. Without waiting for the music, she began to lift up her knees and to step ferociously on the earth around the entrance to the stable where the coming and going of the cows had already worn away the grass. Just by dancing she forced Robert to play a few chords.

Stop! I shouted. The music will tell the others we're here.

The music of the accordion died down. The Cocadrille looked straight at me, unblinking, and slipped her feet back into her clogs. What was disconcerting about her look was its fixity. It was as if her head and neck became suddenly paralysed.

We must be on our way.

Can one of you help me move a barrel? she asked. Robert stepped forward.

Not you, she said, better the one who has just come back from the army.

I shrugged my shoulders and asked my three companions to wait.

Let them go, she said.

Guffawing and making signs with their hands, they left.

Tell La Nan I'm coming to visit her! I shouted after them.

The barrel had oil for the lamp in it. After I had shifted it, the Cocadrille offered me coffee. At first I could hardly see inside the chalet. I stood there, holding the cup in my hands, and she poured *gnôle* into it without asking. To pour *gnôle* into my cup she had to raise her arm higher than her shoulder.

You'd be small enough for a chimney sweep, I said, not knowing what else to say.

I'm a woman, she replied, and I'd shit down their chimneys.

In the very dim light which made her almost invisible, her voice sounded like a woman's.

Are you going away to work in Paris this autumn? she asked.

Yes.

I'll catch a marmot for you to take with you.

How?

That's my secret.

You dig them up when they're asleep?

Will you go up the Eiffel Tower? she asked, ignoring my remark.

The others will be waiting, I said. Thank you for the coffee.

They're singing, she told me. Can't you hear?

No.

She opened the door. They were singing "Mon père a cinq cent moutons."

I'll fetch you some butter, she said.

We don't need any.

You have so much at home that you can refuse butter?

She left me and went through the door into the stable. By now the moon was up, and a little of its light came through the dusty window, no larger than an open book, and down the wooden chimney. There was a pool of moonlight around the dead ashes.

When the Cocadrille came back, I gasped. She had taken off her blouse and chemise. I could see her breasts, each scarcely larger than the bowl of a wooden spoon. She came and stood right in front of me, and I saw that the dark nipples of her breasts were dripping with milk.

It was not until next morning that I reasoned that she must have poured cow's milk over her breasts when she went into the stable. At the time I thought of nothing beyond the thin warm arms she put round me.

We went to lie on the bed, a wooden shelf at the far end of the room. As I caressed her, lying on the bed, I had the impression that she grew larger. She grew as large as the earth upon which I had to throw myself.

How you stir me! she cried, you stir my milk!

The only other time I had been to bed with a woman was in a brothel in the garrison town of L——, and there the lights were pink and the prostitute was as white and plump as a pig. Was that, I asked myself later, why the Cocadrille had asked for the one who had been in the army?

At two in the morning she dressed and reminded me not to forget the butter. As I left, she reached up and pulled the hair at the back of my head, digging her nails into my scalp. I knew the path down by heart.

Suddenly a cloud obscured the moon so that I could see nothing. A noise in the undergrowth made me stop. On every side the low bushes were being trampled. For the third or fourth time that night my heart raced wildly, yet this time, unlike the others, my whole body felt icy. I took to my heels. I ran for ten minutes without stopping, as if I were running from damnation itself.

Later when I reasoned that the Cocadrille must have poured cow's milk over her breasts, I also reasoned that on my way home I had disturbed some sleeping goats.

What was it that made me go back the following evening? Why did I deliberately go up alone, avoiding my companions? She gave no sign of surprise at my arrival.

So you've finished the butter! she said.

Can you give me some more?

Yes, Jean. She pronounced my name solemnly in her deep voice. It was as if she had invented the name herself. Nobody else had ever said my name like that. It disturbed me because it separated me from all other men called Jean or Théophile or François.

She made some coffee. I asked her what she had done and she recounted her day to me. She asked me nothing about myself, but sometimes she looked at me, as if to make sure that I corresponded with the name she had pronounced. We sat across the table, facing each other in the darkness. It was now as dark outside as in. There would be lights in the windows of the other chalets. I knew why she had not lit the lamp: any visitor would conclude that she was already asleep. When a cow moved her head in the stable the note of the bell filled the room, and it was like a reminder of what we were about to do. By now neither of us spoke. I could even hear the breath of the cows. It crossed my mind to leave then and there. Yet it was already too late. Everything outside was already distant, like a coastline seen from the stern of a ship.

She had placed a candle by the bed. Without a word, she lit it. The blanket was white and smelt of sunlight. In the morning, after the cows had grazed, she must have washed the blood from the blanket. I lay there and watched her undress. She threw her clothes onto the table and strode onto the bed.

Stir me! She said this standing over me.

I began to shout at her. I called her obscene names. I referred to parts of her with the words we used for animal parts. All she did was to smile and then, squatting, she sat on me as if I were a horse. I tried to make her fall off and she held onto my shoulders and laughed. Her laughing made me laugh. My shouting stopped. I made a noise like a horse neighing. I neighed and she gripped the hair above my ears as if it were a mane. Later I asked myself how she made me do such things.

We played and made love on the wooden stage of the bed as though we possessed the strength of the whole village. Perhaps that is an old man's boast. I could literally pick her up with one arm, yet every time I tried to put my feet on the floor, she succeeded in pulling me back. It was difficult to believe she was the same woman whom I had passed so often, during the first years of the war, working alone in a field, cursing and already bent with a kind of weariness. I made her laugh by measuring her limb by limb, part by part, against myself. Today I have made a mark on the doorpost of the kitchen to help me recall her real height, before, like all of us, she shrank in old age. One metre, twenty-five centimetres is what I've marked. None of the rest is measurable.

At last we were exhausted and I got up to breathe a little in the fresh air. On the slope behind the Cabrol chalet there is a fold in the earth like a furrow, down which a trickle of water runs. The water makes the flowers grow profusely there, and on both sides of the fold, there are millions of ranunculi, the small, white five-petalled flowers which cows will not eat. I sat down amongst these flowers and the Cocadrille, wearing a man's hat, came out to join me. The other chalets were silent. The crickets had long since stopped. Below were the roofs of the village, no larger than dice.

She lay back among the grasses and ranunculi and looked up at the sky where the stars were the same shape as the flowers, and lying on her back she began to talk. She spoke about herself, about her brother Emile, about the land she would one day inherit, about the cows, about what she thought of the curé, about how she would never marry. At first I listened to what she was saying without much attention. Then gradually it occurred to me that she was saying all this because it might turn out to be otherwise. I became convinced that she was plotting one thing whilst talking about its opposite. It wasn't true that she would never marry. She was plotting to make me her husband. She believed she was now pregnant and so I would be forced to marry her.

Lucie! I interrupted her as we sat there in the firmament of flowers. I do not know why I used her real name.

Yes?

I'm not going to come up again.

I didn't expect you to, Jean.

Her reply confirmed my worst suspicions. It meant that I was already trapped.

Here's the butter, she said, and the way she looked so fixedly at me scared me, making me feel alone and separate, as I had felt when I first arrived and she had used my name in such a strange way.

The next night, asleep in the bed with my brother, I dreamt of her. The Cocadrille came to the house, fearless, eyes blazing. Only one man can be the father of my child, she said in my dream, and Jean is that man! Is it true? asked my own father, turning to me. I couldn't answer. With the Cocadrille! he shouted. No, I don't believe it, he roared. I can prove it, she said. Then prove it! ordered my father. I counted the moles on the small of his back, said the Cocadrille. How many are there? my mother asked. The Cocadrille said a number, and I was forced to take down my trousers in front of the three of them whilst my father counted the moles. You've ruined your life, said my father. Ruined it for nothing! The number was correct. I woke up frightened and sweating.

Many times that summer I was tempted in the evenings to climb up to the *alpage* to discover whether or not she was pregnant. Each time I told myself it was better not. And so I stayed below in suspense. Finally, late in August, I saw her outside the church at a wedding and, to my great relief, she did not single me out in any way.

After I had been in Paris for two winters, Marius à Brine fell sick. It was the month of July and I was back in the village. La Mélanie sat by her husband's bed, lending him what courage she could, and the Cocadrille climbed up to the *alpage* to fetch ice to lay on his burning stomach. There is a cave there, near the horseshoe of rocks where the four of us were going to sing, into which the sun never penetrates. She filled a can with this broken

ice, covered it with a shawl, and ran back all the way down to
Brine. It was the same path I ran down that first night when I
fled from the goats. By the time she arrived, more than half the
ice had melted and there were only rounded slivers left to put on
his pain-clenched stomach. She made three such journeys up to
the cave, and when she came back the third time, in the
midafternoon, Marius was dead.

I went to pay my last respects to him. He was laid out in his
black suit and boots. At the foot of the bed the Cabrol family
kept vigil. The Cocadrille was wearing a widow's dress like her
mother and her face was inclined and invisible. I made the sign
of the cross with the sprig of boxwood over his still heart and
his head with its closed eyes. Edmond, his youngest son, was
only three years old.

Food and drink were laid out for the visitors. The Cocadrille
left the room of the dead and came out to offer me some apple
rissoles. As I ate, she looked up at me. In her drawn, tear-stained
face, framed in black, her blue eyes were even more intense than
I recollected. In April the first forget-me-nots appear in the
grass, like flakes fallen from the sky. Dug up with their roots
and brought inside the house they bring fine weather with them.
Her eyes were the same blue.

So you are leaving us again? she said.

Yes. Not just for Paris, I'm going to South America.

Come back before you die, she said in her deep voice.

Her saying this angered me. I offered my condolences once
more and left. After her father's death the Cocadrille continued
to work on the farm.

In 1936 Emile died as the final consequence of his war
wounds. Two years later La Mélanie followed her husband and
her eldest son into the grave. Henri married Marie, a woman
from the next village. The Cocadrille milked the cows, looked
after the stable, grew the vegetables, collected wood, grazed the
cattle. Marie, her sister-in-law, complained about her:

She's as dirty as a chicken house. And she never lifts a finger
in the kitchen. What sort of woman is that?

The years passed. The Second War broke out.

One morning the Cocadrille was scything between the apple trees with her own scythe which she would never allow anyone else to touch. Over the years its blade had been worn down by whetting and beating until it was scarcely wider than a thumbnail. If you gave me the money, I could never buy another like this, she said. Only the work of twenty summers can make a scythe as light as this. For twenty summers I've cherished this scythe like a son. She was by now known for her original way of talking.

The air was still cooler than the earth under the grass. Far above the orchard, the forest was not yet in the full light of day. Looking up, the Cocadrille saw two men beckoning her from the edge of the trees. Her brothers noticed that she had stopped working and followed her gaze. The two strangers at the edge of the forest must have seen what they took to be a child and two peasants in a hayfield pointing towards them. This was in 1944.

Shit! said Henri.

They're maquisards, said Edmond, who was now as large as a man and already had a knowing expression.

What else could they be? grumbled Henri.

Jésus! don't let anyone else see them.

The Cocadrille pretended to have noticed nothing. It was always Edmond who spoke and Henri who waited, and then it was Henri who prided himself on his cunning.

Marie can give them food and they can go, said Henri after a long pause.

One of the two unknown men started down the slope. Halfway, he emerged from the shadow of the mountain and entered the early morning sunshine. He was short and burly and walked like a peasant.

The two brothers stood absolutely still lest any movement be interpreted by the stranger as a welcome. When he was a few metres away, the stranger said, Good morning.

In the fields deliberate silence is a powerful weapon. Henri said nothing, and withdrew his head back into his shoulders like a dog guarding a doorway. Edmond stood with his hands on his hips, staring insolently.

Two of us need shelter for twenty-four hours, announced the stranger, after allowing the silence to continue long enough to show that he had recognised it.

Who told you to come to our farm?

Nobody. We know who not to go to.

In God's name! muttered Henri. He took out his scythe stone and began sharpening the blade. The noise of the stone on the metal, like the previous silence, was intended to indicate a further refusal to answer.

The stranger strolled over towards the small figure who was still scything between the apple trees.

Good morning, little girl, he said to the Cocadrille.

She turned towards him and he saw that she was a middle-aged woman with a lined face, old enough to be his mother.

I didn't see . . . he excused himself.

This is also my farm, she said.

The stranger made a sign to his companion up by the forest. The second man was limping and carried a gun in each hand.

The two brothers, anxious to prevent the Cocadrille talking to the maquisard, came over to the apple trees.

Where are you from? Edmond asked.

I'm from the Dranse. The SS burnt down my father's farm there.

So you have nothing to lose? remarked Edmond.

Nothing.

The single word contained a threat. This time the silence was filled only with the gasp of the Cocadrille's scythe as it cut the grass.

We'll give you food and after that you must go, announced Henri.

No, we need to stay till tomorrow.

The man who limped and carried the guns joined them. He was young and his unshaven face looked worn and pain-filled.

The best way to hide, said Henri slyly, is to work with us. We need to get the hay in.

The comrade here has a wound that needs dressing, said the peasant from the Dranse.

We are not a hospital!

The Cocadrille leant on her scythe and looked across at the young man. Where is your wound? she asked.

The right thigh, he said.

I will dress it for you.

And if the Germans come? Henri yelled. He can't be in the house.

You are right, interrupted the peasant from the Dranse. It's better if we stay up here.

You mean the Germans *are* looking for you? said Edmond quickly.

Probably.

You came here with a wounded man and with the Germans on your heels and you expect us to risk our lives saving you!

They could hide in the chicken house.

No, we are safer, like you said, working with you. We are your cousins come to help with the hay. Is there anyone down there in the house?

My wife.

So you are four.

With the Cocadrille here, yes.

Can you, Madame, fetch hot water and bandages? Meanwhile we'll hide the weapons.

When she returned from the farm with some strips of linen sheet, she led the wounded man to a flat step of ground by the side of the stream which her grandfather had used to drive the saw. The wound near the top of his thigh was like a wound of any generation.

She knelt in her black dress by his hips and bent over the wound whilst she bathed it with hot water. It took her a long time to get the old dressing completely off. The wound was as red as beef. She diluted some *gnôle* and dabbed it on the wound. When it hurt him, his hand, lying on the grass, found her calf and gripped it through her dress.

Thank you, he said when at last she had bound the wound up again. You have very gentle hands.

Laid out on the grass, his body looked long and his bare legs as thin as those of the body on the cross.

Gentle! she said. They've worked too hard to be gentle. They've been in too much shit.

He shut his eyes.

How old are you? she asked.

Nineteen.

Is your mother alive?

I believe so.

And your father?

He is a judge.

You have such regular teeth. You don't come from here.

No, from Paris.

Have you ever turned hay?

I will do as you do.

She helped him to his feet. After a while, he stopped to wipe his face with the corner of his shirt.

She held out a bottle to him. However much you drink when haymaking, she said, you never piss!

At midday a car drew up at the farmhouse.

Take no notice, ordered the peasant from the Dranse, go on working.

Two men in uniform got out of the car.

They're not the Milice, said Edmond, they're Germans.

The Cocadrille, who was standing beside the young man from Paris, suddenly reached up and slapped the side of his neck with her open hand.

What! he shouted.

A horsefly had been about to bite him.

Soon they could hear the heavy breathing of the Germans whom the slope still hid from view. The first to appear was an officer with a tight belt and straight high cap pulled down over his eyes. Following him came a sergeant holding a sub-machine gun.

Everyone here! shouted the officer. He surveyed the five hay-makers: four peasants and one dwarf woman.

We are looking for six assassins. We know who they are. Who has come by here this morning?

I'll tell you, said the Cocadrille. The brain needs renewing. It wanders. If I had the money to buy a new one and if they sold them, I'd change it tomorrow. She buttoned her dress where it was undone. I did see a car go by this morning—or was it yesterday morning? An army could go by and I wouldn't be sure. When I saw this car I said to myself, that's strange. There was an officer driving it, with a cap like yours, sir— she pointed the prongs of her wooden fork at the officer's face: the sergeant pushed her back. I said to myself, he looks like a man wearing a disguise. Perhaps he was one of the men you are looking for, sir, one of the assassins. His cap came right down over his face like yours, sir, as if he was trying to hide his face. Was it this morning or yesterday morning I saw this car? He could have stolen the car, you see, sir. Was it yesterday? I wish I knew. She put a finger in her ear. You'll do better, believe me, sir, asking my two cousins here. She pointed her fork at the maquisards.

Nobody's passed this way, said the peasant from the Dranse. Not since before it was light. We were up at five. Nobody has come by, unless they stuck to the forest and we didn't see them.

The peasant from the Dranse stared vacantly at the distant snowcovered mountain, white like a pillow propped against the blue sky, and farted.

The officer approached Edmond and gently touched his face so that he could look into the boy's eyes.

They couldn't come here, said Edmond ingratiatingly, they know too well where our sympathies lie.

No, the officer said, you all hate us!

And you? demanded the sergeant, pointing his gun at the young Parisian.

The hay is dry now. He spoke slowly and stupidly as if he were the dwarf woman's son.

What have you seen this morning?

Flies and horseflies.

Has anyone come down from the forest?

Flies and horseflies.

His idiocy provoked the sergeant to jab the muzzle of his gun hard into his stomach. The dwarf woman raised her fork in protest. The officer scowled at the prospect of a brawl on the steep slope which the hay made slippery.

We are wasting our time, he said curtly to the sergeant. To the peasants he said: If you are lying, I can promise you we'll be back, just as we came back to T——.

The previous winter the Germans had come one night to the village of T—— with two armoured lorries, an officer's car, and a searchlight mounted on a sidecar. With their searchlight trained on the doors, they went from house to house. The women they chased into the forest. The men they lined up and shot. Whilst the stables and animals were burning, the German troops sang.

The sergeant left first. The officer, as he went down, dug his heels in so as not to slip, and the dust from the hay coated the backs of his polished boots.

After the car had driven away, there was nowhere any sign of what had happened or of what might happen.

The Aunt here made a fine speech! said the peasant from the Dranse. She scowled in case he was taking her for a fool. During her first life the Cocadrille was never indifferent to what people thought of her.

It's safe now. They won't come back until they've questioned everybody, she said to the one she had bandaged. You can go and rest in the hayloft.

He must work, Henri contradicted, that was the understanding from the beginning. If they come back and find him . . .

His leg needs rest.

Jésus! It's not your farm they'll burn down.

You can lie in the hayloft, and if they come back you can be working on top of the hay, the Cocadrille said.

And if he's asleep?

I'll stay with him.

Stay with him! In God's name! We have this hay to get in.

The Aunt is right, said the peasant from the Dranse, you should listen to her.

Half the hayloft was empty; in the other half the new hay was stacked almost as high as the roof beams. When she shut the door it was like twilight. She told the wounded man, who was young enough to be her son, on no account to hide in the hay, for the previous year a maquisard hiding in another farm had buried himself in the hay and the Italian soldiers had searched the loft, sticking in pitchforks. One of the prongs had wounded him in the neck. He dared not cry out. The Italian soldiers dawdled in the barn, joking with the peasant's wife. And the wounded man bled to death in the blood-red hay.

They know they are defeated now. Couldn't you see it in the officer's eyes? said the young man.

The Cocadrille shrugged her shoulders.

What will you do when the war stops?

I will continue my studies, he said.

And one day become a judge like your father?

No, it is another kind of justice that I believe in, a popular justice, a justice for peasants like you and for workers, a justice which gives factories to those who work in them, and the land to those who cultivate it. As he said this, he smiled shyly, as if confessing something intimate.

Is your father rich? she asked.

Fairly.

Won't you inherit some of his money?

All of it when he dies.

There's the difference between us.

She had a habit of kicking off one sabot and rubbing the bare foot against her other leg.

I shall use that money to start a paper. By then we shall have a free press. A free press is a prerequisite for the full mobilisation of the masses.

Are your feet hot too? she asked.

The hay is dusty, he said. He gravely gave everything he said equal thought.

Meanwhile you are in danger, she commented.

Not more than you.

That is true, today we are equal.

Do your brothers think like you?

I don't think.

I didn't trust them, he said.

They are as straight as a goat's hind leg. You must rest now. Later I will dress your wound again. What is your first name?

They call me Saint-Just.

I have never heard that name. Rest now, Saint-Just.

He slept without stirring. In the evening whilst the others were eating, she took him bread and a plate of soup.

I feel stronger, he announced.

I can dress your wound again.

No, just sit beside me.

When she sat beside him, he laid his head in her lap and she combed his hair with her fingers.

You have very gentle hands, he said for the second time.

It's like raking hay, she said laughing.

She broke off the story there. I do not know whether they made love. Perhaps it is only my own memories which make me ask the question. Yet there was something in the way the Cocadrille recounted her meetings with men which always left you speculating.

The two maquisards departed next day. Within forty-eight hours the village heard that a group of maquisards had been surprised in their camp by the Milice, taken prisoner, transported to A——, and shot in a field there. There were six in the group and they included the peasant from the Dranse and Saint-Just. It was said that the Milice could never have found the camp, unless they had been tipped off by an informer.

The Cocadrille shrieked when she heard the news. At supper that night she was still crying with bloodshot eyes.

In God's name stop it, woman! Henri's wife exclaimed. In any case a woman of your age should be ashamed!

Those who sleep with dogs, wake up with fleas, said Edmond.

That's good! shouted Henri. That's good! Those who sleep with dogs, wake up with fleas!

She never forgave the insult. She began, as she had done when she was a child, to disappear. Without telling her brothers, she would be absent for a whole day, sometimes two days and a night. It became impossible to confide any regular job to her. She gradually withdrew her labour, as job after job appeared to her shameful. Not shameful in itself, but shameful for her to perform for two men whom she could not forgive.

Soon she was no longer on speaking terms with anybody in the house. She slept in the stable. She ate by herself. To save the bother of eating more than once a day, she rolled herself cigarettes. Her brothers were in constant dread that deliberately or accidentally she would set fire to the farm. They threatened to beat her if they found her smoking in the stable. In revenge she put an unlit cigarette in her mouth whenever she saw one of them approaching.

It was Henri who first spoke in the village of the Cocadrille's stealing. She stole, he said, eggs from his wife's chicken house. Since she doesn't work, he added, she has no right to them, and she sells them for money.

Some believed him and sympathised; others argued that she was, after all, his sister and he owed her her share of the inheritance. Gradually it became apparent that she was stealing from other gardens. A few lettuces, some plums, a marrow or two. Nobody, except Henri and Edmond, took these small thefts very seriously. They were humiliated by them.

The end came with the fire. The Cabrol *grenier* burnt down one autumn morning. The two brothers accused the Cocadrille of having deliberately set light to it.

They went to see the Mayor and they told him that they could no longer take responsibility for the actions of their sister, whose unleashed madness was Stealing and Arson. The Mayor was reluctant to refer the matter to any outside authority. It was his wife who thought of the solution which he finally proposed to Henri and Edmond. They accepted it enthusiastically. And with this proposal the first life of the Cocadrille came to an end.

THE SECOND LIFE OF LUCIE CABROL

How long distances seem to a peasant may depend on how he cultivates his land. If he grows melons between cherry trees, five hundred metres is a considerable distance. If he grazes cows on a mountain pasture, five kilometres is not far. To the Cocadrille, who could cultivate nothing, because she now had no land, twenty kilometres became a short distance. She walked fast. When she was an old woman, people still commented on how quickly she disappeared. One moment they saw her on a path: the next moment hillside and skyline were empty. She usually carried a sack and, sometimes, tied across her back, a large blue umbrella.

One September morning in 1967 she set out early. The place she was making for was a high forested plateau, about eight kilometres away from where she now lived. When a pine tree falls in that forest, struck by lightning, or its roots are torn out of the earth by a gale, it lies where it fell until its wood turns grey, stifled by snow in winter and burnt by the sun in summer. There are no paths there. You can see on the fallen tree trunks hundreds of systematically dismantled pine cones, which the squirrels have eaten, undisturbed since the thaw in the spring. Everywhere, climbing over roots and boulders, wild raspberries grow.

The canes were taller than she. As she picked them she crooned. This was to frighten the snakes. With her left hand she bent the canes back so that their undersides, clustered with fruit, were uppermost: then, between the finger and thumb of her right hand she picked, going from cluster to cluster, until she was so far stretched over the cane that she risked falling forward on to her face. Any fruit that failed to come away easily from their white cores she left. Those she picked she put in the palm of her left hand. The berries were warm and granular like nipples. She held them in her calloused dirt-lined palm without squashing them. When she could hold no more she turned round and emptied the handful into a frail made of thin wood. As she moved forward through the forest, she left behind her thousands of white cores from which she had taken the fruit.

I was watching her. I had climbed up to the forest the same morning to look for *bolets* which grow along its upper edge, where the pines stop. To my surprise I saw a very small old woman in black among the trees. Since my return I had only heard about the Cocadrille from others.

After I arrived in Buenos Aires I seldom gave her a thought. If she came to mind at all, I congratulated myself on my luck in escaping her guile. I remained convinced that she had tried to trap me into marriage. Fortunately she had failed—probably because she was sterile. Contrary to what one might expect, as time passed, I thought of her more often. I took for granted my luck in not having become entangled with her. And in the hot airless nights of the city, not far from one of the vilest shanty towns, I used to picture to myself an alpine summer. One of the things I recalled was the long grass beneath the stars beside the Cabrol chalet. And then even her plotting seemed to me to belong to a life that was carefree and innocent.

Among the trees in the forest, she straightened her back from time to time and ate some of the fruit. I hid so she would not see me. I wanted to watch her unawares.

After twenty-five years in the Argentine, I went north to Montreal where, for a while, I was rich. I had my own bar there. Sometimes I would tell my story about the goats in the moonlight and the Cocadrille. Once a client asked me: Was this woman a dwarf? And I had to explain. No, she was not a dwarf, she was tiny, she was underdeveloped, she was ignorant, she was like a dwarf, but she wasn't. If she was physically like a dwarf, the client reasoned, she surely was a dwarf. No, I said.

When I next looked towards the forest, she had disappeared. Not a branch moved. The red cones hung motionless, they were especially, obscenely red that year. I have never seen them so red—as red as the arseholes of baboons. There was no sign of her. I told myself I had imagined seeing her. Yet, when I walked over to where I thought she had been, the raspberry canes were stripped and you could see everywhere the white cores of the fruit she had taken.

A few days previously I had overheard some children coming out of school talking about her.

It makes you frightened just to meet her on the road.

Why does she live up there, so far away, next to the precipice?

Mother says she catches marmots and skins them.

My father says she has a fortune hidden up there.

Why doesn't she have a dog at least to keep her company?

Witches don't have dogs, they have cats.

If she looks at you, you have to open your mouth—have you noticed that—you can't keep it shut!

I was walking with my head down looking for mushrooms. With age I have become somewhat deaf. Something made me look to the side. The woman in the black dress, not more than ten metres away, was squatting at the foot of a tree, holding her dress up over her scratched knees.

The passer-by, she cawed, should always raise his hat to the one who is shitting!

I took off my beret and she cawed with laughter.

I think she didn't recognise me for when she got to her feet and took a few steps towards me, pulling down her skirt, she stopped and exclaimed.

It's Jean!

I nodded.

Do you recognise me?

You're the Cocadrille.

No! she said and her laughter stopped dead.

Why are you following me? she asked.

I came up here to look for *bolets*.

You found some?

What?

Did you find some? she insisted.

I opened my haversack. Her hair was white, the lines to the corners of her mouth were very deep, and down the sides of her face I could see tracks of sweat. Around her lips were spots and traces of dark red from the fruit she had eaten. This, with her lined face and white hair, gave her the macabre air of a prematurely aged child. Or of an old person become childish.

Give them to me. Her eyes were fixed on the *bolets* I had found.

What for?

They are mine! she claimed.

She believed that whatever grew and had not been planted by man, within a radius of ten kilometres of where she lived, was incontestably hers.

I closed my haversack. She shook her head and turned away, cursing quietly to herself.

So you've come back, she said after a minute.

Yes, I've come back.

You were away too long. She stared at me with the intense gaze of her blue eyes, which were no more like flowers but like a stone called kyanite.

I remembered the way up here, I said.

You came up here to spy on me.

Spy?

Spy on me!

Why should I want to spy on you?

Give me the *bolets* then.

No.

Why did I refuse? I had found the mushrooms, therefore they were mine. It was an elementary point of justice. Yet I knew that justice had little to do with my life or hers. I refused out of habit.

She took an empty frail from her sack and began picking. I wondered how I arranged the frails in her sack when they were full so that the fruit would not be damaged.

Whilst you were away, everything changed, she said to me over her shoulder.

A lot must have changed when you left the farm.

I didn't leave it. They disinherited me.

She moved on, following the fruit, away from me. Soon she appeared to forget that I was there. She bent back a stem on which the berries must have been especially closely clustered.

Thank you, little sow, she cawed. Thank you!

Did you marry out there? she shouted.

Yes.

I forced my way through the brambles so as to hear her better. She wore boots with no stockings and her scratched legs were as lean as the forelegs of a cow.

Why did you come back alone then?

My wife died.

You're a widower.

I am a widower.

Do you have children?

Two sons. They are both working in the United States.

Money can change everything, she said. She held up her left hand, full of raspberries, pretending that it was full of coins. He who hasn't got money is like a wolf without teeth. She looked around at the whole forest as if it were the world. And for he who has money, money can do anything. Money can eat and dance. Money can make the dirty clean, the despised respected. Money can even make the dwarf big.

Her using the word *dwarf* shocked me.

I have two million! she cawed.

I hope you keep them in a bank.

Fuck off! she swore. Fuck off and get away!

She pointed as if pointing at a door and ordering me out of a room rather than a forest. Everyone in the village said that she was fearless. I don't think this was true. What she counted on was inspiring fear in others. She knew that people were frightened of her. Now she was angry because she had told me about her savings; she had probably intended to keep this a secret. If I went obediently she might assume that I was not interested. If I insisted upon staying it would be tantamount to admitting my curiosity. So I left.

It is said that large mushrooms are large from the moment they first appear. One morning there is nothing, and the next morning the mushroom is there as large as it will ever be. A small mushroom is not a young large one. It will stay small, as the Cocadrille stayed small.

Occasionally, as I went on looking for my mushrooms, I saw her faded blue sunshade in the distance. Its blue was like the colour of her eyes. They had lost none of their colour with age. They had simply become dry, like stone.

Towards midday I found the largest *bolet* I have ever seen. I looked at it for several minutes before I saw it. Then suddenly it stood out from its surroundings of fern, moss, dead wood, grey pine needles, and earth—exactly as if it had grown from nothing before my eyes. It was thirty centimetres in diameter and thick like a round loaf of bread. Sometimes I dream of finding mushrooms and even in my dream I say to myself: Don't pick them straight away, admire them first. This one weighed two kilos and was still fresh.

I walked to another part of the forest where the pines are not spruce but larches, and where the earth is covered with a carpet of turf as soft as an animal's stomach. There I planned to eat my lunch and afterwards, as has become my habit, to sleep a little. I put my beret over my face to keep the sun out of my eyes. And as I lay there, before I fell asleep, I thought, I must look like an old man who never left his country. This thought along with the mushrooms I had found, the little wine I had drunk, the softness of the turf, was a consolation. I sat up to look once more at the giant bolet in my haversack. It too was a confirmation that I had come home.

God in heaven!

If she hadn't sworn, she wouldn't have woken me. A platoon could march on the turf there without making a sound. She was holding the *bolet* which was as large as a loaf and staring at it.

The strap of my haversack was already over her shoulder. She saw me sit up. This in no way deterred her. With her exaggeratedly long strides she was making off towards the other part of the forest. Why didn't I protest? To lose all the mushrooms I had gathered during the morning, to lose the largest *bolet* I had ever seen, and to lose a haversack into the bargain was a shouting matter. I could have run after her, picked her up, and shaken her. I stayed there on the ground. All the stories I had heard about her were true. She was shameless. She was a thief. I had no doubt she would sell my mushrooms. Why had she not asked me for them once more? I might have given her some. The idea came to me that this time, and this time only, I would let her have what she had taken.

I need my haversack, I shouted.

You know where I live!

She bawled this as if it were a complete justification of what she had done.

A few days later I went to retrieve my haversack. Half an hour's walk along the road which climbs east out of the village brings you to a stone column on top of which is a small statue of the Madonna. She stands there arms relaxed, palms of her hands facing the road as if waiting to welcome the traveller. Either side of the Madonna are railings because, behind her, there is a sheer drop to the gravel of the river Jalent, sixty, seventy metres below.

Around the next bend of the road is the house in which the Cocadrille lived her second life. Beside the house there is a rock, as tall as the roof, with an ash tree growing on top of it. You have the impression that the house is jutting out into the road, edging away from the precipice behind its back. It was originally built before the First World War for a roadmender. He lodged there with his horse during the few weeks of the year when he was working on that isolated stretch of the pass. With the advent of lorries, the house no longer served any purpose and so was locked up and the key kept in the Mayor's office. The Mayor's wife's proposal had been that the Cocadrille should live in the roadmender's house rent-free. There, she would be far enough away from the village to cause trouble to nobody, and the law would not have to be invoked against her.

If you approach the roadmender's house from the opposite direction, you don't see it until you are beside it, for it is completely hidden by the rock with the tree on top of it. The rock is like a second house that has been filled with stone. From the direction I was approaching I could see a window, which had no curtains, in the house which was lived in.

I knocked on the door.

Who is it?

Jean.

You're too late.

It's not half past eight.

The door opened a fraction.

What do you want?

I have come to fetch my haversack.

At this hour!

I won't come in.

Now she opened the door fully.

I'll pay you a coffee.

The room was full of sacks and cardboard boxes, there were two piles of wood and so far as I could see, only one chair at a table, on which there was a pile of old newspapers, a heap of hazelnuts, and some knitting. The blue umbrella stood in a corner. The ceiling was smoked dark brown like the hide of a ham. The room was the size of a small lorry.

She continued doing what she must have been doing before I knocked. She gathered the hazelnuts into a basket and hung them on a pair of scales, the traditional kind made of iron, which, on the banknotes of some countries, the figure of Justice holds up in front of her bosom.

Shit and shit! she grumbled. I can't see in this light.

I put on my glasses and looked over her shoulder to read the markings on the iron bar.

Six kilos, three hundred, I said.

She smelt of the floor of a forest into which the sun never penetrates, she smelt of boar.

After they were weighed she put the nuts into a cardboard box.

I haven't had a visit for three years. I had to strain my ears to hear her. She was speaking as if to herself. The last visitor I had was Monsieur le Curé in July 1964. They put me here to get me out of the way. Why don't you take your glasses off? They make you look like a curé.

If you can't read, you should wear glasses yourself.

Read! she cawed. Read!

From the pocket of her apron she took out a packet of tobacco and slowly rolled herself a cigarette. On the stove she moved a saucepan of milk to get a light from the burning wood.

If I turn my back you spill over, she said to the milk.

A cock came through the door from the adjoining stable. It stood there, one claw poised in the air.

Sit on the chair! she said. It was the last curé, not this one. He was always in bad health. He'd climbed up here on foot on his way somewhere. I offered to pay him a glass of water. Ah, he said, as soon as he came in: You are a child of the earth, Lucie. Without land, I said. You must not harbour resentment, he told me, you have things to be grateful for. I knew what he meant. Like this house you mean—everybody whispers that I don't pay rent for it and what a shack it is! It was built for one man and a horse—she lifted the milk off the fire—and when the horse died it wasn't lived in anymore. I'm the only woman who ever slept in this house. I asked the curé to name one other woman in the village who would live here alone. None of them is a child of the earth, he repeated. I will show you one day what I am, I said, I'm going to surprise you all! It is dangerous—I remember how solemn his voice was—to hope too much; you cannot please the world and there is no reason to envy it. She shooed the cock away into the stable. Father, I said, I believe in happiness! And do you know what happened then? His face went white and he grasped my arm. Lucie, is there a little more water? he whispered. I gave him some *gnôle* and he drank it like water. He started to speak as if he were reading the Bible in church. It is written, sadness has killed many, and there is no profit in it. You are right, my daughter, to believe in happiness. Lie down, Father, I told him, and rest a moment. Where? he asked, I see no bed. I got him to the table. He lay down, closed his eyes, and smiled. The angels, he murmured, who descended and ascended on Jacob's ladder, they had wings, yet they did not fly and they trod the gradual rungs of the ladder. I held the glass for him and undid the buttons where his clothes were too tight. He never opened his eyes. He will be ashamed when he wakes up, I said. He heard me say this because he spoke: I'm ashamed now but I feel better. Slowly, Father, I said, let your strength come back slowly. That was the last visitor I had. She poured out some coffee.

Haven't Henri or Edmond ever visited you?

It was then that she told me the story of her brothers and the maquisards. She told it squatting on a sack beside the stove. The kitchen grew darker and darker. I could see nothing except the orange of the fire in the stove and her white hair which gave off a glimmer of light. Outside there was a hard moon. They are traitors, she added, when she had finished the story.

Traitors?

It was they who informed the Milice.

Have you any proof?

I don't need proof. I know them too well.

Why should they have done that? The war was nearly over. Everyone saw the Germans were losing.

What kind of patriot were you? she hissed. A thousand kilometres away.

Ten thousand, I said.

She spat and rubbed the spittle with her foot on the floorboards.

The only time my brothers came here was when they brought my furniture. They made excuses all day saying they had to finish planting the potatoes. It was in April 1949. Only after they had eaten their soup did they load the cart. Then we set out under cover of darkness. Do you know why? In the daylight they were ashamed to be seen moving their sister out. When we arrived here, it was as dark as it is now. My own brothers, fed on the same mother's milk, sperm of the same father's sperm, left me here in the dark one night. I didn't even have a lamp. Each month they were meant to pay me. Pay my arse! I saw the last of them that same night through the window there.

I watched the cart go, she continued, and when I knew it was far away, I followed it. I went as far as the Madonna. She walked to the dark window in the room and stood looking out through the glass.

There was a long white cloud in the shape of a fish, she went on, I have never seen it again. Where the fish's eye should have been was the moon. I waited there at the foot of the Madonna's column and I spoke to Maman and Papa. You should have known your sons better, I told them. You always thought of them as they were when they were in the cradle. Shit! You didn't know where their evil came from, did you? You died, Papa, didn't you, not knowing that to make a child you need a woman, a man, and the Devil. That's why it's so tempting! I saw what Papa was doing at that very moment when I was standing at the Madonna's feet. He was rutting into Maman. And Maman was pulling him down! When you were alive, you didn't do it enough, did you, you were always too tired and your back felt too broken. Go on. I give you my blessing. Go on, I told them. You have nothing left here. Your sons will give nothing back to you. If you speak out loud, they won't listen. If you stopped and saw me, you'd suffer. I'm not going to let you suffer, Papa, I'm not going to let you suffer, Maman, because I'm going to survive. You carcasses with your backs to everything! I'm not going to let you suffer. I swear it. I'm going to survive.

In the darkness the room smelt of sacks and earth. A car came up the road and its headlights shone straight through the window at which she stood, lighting up the entire room. In this light, the room looked more than ever like a store shed. In the corner, on the far side of the stove, was a ladder and above it an open trapdoor. When the car had passed, the darkness by contrast was total. The noise of the engine died away. In the silence and darkness, the two of us could as well have been in our coffins.

Do you want to eat some soup with me?

I have a bottle of wine.

So you thought you'd stay!

No, I bought it for myself at home.

After forty years' absence, what have you got to show? One litre of wine!

A little more.

What?

Enough to live on till I move to the Boulevard of the Laid Out.

So you've come back to die.

We're not young anymore.

I'm not ready to die yet, she proclaimed.

Death doesn't ask if you are ready.

Are you going to live well? she asked.

I'm not rich. I didn't make the fortune I dreamt of. I was unlucky. Do you always sit in the dark?

What did you find in South America—electricity? I go to bed when I can't see. You're going to keep your mother's house in the village?

I bought it from my brothers.

When did you do that?

This interrogation, during which we were both invisible to the other, reminded me of kneeling before the confession box. I sent them money when I had it.

She must have read my thoughts, for the next question she asked was: Were you faithful to your wife?

What a man does with his own skin, I said, is his own business.

For twenty years I haven't spoken to anyone after nightfall except my chickens and the goat, when I still had one.

Give me my haversack and I'll be going.

No, wait! I'll light the lamp.

She struck a match and made her way over to the cupboard, in which she found a candle.

Are you hot now? she asked the soup, lifting the lid of the saucepan with as much caution as she had first opened the door to me. I can't grow a single potato for you, they've taken every one. Can you lift the lamp down? Otherwise I have to stand on a chair.

The lamp was on the mantelpiece. I lit it. She climbed up the ladder to the loft and came down with a second chair. From the nail in the wall behind the stove she took a pewter ladle and rubbed it against the side of her black dress.

At last we sat down on either side of the table. The soup was steaming in the plates. It must have been past midnight.

So you have brought nothing back with you! She looked into my face.

Not a great fortune.

That's obvious.

She held out her glass for me to fill with wine.

I swore to survive and become rich, and rich I've become, she said. There's no man on earth who has the right to a single glass of vin blanc paid for out of my money! From now on I'm going to drink wine in the evenings.

What time do you get up in the mornings? I asked. I must be going.

In time to milk.

You have no cows.

I get up in time to milk. Every morning for the twenty years since I've been here.

At five?

She nodded.

You have an alarm clock?

In here. She pointed at her white hair.

And tomorrow? I asked.

Tonight is an exception, she said, holding out her glass for me to refill. Tonight I'm going to tell you about the twenty years.

What have they to do with me?

You have come back a pauper yet at least you have seen the world.

When she swore at the feet of the Madonna to survive, she had no clear idea of how to become rich. She knew less than I did when I took the boat to Buenos Aires. All she knew was that she could not become rich in the village.

I have renamed the village, she said. I have renamed it *Chez Cocadrille*! She shook with laughter and licked her colourless lips with her pink tongue.

Fifty kilometres away, just over the frontier, was the city of B——. Marius à Brine had spoken of its wealth, just as his father had done. Marius also said that those who lived in B—— gave nothing away; they were so mean that they melted the snow to give what was left as alms to the poor! The Cocadrille concluded as she watched her two lost parents embracing that the place where money truly existed was B——. Such money as reached the village was vagrant money. She had to go to its home, where money bred.

What could she take to sell in B——? It was the moment for killing kids and she had no goats. It was the time when last summer's cheeses were ready to eat, and she had no cows. It was the laying season for chickens and she had not yet built her chicken run. The solution, obvious as it was, did not come to her immediately. She walked back along the moonlit road from the Madonna's column.

I slept down here the first night, she said. It took me a year to move up to the loft. I missed the animals in the stable, and the idea of sleeping halfway up the sky, in the cold, didn't appeal to me. I prefer to sleep on the ground, don't you?

For a while I lived on the eighteenth storey.

What did it bring you?

She rubbed index finger against thumb in the banknote gesture which signifies money. Then she touched the back of my hand with her fingers.

During the first night in the roadmender's house, she dreamt of the Madonna. The Madonna spoke to her in her dream and told her that everything which people go out to pick, she must pick first and take to the city. This is why the

Madonna's hands were open and pointing to the grass on the verge of the road.

Next day she took the path up to the highest fields of the village. The altitude there is nine hundred metres, and the grass was only just beginning to grow. She picked dandelions for salad, their leaves still very small, their stalks white. She didn't come down until she had picked two kilos. Then she set out for the fields and orchards five hundred metres below, and there, where the dandelions were already flowering and the grass as high as her shins, she hunted for morels. Her fingers led her to them, under the pear trees, among nettles, between the stones of walls.

I still know where a mushroom is waiting, like a bitch in heat for a dog.

By the end of the day she had filled a basket.

At dusk she went out once again to collect violets and primroses at the edge of the forest. The violets she arranged in tiny bouquets with a damp cloth around them, and the primroses she cut out of the earth with their roots and soil attached. When it was fully night, she walked along the road to the Madonna's column and, in the grass at its base, she planted some of the primroses.

A train went to the frontier town which adjoins B——. There was even a song about this train which La Mélanie used to sing. The train in the song left the town at noon, and travelled so slowly, and stopped so often by the river, the smoke from the engine going straight up into the sky, that it never reached the village till it was dark, a fact which delighted lovers because they could caress each other undisturbed in the warm upholstered carriages. La Mélanie used to mime their embraces whilst she sang. The Cocadrille took this train. It was going in the opposite direction to the train in the song and went much faster. The journey lasted less than two hours. What frightened her was its smoothness. She was used to lurches and bumps against which, without thinking, she tensed herself so as not to be bruised against the wood of the cart drawn by the horse. The smoothness of the train made her feel sick: it was as if the earth no longer existed.

When the train arrived at the end of the line, she followed everyone out of the station. She saw no one she knew to ask where the frontier was. She resolved to walk in the same direction as most of the men. It was still early in the morning and she knew that many men went to work for the day in B——.

At the frontier the *douanier* asked her whether she had anything to declare. She looked blank. What have you got with you? he asked. Some morels, she said. I'll sell them to you, if you offer me a good price!

After two hours' searching, she found the market. She walked through it to see whether others were selling the same goods as she had brought. There were no other violets, and she thought she had misread the price of the dandelion leaves. They cost two hundred for a hundred grams. Two thousand a kilo! She understood better the wealth of the city of B——. The morels were selling at five thousand a kilo! She chose a corner in the shade, put her baskets down either side of her feet, and waited for customers to come and buy. She stood waiting all morning. At midday she saw all the other traders packing up their stalls. She had sold nothing. She had not opened her mouth.

On her way back to the frontier she went into a café to ask for a glass of water. Nowhere in the streets had she seen a pump or a fountain. The proprietor peered into her basket of morels. He picked one up without a word, turned it in his fingers.

I'll give you a thousand for the basketful.

There are two kilo there. You can weigh them.

I don't need to.

They're selling for five thousand a kilo in the market, she said, scandalised.

He shrugged his shoulders and turned away. She stared at him, her chin level with the top of his zinc bar. Looking over his shoulder, he opened his silent mouth and guffawed with laughter.

How much do you weigh yourself! he asked. You could throw yourself in for good measure! I'll give you twelve hundred.

She saw that she had to accept the price, it was her last chance.

It took her a year to find her way about B——. In Buenos Aires I saw peasants newly arrived in the city, and all of them had the same air of confusion and extreme timidity. Many of them never got over it. I and the Cocadrille did. Of the two of us, she was the quicker. At home, in the village, it is you who do everything, and the way you do it gives you a certain authority. There are accidents and many things are beyond your control, but it is you who have to deal with the consequences even of these. When you arrive in the city, where so much is happening and so much is being done and shifted, you realise with astonishment that nothing is in your control. It is like being a bee against a window pane. You see the events, the colours, the lights, yet something, which you can't see, separates you. With the peasant it is the forced suspension of his habit of handling and doing. That's why his hands dangle out of his cuffs so stupidly.

Month by month the Cocadrille learnt where she could sell each item in the city, each item which, according to the season, she scavenged from the mountains: wild cherries, lilies of the valley, snails, mushrooms, blueberries, raspberries, wild strawberries, blackberries, *trolles,* juniper berries, cumin, wild rhododendron, mistletoe.

You have to understand that everything you watch in the city is as unimportant as a game. Everything which impresses you about the city is an illusion. It is not easy. To be impressed and unimpressed at the same time! What really happens in a city is hidden. If you want to achieve anything it must be arranged in secret.

She went to cafés, never missing a wink or a nod, never failing to remember a quickly suggested address. She bought a map of the city and on it she marked, with the flowing capital letters which André Masson taught us all, the addresses of her customers.

You'd have to pay to see that map! she cawed.

I poured out the last of the wine.

Do you remember where the cumin grows on the path to the *alpage*? I bring down a *pailler* full on my back and I let it dry there in the stable. I put newspapers underneath for the seeds to fall on to. I can sell a hundred grams of cumin seed for one thousand five hundred!

As she named the price, she tapped with all the fingers of one hand on the edge of the table, and the spoon rattled in her plate. She discovered that there was no need to pay for a ticket to travel to B——. She could stop lorries and cars on the road and they would take her. She went to the city twice a week. All the other days of the year, when there wasn't snow, she scavenged from dawn to dusk.

Drivers came to know me. She touched the back of my hand again. Sometimes they tried to take liberties but they never tried twice.

Réné, the electrician, picked her up one day.

As far as the frontier? she asked.

Réné nodded and she got in the back. He saw her in the driving mirror. It was a new car he had just bought and she sat in the very centre of the shining back seat, bolt upright with her sack on the floor. Réné nudged the apprentice sitting beside him.

Have you heard the story of the he-goat who went mad?
No.
He belonged to a farm where, years before, a cock laid an egg.
How's that?
The peasant's wife was certain because one morning she went into the chicken house and there was the cock on one of the hens' boxes, making laying noises. She shooed him off and there was an egg! Saying nothing to her husband, she took the egg and buried it in the dung heap. Four weeks later . . .

He was interrupted by the noise of something crackling. He turned around. The Cocadrille was lying back with her legs and boots in the air. On the seat beside her, several egg yolks were running down the upholstery. The scraps of newspaper from which she had unwrapped the eggs were still on her lap.

Finish your story, she said. What did the Cocadrille do to the billy goat?

Réné drove on in silence. When the *douanier* at the frontier asked whether they had anything to declare, the Cocadrille leant forward and said:

The two men here have a dozen broken eggs to declare.

Réné shook his head and winked at the *douanier.*

You can count them there on the floor, she insisted, twelve, and they haven't paid me for them yet. A car like this, and they pretend they can't pay an old woman for a dozen eggs!

How did they break? asked the *douanier,* laughing.

A billy goat rolled on them . . . she explained, and, without a thank-you or a good-bye, the Cocadrille got down from the car and followed the tramlines.

She learnt that money did not have the same value on both sides of the frontier. For everything bought, there was a cheap side and an expensive side. She learnt that it was foolish to bring money back; less foolish to bring back what she could sell expensively on her side.

We are surrounded by natural frontiers: snow, mountains, rock walls, rivers, ravines. For centuries we have also lived near an invisible political frontier. Where exactly it runs, changes according to the force of foreign governments and armies. This frontier divides the rich from the poor, and it is the easiest of all to cross. The threat of being flogged, of exile, of execution, of being sent to the galleys, has never deterred men or women from crossing it and smuggling. Many smuggled alone; some formed bands like small armies. The names of the leaders of these bands she knew by heart: Le Grand Joseph, Le Dragon, La Danse à l'Ombre, the great Louis Mandrin who was executed at V——.

What have you got to declare today, Grandma?

Down to there, nothing, she pointed to the pit of her stomach, underneath there is a present for any young man who wants it!

Besides the map which she would not show me, she kept an almanac. In it, each year, she wrote down the date of the month when a crop in a given place was ready for picking. Five days a week, for she was also out scavenging on Sundays, she combed the countryside. Like a crow, she noticed everything.

She knew not only paths but countless clearings, assemblies of rocks, streams, fallen trees, protected hollows, fissures, crests, slopes. It was only for the city of B—— that she needed a map. She knew exactly where to crawl along the border of the forest to find wild strawberries. She knew under which pine trees the cyclamen grow, the tiny cyclamen which are called *pain de porceau* because wild boar eat their roots. She knew on which distant precipitous slope the first rhododendron flower. She knew by which walls whole settlements of snails come out of hiding. She knew where the yellow gentians with the largest roots grow on the mountainside where the soil is least rocky so that digging them is a little easier. She worked and scavenged alone.

I talk to my shadow when the sun is out, and together we calculate the price our loot is likely to fetch. We have become experts, the two of us. And we commiserate together—about the weight of the sack, about the thorns in our hands, about how long we work. Sometimes, like you, we sleep at midday.

Abruptly she pushed back her chair, and went over to the cupboard.

Do you still drink *gnôle*?

It's very late, I complained.

The contempt of her laughter filled the room. She poured from the bottle into the glasses.

I sell a bottle of this for nine thousand!

It was the first gentian which I had tasted since my return. It has a very strong taste. The gentian roots taste of the earth and the earth tastes of the mountain.

She knew where every accessible wild cherry tree was. She carried a small ladder with her, no taller than herself, and this enabled her to get up into the tree. When she was well placed, her back against a branch, her boots on another, surrounded by cherries, and the basket hung from its hook at the right level, she could pick without looking. She could stand in the tree with her eyes shut like an owl, and her fingers would find the stalks, instantly move down them, and break them off at the node four or five at a time. With her eyes half shut she scarcely touched the fruit.

She sold her goods to restaurants, herbalist shops, florists, hotel manageresses.

I'll give you three thousand for the silver thistles, said the manageress, are you deaf, can you hear me? She held out a five-thousand note.

I have no change, said the Cocadrille.

If you never have change, how do you get here every week? demanded the manageress angrily.

By private car!

The manageress was forced to go and change the note. May she rot! added the Cocadrille.

One afternoon there was a cloudburst and she found herself propelled into a crowd of women, who surged through the glass doors of a department store and came to a stop before a glass counter where young women were selling stockings and lace underwear. No sooner had she begun to marvel at the black lace, than she was again pushed from behind, and this time found herself surrounded by other women in a lift. When it went up, she crossed herself and whispered:

Emile, if only you could see me now!

The lift operator, a man of her own age, dressed in a bandsman's uniform, said to her: Coffee, tea, chocolate, *pâtisseries*, Madame. The lift doors slid back and the two carpeted ground levels once more coincided.

For the next ten years, every week, after she had sold her goods, she visited this upper floor tearoom. On her way to the tearoom she went to a tobacconist.

What can I do for you today, Madame?

Give me eight hundred Marlboro.

The tobacconist slipped the four large packets into a gold-coloured plastic bag. Carrying the gold-coloured bag, she entered the department store, crossed to the lift, and waited for the lift-man to address her: Coffee, tea, chocolate, *pâtisseries*, Madame?

On the fourth floor she went to the ladies' room. There she locked herself in the lavatory and pulled up her long black serge skirt. Underneath, at the level of her hips, she wore a cloth band. This bandoleer she had made out of one of La Mélanie's linen chemises. Its pockets were larger than the usual ones for cartridges. Before sewing them she had measured very carefully. Into the double line of pockets she fitted thirty-nine packets of Marlboro.

With these red-and-white packets of what she considered to be tasteless tobacco, she was able to double her income. American cigarettes sold for twice as much on her side of the frontier. After she had arranged her skirt and pulled down her loose cardigan she flushed the toilet and emerged, hat in hand. She arranged her hair in the mirror above the washbasin.

She had the appearance of a pauper and at the same time she looked wilful. Such a combination in a city suggests madness.

The drinking of the chocolate she ordered in the tearoom was a ritual, and was accompanied by her smoking one or two cigarettes from the single packet she had kept out. She preferred the cigarettes she rolled herself. It was her sense of occasion which made her realise it would have been inappropriate to smoke them in such a setting.

This was the only moment of the week when she sat in company, although she spoke to no one except the waitress. Sitting there on one of the gilded wicker chairs, such as she had never seen until her second life began, sipping her chocolate with grated nutmeg sprinkled on its frothy cream, smoking a perfectly cylindrical cigarette with a long filter tip, checking from time to time with her stiffened fingers that her bandoleer was in place, she allowed herself to dream of the fulfillment of her plans. She studied the other customers, nearly all of whom were women out shopping. She noticed their hands, their made-up faces, their jewelry, their shoes with high heels. She had no wish to speak to them and she did not envy them, yet the sight of them gave her pleasure. They were a weekly proof of the extent of what money can do. Each month she saved at least half the money which she received for the cigarettes smuggled across the frontier. Never for an instant did she forget what the total of her savings amounted to. Every week this figure encouraged her. It was like a father. It got her out of bed when it was dark. When she set out, before the sun was up, on her walk of twenty kilometres, and her skirt was drenched by the dew which dripped down her legs into her socks, it reminded her that her dress might dry within an hour, if it didn't rain. When she was hungry, it told her not to complain, for she would eat later. When her back ached and her shoulders were sore and, coming down from the mountain, her knees were knotted and cracked with so much pain that it made her cry out, it reminded her how one day she would buy a new bed. When she talked with her shadow, it promised her that eventually they would move back into the village.

Whilst drinking her chocolate, the total of her savings—she always added on what she was about to receive that day—was as consoling as the music which came out of the loudspeakers high up near the decorated ceiling. Every week, every year, every decade, the amount increased.

When you have enough money, you can stand on your head stark naked!

She said this to a man, accompanied by a woman in a fur coat, who was waiting in the tobacconist's shop. The woman gave a little scream and the man, thinking that she was begging, dug into his trouser pocket for a small coin. The Cocadrille refused it. I have enough! she hissed at him. I have enough, she repeated to me across the table.

She sipped the *gnôle* and rolled herself another cigarette.

Soon it will be winter, she went on. Then I'm alone. And the snow forces me indoors. At Christmas I take mistletoe into B——. I get a thousand for a good bunch. The rest of the time, I knit. I can do nothing else. I never learnt to spin like Maman. Anyway I have no sheep. I knit pullovers and ski caps for a shop in B——.

She gulped back the rest of the *gnôle*.

Next door to the wool shop there is an antique shop. There's a wooden cradle in the window at the moment. If I had mine, I would sell it. Once I went in there and asked the price of a milking stool. Can you guess how much it cost? If it costs that much, I told them, what would I cost? You could sell me piece by piece. You could ask one hundred thousand for a milking hand. You could ask fifty thousand for a milking arm. How much would you get, I asked them, for a real peasant woman's arsehole?

She drew on her cigarette.

All winter I knit. There's nothing here, day after day, except the two needles and me. When a car passes and doesn't stop—and they never stop—I think of shooting the driver. Why not?

Why do you tell me all this?

So that you should know what I'm saying.

Only the corners of the room were still dark. The flame in the lamp looked yellow and daylight was coming through the smeared, dusty windows. She took the lamp and I thought she was going to blow it out. Instead, she walked over to the chimney in the corner and held the lamp above her head.

Look! she ordered.

On the mantelpiece were several porcelain plates decorated with cherries and flowers, a statuette of a chamois standing on a rock with his head high in the air, and a white bust in porcelain of St. François de Sales. Unlike everything else in the room, these objects were dusted, carefully arranged, and shining.

Have you really saved two million? I asked.

She cocked her head on one side, like a blackbird when it is about to smash a snail against a stone.

I have been listening all night, I said. It's not as if you're hiding things from me!

She blew out the lamp, turned her back, and refused to utter another word.

Three days later, on returning home in the evening, I found a note rolled and put into the keyhole of my door. The Cocadrille must have passed through the village and found the door locked. The note, written in her large flowery hand, simply said: *If you want to hear more, I have more to tell you.* It was useless to visit her in the daytime for she might be anywhere in her vast territory, and so the following evening I took the road past the Madonna's column. When I turned the corner I saw to my surprise that there was already a light in the window of the roadmender's house. I knocked at the door.

Who is it?

Jean! I replied. Are you alone?

She undid the lock.

I wasn't expecting you.

I found your note.

What note?

The note you left in my door yesterday.

I wasn't in the village yesterday.

Who else could it have been?

Was it signed?

She demanded this mischievously as though she already knew or had guessed the answer.

No, it wasn't.

The storeroom was unchanged, except that there were several bulging sacks in the corner under the ladder, and from their smell I knew they were full of gentian roots. Like roots, her own hands were caked with earth.

What have you done? she asked.

I was at the fair at La Roche.

I was by Le Forêt du Cercle.

In my head I tried to work out who, if not the Cocadrille, might have written the note. Whoever it was intended that I should believe it was written by the Cocadrille; it must have been written by somebody who knew that I had already visited her.

Why have you lit the lamp so early? I asked.

I was going to write.

Another note to me?

To somebody else.

It then occurred to me that, contrary to what she said, the Cocadrille was in the habit of receiving other visitors. And they were men, I felt sure of that. She used her jokes and stories as a bait to attract some company for a little while, to drink across the table—this is why she had commented on my bringing only one bottle of wine—and perhaps also out of a kind of malice, to make a little mischief with the men's wives. It was a previous visitor who must have written me the note.

Sit down, she said, I'll heat the soup.

I can't stay long.

You have so much to do!

She knelt down to blow into the fire and whisper into it: there is something I want to ask you. It was not clear whether she said this to the fire or to me.

She went out to the stable and I heard her washing her hands in a bucket of water.

What can I pay you? she asked when she came back.

A little red.

I carry everything up here on my back!

Is the white wine lighter?

She laughed at that, and glanced at me conspiratorially.

Wait! she ordered and climbed up the ladder.

The wood cracked as it caught fire in the stove. I went over to smell the soup—with age I have become greedy: not that I eat so much and not that, living alone, I cook special dishes for myself, it is simply that I think more about food, thoughts about food pester me like cats that have not been fed. I glanced up at the mantelpiece and the shining porcelain plates decorated with cherry-tree branches. I rubbed my finger on the shelf to check whether it had collected dust and I thought: How unpredictable the Cocadrille is!

Outside, the sun had set behind the Roc d'Enfer, I could tell because the distant rockface, where the cumin grows, had turned pink, the colour of pale coral. Usually it is as grey as wood ash. I went out of the door onto the ledge. I could hear the Jalent below. They said in the village that the Cocadrille seldom washed her clothes; when a garment was rotten with dirt she simply threw it over the edge.

On the other side of the river were orchards and meadows with cows in them. They looked like a picture engraved on a wooden mould for butter. La Mélanie had had just such a mould showing a river at the bottom, two cows in the middle, and some apple trees in the distance. This was the mould the Cocadrille used in the *alpage* fifty years before.

I looked behind the chicken hutch, I walked right round the rock house with the tree on top of it, I went down the road as far as the corner, I surveyed the mountain above. Nobody was there. Whoever had written the note was going to play no practical joke tonight. I was slightly disappointed for had he come, we could have talked there on the road about the Cocadrille's stratagems. The air was turning cold, and I returned indoors.

The saucepan was steaming on the stove.

So you've seen the ledge I live on!

I looked up. She was standing halfway down the ladder. She had changed her clothes. She was wearing shoes, not sabots, some kind of silk stockings instead of woollen ones, a black heavy silk skirt, a white blouse, a jacket to match the skirt, and around her head and shoulders a white tulle veil. She was dressed in the clothes in which women go to church to be married.

In God's name, what do you think you are doing! I shouted.

Her eyes were so intense that they forced you to share in their madness. I remember thinking: For the first time I understand why you are called the Cocadrille. Her eyes made both our long lives seem no more than a moment.

My poor Jean! You're shitting in your pants!

She came down the ladder, went over to the stove, and dipped the ladle into the saucepan. Years before, her entry from the stable had so surprised me that I did not fully understand what she had done until the next day; it was only then that I realised how she must have sprinkled cow's milk on her breasts. This time I was more percipient. Clearly she had spent several evenings sewing the black silk costume. Even if, as was likely, she had inherited it from Mélanie, it would have been too large for the Cocadrille and would have required drastic alteration. She must have prepared this scene. It was part of a plan.

You certainly have a taste for theatre! I muttered.

There is no theatre in what I do.

Why do you dress up then?

The last time I undressed! She put her hands on her ribs as though to quieten the cackling of her own laughter.

We broke the bread and put it in the soup. Neither of us spoke and the silence was filled with the sound of her sucking from her spoon. She had fewer than half her teeth left. When she had finished, she pushed her plate away, got up, and came back with a bottle of *gnôle*. Of all the stories I had heard about her, none hinted that she was normally in the habit of drinking. Her shoes were brand new—as indeed they must have been, for nobody else's would have fitted her.

Do you dress up like this every time you invite a man up from the village?

Abruptly she drank back the *gnôle* in her glass. She drank it back like a chicken drinks, with a quick stupid toss of its head.

If I didn't have enough, she cried, I could go on for another ten years. I do have enough. I have scavenged for twenty years. I want to enjoy the rest of my life. I want to move back into the village. You have a house in the village and you haven't much else. I'm prepared to buy now a share of your house until I'm dead, and I will pay you straight away. The rest of my savings I'm keeping for myself. Does that interest you?

The house is too small.

I know.

The way you live—I looked deliberately round the kitchen— is not the way I could live. At my age I'm not going to change.

I can change. That's why I showed you the plates and the chamois.

I shook my head. Why don't you rent a whole house to yourself?

There are none. And it would be a waste of too much money.

Have you asked anyone else to take you in?

Only *you* know me! She whispered this as though we were not alone in the lonely house on the deserted road which led over the empty pass.

Was it you who wrote the note?

She nodded. I was writing to you again tonight.

What you really want, I shouted, is for me to marry you! That's what you have always wanted!

Yes, she said. In church, with this veil.

You are out of your mind.

There's no one to stop you this time. You are alone, she said.

God protect me.

I will pay you separately for the marriage, I'll give you a dowry.

You can't be that rich!

We can talk about money as soon as we agree in principle. She laid her hand on the back of mine.

I can't marry you.

Jean!

Again she said my name as she had said it forty years before and again it separated me, marked me out from all other men. In the mountains the past is never behind, it's always to the side. You come down from the forest at dusk and a dog is barking in a hamlet. A century ago in the same spot at the same time of day, a dog, when it heard a man coming down through the forest, was barking, and the interval between the two occasions is no more than a pause in the barking.

In the pause between her twice saying my name in the same way, I saw myself as the young boy I had once been, encouraged by Masson to believe that I was more than usually intelligent, I saw myself as a young man without prospects, because I was the youngest, but with great ambitions, my first departure for Paris which so impressed me as the centre, the capital of the globe, that I was determined to take one of the roads from l'Etoile across the world, the last good-byes to my family, my mother imploring me not to go all the time that I harnessed the horse and my father put my bag in the cart. It is the Land of the Dead, she said. The voyage by the boat on which each day I dreamt of how I would return to the village, honoured and rich with presents for my mother, I saw myself on the quayside where I did not understand a single word of what was being said, and the

great boulevards and the obelisk, the grandeur of the packing
plants which I tried to describe in a letter to my father, for
whom the selling of one cow for meat was the subject of a
month's discussion, the news of my father's death, the noise of
the trains through the window of the room where I lodged for
five years, Carmen's tantrums and her plans to open a bar of her
own, her black hair the colour of the coal I shovelled, the epi-
demic in the shantytown, the land of straight railways so flat
and going on forever; I saw myself in the train going south to
Río Gallegos in Patagonia, sheepshearing and a wind that, like
my homesickness, never stopped, I saw my wedding in Mar del
Plata with all seventy-three members of Ursula's family, the
birth of Gabriel six months later, the birth of Basil eighteen
months afterwards and my fight with her family to christen him
Basil, Ursula's dressmaking, her mother's debts, my friendship
with Gilles and the pleasure of speaking my own language
again, I saw Gilles' death, Ursula refusing to go to his funeral or
to let the boys go, the flight to Montreal, the boys learning
English which I could never speak, the news of my mother's
death, the news of Ursula's death, the fire in the bar, the police
investigations, I saw myself working as a night-watchman, my
Sundays in the forest, the buying of my ticket home, I saw forty
whole years compressed within the pause.

What separated me this time from all other men called Jean
or Théophile or François was not desire, which is stronger than
words, it was a sense of loss, an anguish deeper than any understanding. When she said my name the first time in the chalet in
the *alpage,* she offered another life to the one I was about to
live. Looking back I saw, now, the hope in the other life she
offered and the hopelessness of the one I chose. Saying my name
the second time, it was as if she had only paused a moment and
then repeated the offer; yet the hope had gone. Our lives had
dissolved it. I hated her. I would gladly have killed her. She made
me see my life as wasted. She stood there and everything I saw—
her wrinkled cider-apple of a face, her stiff swollen hands which
grabbed and rooted the region like a boar's tusks, placed now

with their palms to her breast as if in supplication, the frail veil, the morsel of cigarette paper stuck to her lip, were all proof of the dissolution of the offer. Yet I was forced—for the first and last time in this life—to speak to her tenderly.

Give me time to think, Lucie!

My using her proper name caused her to smile and brought tears to her eyes. For a moment their extraordinary sharpness was clouded and the thousands of lines around them were doubled as she screwed them up.

Come and tell me when you want to, Jean.

Before I gave her my considered answer, she was dead.

Her body was discovered by the postman, who noticed that the window onto the road was broken and swinging on its hinges. The second morning he knocked and went in. She had been felled with an axe. The blade had split her skull. The signs were that she had put up a fight and had thrown a bottle through the window. Despite extensive searches, her fortune was never found. The most likely explanation was that the murderer came to steal her savings, had been surprised by her when he was leaving, and had killed her. The axe was her own which he had taken from the stable. The police cross-questioned almost everybody in the village, including myself, yet they made no arrest and the murderer was not identified.

She was buried a month before La Toussaint. There were fewer than a hundred people at her funeral; her death was a kind of disgrace for the village. She had been killed for her fortune and only somebody from the village was likely to have known about it. There were many flowers placed on her coffin, and the large unsigned wreath I ordered was not immediately remarkable.

THE THIRD LIFE OF LUCIE CABROL

One morning when I was six my father said to me: When you let out the cows, keep Fougère behind, she's going to the abattoir today. I undid the chains of the other cows—I could just reach the locking links with my arms above my head—and the dog chased them out. Later I would take the cows to the slopes by the place which we called Nîmes. Left alone in the stable, Fougère looked anxiously around her, her ears full out like wings. By this afternoon, I said, you will be dead. She started to eat the hay in the manger. After pulling out several mouthfuls, each with a toss of her head, she looked around again and lowed. The other cows were already grazing outside. I could hear their bells. The sunlight coming through the holes in the planks of the stable walls made beams in the dust which I raised as I swept. My father unbuckled the wide leather collar Fougère was wearing. Attached to this collar was her bell which weighed five kilos. Before he turned away to hang the collar and the bell on the wall, he looked at the beast and said: My poor cuckoo, you'll never again go to Nîmes.

Whilst the funeral service was being performed inside the church, most of us men stood outside. This group of standing figures, solemn and still, always looks dwarfed by the mountains. We spoke in low voices, about the murder. Everyone was agreed that the police would never discover who the assassin was. Each said this as if he himself had a clear idea of the truth. She was fearless, they said, this had been the Cocadrille's trouble.

When the coffin came out of the church, the crowd followed it in procession through the cemetery. Nobody spoke now. The coffin was so small that it made you think of a child's funeral. It was in the cemetery that I first heard her voice. I had no difficulty in hearing what she said, although she was whispering.

Do you want me to say who it is? He's among you, he's here in the cemetery, the thief.

The murderer, I muttered.

It's the thief whom I cannot forgive!

Her voice made me frightened. I realised that the others could not hear it. My fear was that she would shout, and it would become obvious by my reactions that I could hear something.

What would you do if I shouted his name? she said, realising my thoughts.

They won't hear.

You will hear me, Jean, you can hear me if I say Jean, can't you.

Yes, I said, and made the sign of the cross over her coffin.

When once the coffin was passed, the procession shuffled forward more quickly.

It wasn't me.

You thought of killing me.

Outside the cemetery gate her brothers Edmond and Henri stood by the wall traditionally reserved after funerals for the closest of kin. If stones could feel, the stones there would be blood-red from the pain felt by many of those who have leant against them.

My brothers look solemn and hopeful, don't they? Solemn and hopeful!

The crowd dispersed and the men went to drink in the cafés. I declined several invitations and hurried away in order to lead her voice back home, where we would be unobserved.

In the house, the same house in which she had planned that we should live after we had married, I spoke to her. She did not reply. Indeed I had the impression she had not accompanied me. Perhaps she had gone to the cafés.

I awoke early next morning and went to look out of the window. The valley below was filled with opaque white mist; where it ended, little trails of transparent cloud blew off like steam into the sky. The valley was like a laundry, the endless laundry of the damned, steaming, soaping, billowing, working against the bath of the rockfaces in total silence. The lichen on the rocks were the voices of the damned.

Did you decide not to marry me?

I hadn't decided.

Then I'll leave you till you've made up your mind.

At La Toussaint the cemetery was full of flowers, and many people stood at the feet of the graves of their loved ones trying to listen to the dead. That night I heard her voice again. It was as close as if it were on the pillow beside mine.

I've learnt something, Jean. All over the world the dead drink at La Toussaint. Everyone drinks, no one refuses. Every year it is the same, they drink until they're drunk. They know that they have to visit the living. And so they get drunk!

On what?

On *eau de vie*! She spluttered with laughter and I felt her spit in my ear.

When she had got her breath back, she continued: And so they never know whether the living are as boneheaded as they seem, or whether the dead only have that impression because the dead are so drunk!

You sound drunk now.

Why did you think of killing me?

You know it wasn't I who stole your savings?

What did you want to kill me for?

You are drunk.

I tell you, nobody comes today if they are sober.

Has La Mélanie come?

She's making some coffee.

That will sober you up!

Not the black coffee of the dead won't. She cackled with laughter once more.

So you're drunk, every time you talk to me.

No, the dead forget the living, I haven't forgotten yet.

How long does it take to forget?

I know why you thought of killing me.

Why do you ask then?

I want to hear you say it.

Are you alone, Lucie?

You can see.

I can see nothing in the dark.

Admit the truth to me and you'll see.

Yes, I thought of killing you the night you dressed up.

I heard her get out of the bed and the floorboards creaked under her feet.

Have you been to see the man who did kill you?

It doesn't interest me.

You said you could never forgive the thief.

I've changed my mind. I don't need my savings now. Why did you think of killing me?

You were going to force me to marry you.

Force you! Force you! What with?

Then she went.

The room smelt of boar. Otherwise there was no sign that she had been there.

The thirteenth of December was her name day, *Sainte Lucie*. According to the old calendar—I read this in an almanac— Saint Lucie's day used to be the twenty-third, just after the winter solstice.

From the day of Saint Lucie
the days lengthen by a flea's width.

On neither the thirteenth nor on the twenty-third of December did she come back. The days grew longer.

At last the weather turned warm. My circulation improved. The old man's blood responding a little to the sun. The apple trees blossomed, the potatoes were planted, the cows were put out in the pastures. The hay was cut. One evening when the valley, full of clouds and torn mists, had its look of being the laundry of the damned, I told myself: on the next fine day I will climb up to Nîmes and pick some blueberries.

The sky was clear, and its peacefulness extended further than the furthest range of snowcapped mountains. The blueberries grow above the tree line, usually on slopes facing east or west. The southern slopes have too much sun. My mother used to dry whole sprigs of blueberries with their leaves to give to the cows when they had diarrhoea.

From the slope where I began picking, I could see the Cabrol chalet, a little to the right and below. The chalet will scarcely outlast me, I said to myself. It must be years since Henri or Edmond have done anything to it. Instead of bringing their cows up, they rent extra pasture below. There are holes in the roof and many of the shingles need replacing. The snow will be driven in, the beams will rot, and one day one end of the timberwork will fall. The following winter it will look like a shipwreck; the wind, the snow, the slope, the summer sun, which burns the wood black, wear away the timber just as the sea and waves do.

The Cocadrille used a comb to pick her blueberries. When we were young, the comb didn't exist. It is like a bear's paw, made of wood and nails. It scoops up berries between each claw, and working with it is ten times as fast as picking each berry separately between finger and thumb. It collects indiscriminately: anything that passes between its nails, it keeps in its wooden paw. As well as ripe berries, you find green ones, leaves, the ends of twigs, tiny white snails, and the pods of flowers. Later, to separate them, you set up a plank at an angle to the ground, wet the plank with water, take a handful of fruit from the bucket and pour them so that they roll down the wet plank; the ripe fruit roll to the bottom into the pan, and most of the leaves and the twigs and the grass and the snails stick to the wood.

The Cocadrille set up her plank on the ledge of ground behind the roadmender's house. It is a tedious operation if you are alone. You need one person to roll the fruit, and another to check in the pan below and take out the green ones which didn't stick to the wood. She must have rolled a few handfuls and then gone to squat by the pan on the ground, then rolled a few more, then gone to squat by the pan and so on.

Bent forward towards the slope, my face close to the ground, I could see the grasshoppers. There were a couple mating. Their bodies are bright green with streaks of white yellow. They are about three centimetres long, and the noise they make consists of three soft chuffs and then a long drawn-out hiss like a snake.

Tchee tchee hissssss.

When she rolled the blueberries down the wet plank, she must have heard the roar of the Jalent at the bottom of the ravine and the tinkle of the blueberries as they fell into the pan.

When blueberries are wet they darken to the colour of ink. Warm and dry in the sun they almost have a bloom like grapes. As you comb, you notice others a little higher up or a little to the side, and so you move towards them to comb them too with the bear's paw, and they in turn lead you to others and the others to others. Picking blueberries is like grazing.

As she sorted the fruit she must sometimes have gazed at the orchards and fields on the other side of the ravine, a reminder of all she had lost in her second life.

My bucket was half full. I had climbed out of sight of the place where I had begun.

Jean!

I wasn't convinced that I had heard her.

How many have you picked?

Half a bucket.

As slow as ever! she mocked.

I have calluses under my chin, I shouted, because all my life I have rested it on the handle of a shovel.

I thought this made her laugh. I could not be sure because there was a jackdaw flying overhead. And the laugh I heard might have been his cry: Drru krrie kriee! Drru krrie kriee!

Shall I help you pick?

If you wish.

I went on picking, and I heard no more, only the grasshoppers, the jackdaw, and occasionally very distantly, when the wind blew, the sound of cowbells.

I learnt what the cowbells said as a boy:

It's mine! It's mine! Can it go on? Can it go on? It can't! It can't!

I combed with the bear's paw, following the trail of the berries, grazing higher and higher. The next time I emptied the paw into the bucket, I had the impression that the level of the fruit had mounted twice as fast as before.

I straightened my back and, for the first time since her death, I saw her. She was combing, leaning against the green slope, with her head above the skyline, silhouetted against the blue sky. A scarf was tied round her head. As I watched, she climbed and went over the skyline.

She's as easy to lose as a button, La Mélanie said.

I left my bucket and climbed up to the crest. She lay there on the other side as if dead. She lay there on the soft turf between the rhododendron bushes whose flowers were finished, and she wore a scarf round her head, a crumpled black dress, socks, and boots. Her shins were bare and scratched. Her eyes were shut and her arms were crossed exactly as if she were dead. It is strange I thought that, for I knew she was dead. I had seen her coffin lowered into the earth. Now there was no coffin lid, no earth, nothing but the blue sky above her.

Without thinking I took off my beret and stood there holding it in my clasped hands as I gazed down at her. Her face was grey like the outcrops of limestone. She was as motionless as a boulder. I know that it is easy in the mountains to see things that others cannot see. And then I noticed the fingers of her hands. They were stained an inky blue-black. They were like any of our fingers in André Masson's class. This was proof that she had indeed been picking blueberries this morning. In September when she was murdered there were no blueberries.

Can you see me now? I heard her say this, although her lips didn't move.

Without answering, I lay down beside her and gazed up into the sky. The sky was benign and the jackdaws were still circling in wide circles above us.

How old am I? she asked.

You were in the class of 1920. That makes you sixty-eight. No, sixty-seven.

I was born in the morning. My father was milking in the stable. White cloud like smoke was blowing through the door. My mother had her sister and a neighbour with her. I was born very quickly. The neighbour held me up feet first and cried, It's a girl. Give her to me, my mother said and then she screamed, Jésus forgive me, she screamed, she is marked with the mark of the craving, Jésus! I have marked her with the mark of the craving. Mélanie, said the neighbour, be calm. It is not the mark of the craving.

You know everything about your life now, I said.

If I told you all that I know it would take sixty-seven years.

I turned my head towards her, she was smiling at me, her blue eyes open, dirt smudged on her cheek, a few black hairs escaping from her scarf; she had the face of the Cocadrille at twenty. I moved my arm away from my body to find her hand. When I touched it, I remembered.

She led me by the hand towards the side of the mountain. Crossing an outcrop of rock she stopped, and pointed with the toe of her boot.

Cherry stones in the bird shit! She laughed. They fly with them all the way up here.

I did not recognise the path we took. At first I blamed my memory. Forty-six years is a long time. Soon I doubted whether it was a path at all. The going became steeper and steeper, and we had to push our way through pine trees which grew so close together that no sunlight ever reached the ground. There were centuries of pine needles and my boots sunk into them up to the ankles. I could feel them working their way through the wool of my socks. The needles were either ashen grey or black, they had no more colour than the lower branches of the trees. To prevent ourselves slipping we held on to the branches like ropes.

She led the way and I followed. At one point the slope was so steep that it was like climbing down the trunk of the tree itself. I suddenly remembered the porcelain chamois on her mantelpiece. I wondered whether it was still there. At least three men had fallen to their deaths whilst hunting chamois on this mountain. I hoped that she knew exactly where we were going. I doubted whether I would be capable of climbing up again. My legs were already shaking out of weakness. When I was twelve, Sylvestre, an old man, was trapped on the mountainside. He could neither climb up nor continue down. The alarm was given just before nightfall. Twenty of us with lamps set out to try to find him. If the Cocadrille disappeared, I would be like Sylvestre.

When the Devil grows old, she shouted back at me, he becomes a hermit!

Sylvestre was dead when we found him.

Fortunately she knew the path as she knew all paths. There was not a slope or crag or stream on this mountainside that she did not know. We emerged from the trees into the sunlight. We were at the top of a long bank of grass on which the paths the cows had traced over generations were like steps for us to walk down. A man in Montreal who worked for the radio once sent me a postcard of an ancient Roman theatre. The steps down the grass were like the seats of that theatre. At the bottom was a large pasture bordered by a forest. In front of the forest I could see men working.

Descending the grass steps I suddenly felt as carefree as I did before I was fully grown. Opposite Saint Lucie beside the shortest day, there is Saint Audrey beside the longest. You put on a clean shirt, newly ironed by your mother—it touches your shoulders like the face of a flat iron gone cold—you comb your hair and look at yourself in the mirror, what you see is a sixteen-year-old to whom anything may happen this Sunday. You join friends walking down to the village. You wait in the square. Everything which occurs is part of a preparation. You drink in the café. You read the signs of the future—so many of them are jokes—and yet you remain ignorant. This ignorance makes the time easy and long. You walk to the next village. There is a fight. You notice the consequences of your smallest actions and these consequences never reinforce each other. You walk back by moonlight. The girls flounce their skirts. Almost everything talked about has not yet happened. Father is asleep, beneath the smoked sausages hanging from the ceiling. You fold your trousers with care, scratch your balls, and fall asleep. Sunday follows Sunday, season follows season, and you go from tree to tree: there is as yet no forest. Then a day comes when there is only a forest and you have to live in it forever: then all the days, both summer or winter, are short. I never expected to emerge from that forest, yet there I was, walking down the grass steps as if my life lay before me.

I first singled you out at school, said the Cocadrille, you made less noise than the other boys and you were methodical. You always carried a knife in your hands, always carving a stick. Once you cut yourself, and I saw you peeing over your cut to disinfect it.

Amongst the flowers in the grass there were red campions. Their pink is like the pink of paper flags all over the world when there is a fiesta.

Where are we?

This is where I am going to build.

Who does it belong to?

Me.

You!

The dead own everything, she said.

So you have land now.

Land but no seasons.

How do you plant?

We don't, we have no reason to, we have access to all the granaries in the world, they are all full.

And when they are empty?

They are full forever.

Why don't you give potatoes to the hungry then?

We can't.

You could smuggle some across.

I chose a smoked ham for you last winter, it weighed seven kilos and was beautifully dry, I stood by when it was being smoked for two days, I was there when Emile cut the juniper bushes and when he threw water on the burning branches to make more smoke, six weeks earlier I led the pig to have her throat cut, I put my hands over her eyes so she became calm when the life flowed out of her, I gave her to the sow to suckle the day she was born, and I carried the ham to your house and I hung it in the cellar, wrapped in muslin, and when you found it two days later it was a bone, even the string had rotted and you found it in the earth in which you bury your white beet so they stay white on the cellar floor.

That bone! I muttered.

And you said: It could be the ham of a pig we killed when I was a child. I heard you say that and I knew then I could give you nothing.

You are lying.

You didn't say that and you didn't throw it over the wall?

Yes I did.

She shrugged her shoulders.

The figures I had seen from afar were working on timber, hammering nails into the joints of three vast frames which lay flat on the ground and which, when raised, would hold the walls and roof of a chalet. Each frame had five vertical columns, each column as thick as a sixty-year-old tree and twelve metres high.

They felled the trees last September, the Cocadrille said, on the day I was killed with the axe. The sap was rising.

The frames laid out on the ground were the colour of stripped radiant pine. One of the men who was hammering straightened his back. It was Marius Cabrol. I had seen him last on his deathbed. I had made the sign of the cross with a sprig of boxwood dipped in holy water over his heart. It was his daughter who had laid him out and dressed him. The way he now greeted us disconcerted me for he gave no sign that he remembered or recognised any of this. He grinned as if we had just drunk a glass together.

Fifteen spruces for the columns, he said, a dozen for the purlins, forty twenty-year-old trees for the rafters, I forget how many for the planks. We cut them all down when the axe entered her head. She told us afterwards she heard us sawing in the forest.

The first thing I did, wasn't it, was to bring you all cider and cheese and bread. I knew exactly where you were.

We were getting hungry, said Marius, smiling.

She took my hand and we stepped over the columns of the nearest frame. She was a young woman leading an old man. The men sat astride the frame as they hammered, the nails were big and they launched them into the wood with blows from the shoulder.

All right, Lucie? The hammerer who shouted this with virile impertinence was Armand who had been carried away by the Jalent and drowned. Next to him hammered Gustave who had fallen from the mountain. Georges, who hanged himself because he knew that he would become a pauper, was sewing paper flowers to the branches of a tiny spruce; the flowers were white like silver and yellow like gold. Adelin, who was killed by a tree in the forest, was tying a rope. Mathieu who was struck dead by lightning was measuring with a yellow ruler. Then I recognised Michel who died of internal bleeding after being kicked by a horse, and I saw Joset who was lost in an avalanche.

Why are they all here? I demanded.

They have come to help us, each of them brought food and drink for the meal tonight, they are good neighbours.

Why only—

Only what, Jean?

The ones who died violently.

They are the first you see.

And those who died peacefully?

There are not so many who die in their beds. It's a poor country.

Why first—? My fears that I had been led into a trap were increased.

Bend down.

She kissed me on the cheek and my fears became ridiculous. Her mouth was full of white teeth and she smelt of grass. Was it really she who fifty years ago nobody in their right mind would have thought of marrying?

They all say your trouble was that you were fearless.

I knew what I wanted.

She laughed. Between the buttons of her shirt I could make out the slight, barely noticeable rise of her breasts. Like two leaves on the earth.

Do you know, it took me no longer to learn my way around here among the dead than it took me to learn my way around the city of B——.

As she said this, her voice aged and became hoarser. I glanced at her. She was an old woman with a sack on her back and she looked mad.

Who is going to live in the chalet?

Somebody from behind pushed my beret over my eyes. It was Marius, her father. Once again he was grinning.

You are warmer in bed with a wife. The whole war I thought of nothing else, I thought only of caressing Mélanie in bed. The way Marius spoke had the unctuousness of a caress. There were some who had intercourse with donkeys, it never interested me, a beast isn't soft enough, when at last I came home I took her to bed and we had our fourth child. Even when I was old and lost my warmth, I thought of going to bed when I was working alone in the fields, sometimes thinking about it made me warm. There are those who call me lazy. It was my idea of happiness, you'll see for yourself, if you don't see now—it's better than sleeping alone.

The Cocadrille walked away, across her back was tied the blue umbrella and over her shoulder she carried a sack.

Aren't you forgetting that your daughter has been a spinster all her life? I asked.

Ah! my poor Jean, my poor future son-in-law, it's now that she's at the marrying age. Why else would I be building a chalet for her?

You were never a carpenter, I pointed out, and sixty-eight is no marrying age!

We can become anything. That is why injustice is impossible here. There may be the accident of birth, there is no accident of death. Nothing forces us to remain what we were. The Cocadrille could be seventeen, tall, with wide hips, and with breasts you couldn't take your eyes off—only then you wouldn't know her, would you?

Once more I had the feeling of not yet having entered the forest, of all my life being in front of me.

All the men you see working here, whispered Marius—I remembered the milk running off her breasts—have married her!

Not Georges! I exclaimed.

Georges was the first. He married her the day after her funeral. The bridesmaids took the flowers from the grave. Those who die violently fall into each other's arms.

Am I to die violently? I asked.

Do you want to marry her? His smile had now become a leer.

Everything's ready! a man shouted.

The frame lay on the ground, constructed, finished, waiting to be lifted up into the air. To lift such a frame, thirty-five or forty men are needed. They came from every direction. All those whom I recognised were among the dead. Some carried ladders. Some were speaking and joking to one another and I could not hear their words. All of them greeted Marius à Brine who stood beside the *sablière,* which is the horizontal timber on the ground into which the frame, when vertical, has to be fitted. He who was no carpenter had become the master builder.

The wood of the frame smelt strongly of pine resin. Mixed with wax, this resin makes a good poultice for the cure of sciatica, a complaint from which many of us suffer as a result of carrying heavy loads on the slopes. We bent down together to lift the frame with our hands.

Marius was shouting so that everyone lifted at the same moment.

Tchee! Tchee! Lift!

And again. Tchee! Tchee! Hissssss!

The dead got their forearms under the frame. Bent double over the ground, they cradled the wood as you cradle a baby.

Tchee! Tchee! Hissssss!

Wood is to us what iron has been to others for two thousand years. We even made gearwheels out of wood.

With each heave we raised the frame a little higher. We could just rest our forearms on our thighs. The dead who were lifting the king-post, the vertical beam which holds the point of the roof, were now able to slip their shoulders under it, bundling together like bearers carrying a coffin.

When the frame was too high for us to lift with our hands, we thrust with poles. There was a pole tied to each column.

Half a dozen or so men gathered around each pole, thrusting it up, their grasping hands overlapping. Ten hands, fifty fingers, they were indistinguishable one from the other except where there was a scarred severed finger. How many of our fingers have been cut off by saws! Yet better a finger than a life, the living had a habit of saying.

With each thrust we grunted. The grunts came from the pit of the stomach. Sometimes a dead man farted with the effort. The Cocadrille had come back and was standing by my side, the same scarf round her head, white hairs straggling out of it.

Why do you want a hayloft, you have no land? I gasped.

Tchee! Tchee! Hissssss!

The gigantic frame which was going to span three rooms, a stable, and a hayloft—a hayloft such as a hundred haycarts, pulled across the wooden floor by the mares, would scarcely fill—shook with each heave. Or, rather, it was we who shook.

To store our hay, she said.

You have no cows.

To have thirty-five litres of milk a day for butter and cheese.

Tchee! Tchee! Hissssss!

You don't need to eat, I said.

To support ourselves and to have something to hand on to our children! She smiled, as she had when she handed me the butter fifty years before.

The faces of the dead were red with the effort of grasping, heaving, and holding, their mouths were strained, their eyes bulged, the muscles and veins on their necks stood out like ropes and cords beneath the skin.

I was always told the dead rest after a lifetime's work, I muttered.

When they remember their past, they work, she said. What else should they remember?

The shoulders of those who had taken off their shirts glistened with sweat, yet the frame was still below the angle of forty-five degrees.

Again! Tchee! Tchee! Lift!

The gigantic naked frame scarcely stirred. It was as if another forty men were pushing it down against us.

We need more help, go and fetch some others, round up the neighbours!

Jésus, Marie, and Joseph!

A ménage à trois!

Be quick about it!

The Cocadrille ran towards the forest. It was not possible to lay the frame down on the ground. It is easier to raise such a weight than to lower it, and in lowering it there is the risk of somebody being trapped beneath it. Pierre, who was on the next pole, had been trapped under a frame, with both his legs broken, and had died two years later.

No man should suffer the same thing twice.

We were able to prop several poles against the ground. We wedged in several ladders. Most of the weight was taken off us, yet nobody took their hands off the poles. The great frame pointed into the sky, not into the dark blue sky above us, it pointed towards the pale sky beyond the distant mountains. A jackdaw—I cannot say whether he was the same one—was circling above the frame. At one moment I thought he was going to alight on it. Everything was still, none of the dead was moving.

When the Cocadrille came back from the forest, she was young; several men followed her. As so many years before, I was astounded by how fast she ran.

Yes, I should have married her! I said it out loud. The dead were lost in their own thoughts. Nobody responded.

The newcomers joined the groups round each pole.

Tchee! Tchee! Hissssss!

The frame shifted up five or six degrees. Together we were going to master it. As soon as it passed the halfway mark of forty-five degrees it would become easier.

As a precautionary measure some men were already holding the ropes in case the almost vertical frame should incline too far and fall inwards. When the frame was vertical its tusk tenons had to be slotted into the mortices of the *sablière*. Human geometry had to replace the original strength of the trees. The tusks entered the mouths of the *sablière,* all five at almost the same moment.

I will marry you, I said, turning towards her.

To my horror 'Mile à Lapraz was standing beside her. He was flushed and looked as if he had been drinking. I had seen him only a week before in the village. It occurred to me then that all the men she had brought back running with her were among the living.

You will be a witness, she said to 'Mile.

Where are we? I mumbled. Aren't we far from the village?

We are outside the church, Jean, where the men stand at funerals and the newly married are photographed.

My face must have shown my consternation.

He's so careful, slurred 'Mile à Lapraz, nodding in my direction, he wipes his arse before he has shat!

You should talk, the Cocadrille snapped back at him. You've lived alone all your life, you get drunk alone, your bed smells like a distillery. Jean has been to the other side of the world, he married, he had children, he came back, he picks blueberries very slowly, all right he pretends to be deaf, he wanted to kill me, he has taken his time, but now at the last moment, the very last moment, he has agreed to marry me, you would never have the spunk to do that, 'Mile.

Now that the first frame was in place, she went from man to man with a bottle and a glass offering them to drink.

After we had rested, Marius à Brine called us to start raising the second frame. Encouraged by the sight of the first, upright, its columns as thick as trees, its white wood framing triangles of deep blue sky, we lifted the second frame, call by call:

Tchee! Tchee! Hissssss!

We lifted it without stopping, and the tusks of its columns entered the mouths of the *sablière.* We raised the third frame even quicker than the second. Some said this was because the wood was less green and so lighter.

Fifty men stood looking up at the three frames which indicated the full dimensions of the chalet; it was an outline drawing in white on the green pasture, the dark forest, and the blue sky.

No one will kill themselves in this chalet, she said.

The men whom the Cocadrille had brought from the village announced that, if they were no longer needed, they would return. Marius à Brine did his best to persuade them to stay for the feast they would have as soon as the work was over. They said they must go.

Come back later, insisted Marius, come back with your women for the feast!

The villagers were noncommittal.

Several of the dead came over to thank them. At least let us pay you another glass, they said.

No need to thank us, answered the living, you'd do the same for us.

That goes without saying, whenever a house is built some of us are there.

I watched the villagers walk away into the forest. Gradually they formed a single file, each one walking by himself. Their going disturbed me: I was alone again with the dead. At the same time I was relieved by their going; I would have no questions to answer. What language do they speak in Buenos Aires? How long have you been a widower? Are you really thinking of remarrying? How did she persuade you?

The work which remained to be done was now more divided and less anxious. We had to lift the purlins, the beams which run the length of the roof, into their positions, fit their joints and nail them. Every purlin was numbered with a numeral, written as André Masson had taught us all at school, and every joint was indicated twice on each piece of wood, with a capital letter. Some of the dead were on ladders and some worked on the ground. They made more comments than before and more jokes. Those on the ground fixed temporary bars at an angle to the future walls, like buttresses. Along these they pushed and pulled the purlins up with ropes.

The first to be fixed in place was the lowest, the timber bordering the overhanging roof. Against the wall beneath this overhanging roof, the wood for the stove would be stacked, sheltered from the snow and the rain. Against the southern wall protected by the roof she'd plant lettuces and parsley, and, along the edge of the same bed, multicoloured pansies, which have the colours of most of the precious stones in the world. Under the roof behind the first purlin, sparrows would nest and on the posts of the fence, for which the stakes have not yet been cut or pointed, a pair of crows would sit, waiting for her to come out to feed the chickens. I heard her calling them.

She took my hand in her stiff, calloused, grabbing, picking, old woman's hand. It was no longer possible for me to think of her as young.

There is no need for you to work, she said, they have enough help, we can sit in the sun.

And the food? I asked. Is everything prepared?

Everything.

I don't see any tables or benches.

They are in the church, it'll only take a minute to bring them out.

At her funeral when people were still filing out of the cemetery, the Mayor told the local veterinary surgeon: And so we gave her the roadmender's house, it was the best we could think of. You have to reckon with the fact that if she'd lived in a city, she would certainly have been put in an institution many years ago . . .

Look! she said, tapping my shoulder, they will soon be finished.

We were sitting there side by side, watching the mountains, and the men working. We were the eldest, all the working dead were younger than us. The Cocadrille's features and the backs of my own hands were a reminder of our age. The Cocadrille was sixty-seven when she was murdered, and I was three years older.

So, my contraband, I've smuggled you here, she said. An unlit cigarette was stuck to her lower lip which protruded and was blueish from the blueberries she had eaten.

The feeling of endless promise such as I hadn't experienced since I was young bore me up, cradled me. I saw my father making rabbit hutches, and myself handing him the nails. I must have been eleven the year when, under my mother's careful supervision, I bled and skinned my first rabbit. At the catechism class the Cocadrille knew by heart the answers I could not remember.

What is avarice?

Avarice is an excessive longing for the good things of life and particularly money.

Is love of the good things of life ever justified?

Yes, there is a justified love of the good things of life and this love inspires foresight and thrift.

On feast days in the Argentine the *peones* killed and ate turkeys: emigration offered me no new promises. The promise of the Place d'Etoile and the promise of the Arenne Corrientes in Buenos Aires were simply revivals of what I had already hoped in the village. I couldn't have imagined those places from the village, yet I did imagine my pleasure, the same pleasure they promised and didn't give me.

Pleasure is always your own, and it varies as much and no more than pain does. I had become accustomed to pain, and now to my surprise the hope of pleasure, the hope I had known when I was eleven, was coming from the old woman with the unlit cigarette who called me her contraband. Where had my life gone? I asked myself.

The dead were nailing the rafters. By the time all forty were in place, the sun was low and the bars of the roof cast a shadow on the grass beside the chalet which looked like a dark cage. The bars were the shadows.

Do you want to nail the bouquet? shouted Marius à Brine.

She waited for me to answer. I could feel her gaze through her half-shut eyes. The force of my reply surprised me.

From the corner of each of her puckered, squeezed eyes a tear came like juice. She crossed her arms to grasp her flat chest with her stiff hands. Her mouth stretched in a smile. Her tears ran down the deep lines to the corners of her mouth and she licked her upper lip.

Go, she said to me.

Marius handed me the hammer and the nails and I walked over to the foot of the first ladder. There was Georges, who hanged himself because he knew he was to become a pauper and would be sent in the winter to the old people's hostel where half the inmates were incoherent. The money to build this hostel had been donated by a rich engineer from the region who had built many bridges for roads and railways far away. Georges planned his suicide as carefully as the engineer planned his bridges, he fixed a hooked wire to a tall wooden pole, ran the wire down it and with the help of this pole touched a high-tension wire, near the centre of the village, in a place where he would disturb no one. At the instant he died, all the lights in the village went out. Now Georges handed me the spruce to which he had attached the yellow and white paper flowers shaped like roses. With this bouquet across my shoulder, like a sweep's brush, I climbed the ladder, which Georges held for me.

At the top a man I did not know was sitting on a cross beam. He put out his hand to steady me as I stepped off the ladder. I shook my head. It was a long time since I'd been on a roof and I needed no help. Like all of us I was born to it. Why were so many of us obliged to go to Paris as chimney sweeps? We lived on a roof; almost the first steps we take are on slopes as steep as our roofs. As long as I can climb up a ladder and lift one foot above the next, I need no help.

Who are you? I asked, you're not from here.

Lucie knew me as Saint-Just, he replied.

You were in the maquis!

We were ordered to dig our graves and we were shot.

I will tell you something, I said. There were Nazis who escaped after the Liberation and came to the Argentine, they changed their names and they lived off the fat of the pampas.

They only escaped for a moment.

You can't be so sure, can you?

Justice will be done.

When?

When the living know what the dead suffered.

He said this without a trace of bitterness in his voice, as if he had more than all the patience in the world.

I climbed a second ladder with the tree across my shoulder, and sat astride the roof. There was a slight breeze; I felt it on my forearms. I could see the trees in the forest. In the east the snow on the mountains was turning a very diluted rose, no redder than the water of a stream when an animal has been killed. I looked down through the open roof into the upturned faces of the dead who had assembled to watch what I was going to do.

It was then that I noticed the band. They were standing at the end of the chalet, by the first frame. They were like the band I had joined as a drummer when I was fourteen. The band that played the soldiers out of the village. The sun was by now too low in the sky for the brass and silver instruments to dazzle. Their metals shone only dully like water in a mountain lake.

I began to make my way—not without some difficulty— along the ridge of the roof. When I reached the end, I looked down on the upturned faces; they were grinning like skulls. I lifted the tree off my shoulder and held it upright. What I had to do now was to nail it to the king-post. Suddenly from behind two thin arms clasped me round the ribs.

Hold the tree, I said.

She couldn't reach it.

I'll sit on your shoulders, she said.

The onlookers below started to cheer. All the remembered dead of the village were there, women and children as well as men. She held the tree and I drove in four nails.

The little tree pointed up into the sky. She sat behind me, her arms relaxed. We were like a couple riding on their horse going to work in the fields. Her hands lay in my lap.

The bandsmen raised the instruments to their mouths, the drummers lifted their sticks. For a moment they remained transfixed and still, then they started to play.

The sign of the tree nailed to the roof was in honour of a work completed. All that remained to be done was to cover the roof with *bûchilles* cut from the beams, to lay the floors, nail boards on the walls, make and fit the doors and windows, construct the chimney, build the cupboards, make the shelf for the bed. It was the work of months. Yet the whole weight-bearing frame which promised shelter was there.

How can I tell you what the band played. I could hum the melody and you would not hear it. The bandsmen were dead and they played the music of silence. On Ascension Day the village band goes out into the country across the slopes, between the orchards, and, wherever there are two or three farms, it stops to play. Three summers I went out with them as drummer before I had to leave to find work. The music drowns the noise of the water in the *bassin,* it drowns the streams, it drowns the cuckoo. At each farm they gave us cider or *gnôle* to drink. The saxophonist, who played like a bird, always got drunk. Sweating under our peaked caps and in our brass-buttoned jackets we played as well and as loudly as we knew how, and the louder we played, the more still became the mountains and the trees of the forest. Only the deaf butterflies continued to flutter and climb, close and open their wings. On Ascension Day we played to the dead, and the dead, behind the motionless mountains and the still trees, listened to us. Now everything was the other way round, it was the dead who played at the foot of the chalet, and I, astride the roof, who was listening.

The village began to dance to the music, on the grass under the roof timbers. The Cocadrille beat her hands on my thighs to the rhythm of the music. I saw that my blood had not turned as cold with age as I thought it had. When the music stopped she kept her hands there.

The band started up again.

Wait for me, she whispered.

Climbing to her feet, she walked along the ridge of the roof like a chamois. As she went down I prided myself on having learnt from experience. Her return would be startling and unexpected. Still aroused, I tried to foresee how she would come back: perhaps she would come back aged twenty and naked as though she had been bathing in a river.

It was impossible to make out the uniforms of the bandsmen. Occasionally an instrument glinted like an ember when you blow on it. They knew the dances they were playing by heart, for it was too dark to read the notes on the music cards clipped to their instruments. The dancers, as the light disappeared, packed closer and closer together into the chalet.

I peered down, looking for the Cocadrille. The darkness was not so total that the whiteness of her body would not give off a certain light, like the white flowers sewn on to the tree did.

I felt my way down the first ladder. The dancers were now packed together in the area which would be the stable, where we would milk the cows. The cows were there. One was licking the head of her neighbour. Her tongue was so strong that when she licked round the eye, it pulled it open, revealing the eyeball, as you must do if you are looking for something which has entered the eye and is hurting it.

Seeing that eye, I saw the truth. The Cocadrille was not going to come back. Or if she came back, she would come back as nothing.

Lucie! Lucie!

Beyond the timbers of the roof the stars were shining. They shine over some oceans like they shine over the *alpage*. They are very bright and the similarity isn't in their brightness; it is simply that their distance isn't confusing. The Milky Way was folded into the sky like the ranunculi bordering the stream are folded into the hill beside the abandoned Cabrol chalet.

I missed my footing, rolled, like a log, down a precipitous slope. What saved me were some rhododendron bushes at which I instinctively, unthinkingly, grasped. I never lost consciousness. Ten metres further down was a sheer drop of a hundred metres. I had a broken arm and shoulder. When it was light, I somehow made my way down the path where the cumin grows, my arm hanging loose like the tongue of a bell.

Ten days later I met 'Mile à Lapraz in the village.

Where were you, 'Mile, ten days ago?

At home.

Where exactly, doing what?

The Friday, you mean?

Yes, the Friday.

Wait, Friday. I remember, I was ill in bed. I had terrible pains in the stomach. A white weasel was eating it. I swear to you I thought it was the end. As it turned out, he didn't want me, and so here I am. I'll pay you a drink.

Standing by the counter of the café, he clinked glasses and said conspiratorially: To the two of us they didn't take!

Later when my arm was still in plaster, I walked up to the roadmender's house. The weight of the plaster round my arm was as heavy as iron. I climbed slowly, letting one leg follow the other: the body becomes accustomed to a rhythm not unlike that of a cradle being slowly rocked from side to side. After an hour or two of such climbing you promise yourself a pleasure: the pleasure at night of lying absolutely still.

The hospital had discovered nothing with X-rays, yet I was convinced that at least one of my ribs was fractured. With each breath it stabbed me on the left-hand side, near the heart. I stopped once and looked down at the valley and the road that led away. I remembered the Cocadrille's story of the curé climbing up to the house and being taken ill. What was it that he muttered when she loosened his clothes on the table?

I had not been to the Cocadrille's house since the night when she came down from the loft wearing her wedding veil. The chicken hutches had been taken away from the ledge, and the door was ajar. I knocked. I could hear only the Jalent below. I pushed the door open. The table and chair were still there. There was nothing on the mantelpiece. Who had taken the plates? I opened the stove. It was stuffed with the recent remains of a picnic. On the wall by the cupboard some initials had been scratched, neither hers nor mine, and beside them was a drawn heart, the shape of an owl's face, with an arrow through it.

In the stable I found some sacks and the bear's paw. There was no sign of the blue umbrella. I climbed up the ladder to the loft. She dreamt about that ladder. She was in her bed in the loft and a young man climbed up and started to undress to get into bed with her. She could see that he was beautiful. He slipped between the blankets beside her and just as she felt his warmth, she woke up. The bed too had gone.

Before I was six, before I looked after the cows, perhaps I was only two or three, I used to watch my father in the kitchen on winter mornings, when it was still as dark as night. He knelt by an iron beast, feeding it. If I came near, he shouted at me. He knelt down at one side of the animal, between its iron legs and, breathing deeply, he whispered to it. I saw my father praying in church. In the kitchen he prayed in long breaths, blowing and sighing. I never saw the iron animal's face, which was inside its stomach. After a while I could feel the warmth filling the kitchen, and my father would sit beside the animal, warming his feet between its legs, before putting his boots on and going to feed the other animals. Now when I light the stove in the morning, I say to myself: I and the fire are the only living things in this house; my father, mother, brothers, the horse, cows, rabbits, chickens, all have gone. And the Cocadrille is dead.

I say that, and I do not altogether believe it. Sometimes it seems to me that I am nearing the edge of the forest. I will never again be sixteen; if I am to leave the forest, it will be on the far side. Do I feel this because I am old and tired? I doubt it. The old animal when he feels his strength disappearing hides himself in the very centre of the forest, he does not dream of leaving it. Is it a longing for death such as an animal never feels? Is it only death that will at last deliver me from the forest? There are moments when I see something different, moments when a blue sky reminds me of Lucie Cabrol. At these moments I see again the roof which we raised, built with the trees, and then I am convinced that it is with the love of the Cocadrille that I shall leave the forest. ∾

INTERPRETIVE QUESTIONS
FOR DISCUSSION

Why is Jean haunted by Lucie Cabrol throughout his life?

1. Why is the young Jean so fearful of marrying the passionate, hardworking Lucie? Why does he dream that she entraps him—with the same cunning that she would use to catch a trout—into a marriage that ruins his life? (101; cf. 84)

2. When making love to her for the first time, why does it seem to Jean that Lucie grows larger, "as large as the earth upon which I had to throw myself"? (98) Why does he go back to Lucie's chalet a second time, but not again?

3. Why does Jean grow more nostalgic about Lucie as he grows older? (113) Why does he obey her command to return to the village before he dies? (102, 123)

4. Why does Lucie still want to marry Jean when they are both old? Why does Jean feel that when Lucie speaks his name, it marks him out from all other men? (140–141; cf. 99)

5. Why does Jean see the failure of his life in the pause between Lucie's twice speaking his name? Was Lucie's life wasted, too, lived without Jean? (140–142)

6. Why does Lucie's offer of marriage—and the sense of loss it makes him feel—make Jean want to kill her? (141) Why, instead of showing his rage, does he feel forced to respond to her proposition tenderly and indefinitely? (142)

7. Why does Lucie speak to Jean after her death and appear before him as a desirable girl of twenty and an old, mad-looking woman? (150, 155, 158) Why do they pick blueberries together? (148)

8. Why does Lucie learn Jean's true feelings in her third life? Why does Jean tell Lucie's ghost that he hadn't made up his mind whether or not to marry her? (144)

9. Why does Jean's vision of the dead building a chalet for Lucie lead him to conclude that he should have married her? (158)

10. Why does his vision of the dead make Jean feel that he had not yet entered the forest—that his life was in front of him? (151, 155) After the vision is over, why is Jean convinced that he will leave the forest—he will die—fortified by the love of Lucie Cabrol? (168)

Suggested textual analyses

Pages 98–101: beginning, "When the Cocadrille came back," and ending, "she did not single me out in any way."

Pages 140–142: beginning, "In the pause between her twice saying my name," and ending, "she was dead."

Why does the author have Lucie Cabrol brutally and mysteriously murdered?

1. Why does Lucie receive a nickname, the Cocadrille, that is born of both hatred and love? Why is it Henri who gives her the name, but her father who makes it stick? (86–90)

2. Why is Lucie portrayed as a midget who is as strong and tireless as a man? Why does Jean characterize her body as that of "the ideal servant, tiny but active, without age or sex"? (96)

3. In contrast to her two brothers, why is Lucie willing to risk her farm and her life to save the maquisards from the Nazis? Why does she outwit the Nazis by posing as a fool? (107–108)

4. Why does the Cabrol farm end up in the hands of the men who did not fight in the world wars?

5. Why does only Jean suspect that Lucie is not fearless, but that she counts on inspiring fear in others? (116) Why do the villagers believe that Lucie's fearlessness was the cause of her trouble? (143)

6. Why is Lucie murdered before she is able to achieve her goal of moving back into the village a rich woman?

7. Why does Jean tell Lucie's ghost that he did not kill her or steal her savings? Why does Lucie's ghost remind Jean that he *thought* about killing her? (144–145)

8. Why does Lucie's ghost at first say that she forgives her murderer, but not the thief? (143)

9. Why does Lucie's father say that, in death, one "can become anything"? (155)

10. Why do we never learn who murdered Lucie?

Suggested textual analyses

Pages 86–90: beginning, "It was in her last year at school," and ending, "The Cocadrille! The Cocadrille!"

Pages 142–146: beginning, "One morning when I was six," and ending, "Then she went."

Why do the dead build a huge chalet for Lucie and Jean in Lucie's third life?

1. Why does Lucie believe in happiness, even toward the end of her second life? (120)

2. Why do the dead slaughter animals and build chalets, the work they did when alive? (152–153, 157)

3. Why is Lucie married many times in her third life? Why is it suggested that only those who die violently may marry Lucie? (155–156)

4. Why does Lucie tell Jean that the chalet is intended to support them and give them something to hand on to their children? Why does Lucie appear to Jean as the murdered old woman when she tells him this? (157)

5. Why does Lucie bring a group of living men to help the dead raise the chalet?

6. Why does Lucie say that no one will kill themselves in the chalet built for her by the dead? (160)

7. Why does Jean experience a feeling of endless promise as he watches the dead doing the work of the village? (161)

8. Why in Lucie's third life is the ritual of Ascension Day reversed— the dead play music for the living? (165)

9. Why does Jean see the truth in the eye of a cow in his stable— that Lucie is not coming back to him? Why does Jean's vision end before his marriage with Lucie takes place? (166)

10. Why does the vision of Lucie's third life cause Jean to recall his youth and long for his death?

Suggested textual analyses

Page 151: beginning, "Descending the grass steps," and ending, "as if my life lay before me."

Page 168: from "Before I was six," to the end of the story.

FOR FURTHER REFLECTION

1. Is Lucie right when she says that "money can change everything"?

2. Is Lucie an attractive character or do her avarice and crudeness make her repellent? Was her avarice a vice or a courageous means of survival?

3. Was Jean weak for not wanting to marry Lucie?

4. Do our childhood and youth leave a mark on us—a "craving"— that must be reconciled in our adult lives?

5. Is it easier to find peace in life when one is older and facing death?

HAPPINESS

Mary Lavin

MARY LAVIN (1912–1996) was born in
Massachusetts, but grew up in Ireland.
One of Ireland's most respected contemporary authors, Lavin was one of the few Irish
women writers of her generation who
remained in Ireland and made it the focus
of their fiction. She served as president of
the Irish Academy of Letters and the Irish
P.E.N., and received many awards and prizes,
including three Guggenheim Fellowships
and the Katherine Mansfield-Menton Prize.
Lavin published ten collections of short
stories, including *Happiness* in 1969,
as well as four novels.

MOTHER HAD a lot to say. This does not mean she was always talking but that we children felt the wells she drew upon were deep, deep, deep. Her theme was happiness: what it was, what it was not; where we might find it, where not; and how, if found, it must be guarded. Never must we confound it with pleasure. Nor think sorrow its exact opposite.

"Take Father Hugh," Mother's eyes flashed as she looked at him. "According to him, sorrow is an ingredient of happiness— a *necessary* ingredient, if you please!" And when he tried to protest she put up her hand. "There may be a freakish truth in the theory—for some people. But not for me. And not, I hope, for my children." She looked severely at us three girls. We laughed. None of us had had much experience with sorrow. Bea and I were children and Linda only a year old when our father died suddenly after a short illness that had not at first seemed serious. "I've known people to make sorrow a *substitute* for happiness," Mother said.

Father Hugh protested again. "You're not putting me in that class, I hope?"

Father Hugh, ever since our father died, had been the closest of anyone to us as a family, without being close to any one of us in particular—even to Mother. He lived in a monastery near our farm in County Meath, and he had been one of the celebrants at the Requiem High Mass our father's political importance had demanded. He met us that day for the first time, but he took to dropping in to see us, with the idea of filling the crater of loneliness left at our centre. He did not know that there was a cavity in his own life, much less that we would fill it. He and Mother were both young in those days, and perhaps it gave scandal to some that he was so often in our house, staying till late into the night and, indeed, thinking nothing of stopping all night if there was any special reason, such as one of us being sick. He had even on occasion slept there if the night was too wet for tramping home across the fields.

When we girls were young, we were so used to having Father Hugh around that we never stood on ceremony with him but in his presence dried our hair and pared our nails and never minded what garments were strewn about. As for Mother—she thought nothing of running out of the bathroom in her slip, brushing her teeth or combing her hair, if she wanted to tell him something she might otherwise forget. And she brooked no criticism of her behaviour. "Celibacy was never meant to take all the warmth and homeliness out of their lives," she said.

On this point, too, Bea was adamant. Bea, the middle sister, was our oracle. "I'm so glad he *has* Mother," she said, "as well as her having him, because it must be awful the way most women treat them—priests, I mean—as if they were pariahs. Mother treats him like a human being—that's all!"

And when it came to Mother's ears that there had been gossip about her making free with Father Hugh, she opened her eyes wide in astonishment. "But he's only a priest!" she said.

Bea giggled. "It's a good job he didn't hear *that,*" she said to me afterwards. "It would undo the good she's done him. You'd think he was a eunuch."

"Bea!" I said. "Do you think he's in love with her?"

"If so, he doesn't know it," Bea said firmly. "It's her soul he's after! Maybe he wants to make sure of her in the next world!"

But thoughts of the world to come never troubled Mother. "If anything ever happens to me, children," she said, "suddenly, I mean, or when you are not near me, or I cannot speak to you, I want you to promise you won't feel bad. There's no need! Just remember that I had a happy life—and that if I had to choose my kind of heaven I'd take it on this earth with you again, no matter how much you might annoy me!"

You see, annoyance and fatigue, according to Mother, and even illness and pain, could coexist with happiness. She had a habit of asking people if they were happy at times and in places that—to say the least of it—seemed to us inappropriate. "But are you happy?" she'd probe as one lay sick and bathed in sweat, or in the throes of a jumping toothache. And once in our presence she made the inquiry of an old friend as he lay upon his deathbed.

"Why not?" she said when we took her to task for it later. "Isn't it more important than ever to be happy when you're dying? Take my own father! You know what he said in his last moments? On his deathbed, he defied me to name a man who had enjoyed a better life. In spite of dreadful pain, his face *radiated* happiness!" Mother nodded her head comfortably. "Happiness drives out pain, as fire burns out fire."

Having no knowledge of our own to pit against hers, we thirstily drank in her rhetoric. Only Bea was sceptical. "Perhaps you *got* it from him, like spots, or fever," she said. "Or something that could at least be slipped from hand to hand."

"Do you think I'd have taken it if that were the case!" Mother cried. "Then, when he needed it most?"

"Not there and then!" Bea said stubbornly. "I meant as a sort of legacy."

"Don't you think in *that* case," Mother said, exasperated, "he would have felt obliged to leave it to your grandmother?"

Certainly we knew that in spite of his lavish heart our grandfather had failed to provide our grandmother with enduring happiness. He had passed that job on to Mother. And Mother had not made too good a fist of it, even when Father was living and she had him—and, later, us children—to help.

As for Father Hugh, he had given our grandmother up early in the game. "God Almighty couldn't make that woman happy," he said one day, seeing Mother's face, drawn and pale with fatigue, preparing for the nightly run over to her own mother's flat that would exhaust her utterly.

There were evenings after she came home from the library where she worked when we saw her stand with the car keys in her hand, trying to think which would be worse—to slog over there on foot, or take out the car again. And yet the distance was short. It was Mother's day that had been too long.

"Weren't you over to see her this morning?" Father Hugh demanded.

"No matter!" said Mother. She was no doubt thinking of the forlorn face our grandmother always put on when she was leaving. ("Don't say good night, Vera," Grandmother would plead. "It makes me feel too lonely. And you never can tell—you might slip over again before you go to bed!")

"Do you know the time?" Bea would say impatiently, if she happened to be with Mother. Not indeed that the lateness of the hour counted for anything, because in all likelihood Mother *would* go back, if only to pass by under the window and see that the lights were out, or stand and listen and make sure that as far as she could tell all was well.

"I wouldn't mind if she was happy," Mother said.

"And how do you know she's not?" we'd ask.

"When people are happy, I can feel it. Can't you?"

We were not sure. Most people thought our grandmother was a gay creature, a small birdy being who even at a great age laughed like a girl, and—more remarkably—sang like one, as she went about her day. But beak and claw were of steel. She'd think nothing of sending Mother back to a shop three times if her errands were not exactly right. "Not sugar like that—that's *too* fine; it's not castor sugar I want. But *not* as coarse as *that,* either. I want an in-between kind."

Provoked one day, my youngest sister, Linda, turned and gave battle. "You're mean!" she cried. "You love ordering people about!"

Grandmother preened, as if Linda had acclaimed an attribute. "I was always hard to please," she said. "As a girl, I used to be called Miss Imperious."

And Miss Imperious she remained as long as she lived, even when she was a great age. Her orders were then given a wry twist by the fact that as she advanced in age she took to calling her daughter Mother, as we did.

There was one great phrase with which our grandmother opened every sentence: "if only." "If only," she'd say, when we came to visit her—"if only you'd come earlier, before I was worn out expecting you!" Or if we were early, then if only it was later, after she'd had a rest and could enjoy us, be *able* for us. And if we brought her flowers, she'd sigh to think that if only we'd brought them the previous day she'd have had a visitor to appreciate them, or say it was a pity the stems weren't longer. If only we'd picked a few green leaves, or included some buds, because, she said disparagingly, the poor flowers we'd brought were already wilting. We might just as well not have brought them! As the years went on, Grandmother had a new bead to add to her rosary: if only her friends were not all dead! By their absence, they reduced to nil all *real* enjoyment in anything. Our own father—her son-in-law—was the one person who had ever gone close to pleasing her. But even here there had been a snag. "If only he was my real son!" she used to say with a sigh.

Mother's mother lived on through our childhood and into our early maturity (though she outlived the money our grandfather left her), and in our minds she was a complicated mixture of valiance and defeat. Courageous and generous within the limits of her own life, her simplest demand was yet enormous in the larger frame of Mother's life, and so we never could see her with the same clarity of vision with which we saw our grandfather, or our own father. Them we saw only through Mother's eyes.

"Take your grandfather!" she'd cry, and instantly we'd see him, his eyes burning upon us—yes, upon *us,* although in his day only one of us had been born: me. At another time, Mother would cry, "Take your own father!" and instantly we'd see *him*—tall, handsome, young, and much more suited to marry one of us than poor bedraggled Mother.

Most fascinating of all were the times Mother would say, "Take me!" By magic then, staring down the years, we'd see blazingly clear a small girl with black hair and buttoned boots, who, though plain and pouting, burned bright, like a star. "I was happy, you see," Mother said. And we'd strain hard to try and understand the mystery of the light that still radiated from her. "I used to lean along a tree that grew out over the river," she said, "and look down through the grey leaves at the water flowing past below, and I used to think it was not the stream that flowed but me, spread-eagled over it, who flew through the air! Like a bird! That I'd found the secret!" She made it seem there might *be* such a secret, just waiting to be found. Another time she'd dream that she'd be a great singer.

"We didn't know you sang, Mother!"

She had to laugh. "Like a crow," she said.

Sometimes she used to think she'd swim the Channel.

"Did you swim *that* well, Mother?"

"Oh, not really—just the breaststroke," she said. "And then only by the aid of two pig bladders blown up by my father and tied around my middle. But I used to throb—yes, throb—with happiness."

Behind Mother's back, Bea raised her eyebrows.

What was it, we used to ask ourselves—that quality that she, we felt sure, misnamed? Was it courage? Was it strength, health, or high spirits? Something you could not give or take—a conundrum? A game of catch-as-you-can?

"I know," cried Bea. "A sham!"

Whatever it was, we knew that Mother would let no wind of violence from within or without tear it from her. Although, one evening when Father Hugh was with us, our astonished ears heard her proclaim that there might be a time when one had to slacken hold on it—let go—to catch at it again with a surer hand. In the way, we supposed, that the high-wire walker up among the painted stars of his canvas sky must wait to fling himself through the air until the bar he catches at has started to sway perversely from him. Oh no, no! That downward drag at our innards we could not bear, the belly swelling to the shape of a pear. Let happiness go by the board. "After all, lots of people seem to make out without it," Bea cried. It was too tricky a business. And might it not be that one had to be born with a flair for it?

"A flair would not be enough," Mother answered. "Take Father Hugh. He, if anyone, had a flair for it—a natural capacity! You've only to look at him when he's off guard, with you children, or helping me in the garden. But he rejects happiness! He casts it from him."

"That is simply not true, Vera," cried Father Hugh, overhearing her. "It's just that I don't place an inordinate value on it like you. I don't think it's enough to carry one all the way. To the end, I mean—and after."

"Oh, don't talk about the end when we're only in the middle," cried Mother. And, indeed, at that moment her own face shone with such happiness it was hard to believe that earth was not her heaven. Certainly it was her constant contention that of happiness she had had a lion's share. This, however, we, in private, doubted. Perhaps there were times when she had had a surplus of it—when she was young, say, with her redoubtable father, whose love blazed circles around her, making winter into summer and ice into fire. Perhaps she did have a brimming measure in her early married years. By straining hard, we could find traces left in our minds from those days of milk and honey. Our father, while he lived, had cast a magic over everything, for us as well as for her. He held his love up over us like an umbrella and kept off the troubles that afterwards came down on us, pouring cats and dogs!

But if she did have more than the common lot of happiness in those early days, what use was that when we could remember so clearly how our father's death had ravaged her? And how could we forget the distress it brought on us when, afraid to let her out of our sight, Bea and I stumbled after her everywhere, through the woods and along the bank of the river, where, in the weeks that followed, she tried vainly to find peace.

The summer after Father died, we were invited to France to stay with friends, and when she went walking on the cliffs at Fécamp our fears for her grew frenzied, so that we hung on to her arm and dragged at her skirt, hoping that like leaded weights we'd pin her down if she went too near to the edge. But at night we had to abandon our watch, being forced to follow the conventions of a family still whole—a home still intact—and go to bed at the same time as the other children. It was at that hour, when the coast guard was gone from his rowing boat offshore and the sand was as cold and grey as the sea, that Mother liked to swim. And when she had washed, kissed, and left us, our hearts almost died inside us and we'd creep out of bed again to stand in our bare feet at the mansard and watch as she ran down the shingle, striking out when she reached the water where, far out, wave and sky and mist were one, and the greyness closed over her. If we took our eyes off her for an instant, it was impossible to find her again.

"Oh, make her turn back, God, please!" I prayed out loud one night.

Startled, Bea turned away from the window. "She'll *have* to turn back sometime, won't she? Unless . . . ?"

Locking our damp hands together, we stared out again. "She wouldn't!" I whispered. "It would be a sin!"

Secure in the deterring power of sin, we let out our breath. Then Bea's breath caught again. "What if she went out so far she used up all her strength? She couldn't swim back! It wouldn't be a sin then!"

"It's the intention that counts," I whispered.

A second later, we could see an arm lift heavily up and wearily cleave down, and at last Mother was in the shallows, wading back to shore.

"Don't let her see us!" cried Bea. As if our chattering teeth would not give us away when she looked in at us before she went to her own room on the other side of the corridor, where, later in the night, sometimes the sound of crying would reach us.

What was it worth—a happiness bought that dearly.

Mother had never questioned it. And once she told us, "On a wintry day, I brought my own mother a snowdrop. It was the first one of the year—a bleak bud that had come up stunted before its time—and I meant it for a sign. But do you know what your grandmother said? 'What good are snowdrops to me now?' Such a thing to say! What good is a snowdrop at all if it doesn't hold its value always, and never lose it! Isn't that the whole point of a snowdrop? And that is the whole point of happiness, too! What good would it be if it could be erased without trace? Take me and those daffodils!" Stooping, she buried her face in a bunch that lay on the table waiting to be put in vases. "If they didn't hold their beauty absolute and inviolable, do you think I could bear the sight of them after what happened when your father was in hospital?"

It was a fair question. When Father went to hospital, Mother went with him and stayed in a small hotel across the street so she could be with him all day from early to late. "Because it was so awful for him—being in Dublin!" she said. "You have no idea how he hated it."

That he was dying neither of them realized. How could they know, as it rushed through the sky, that their star was a falling star! But one evening when she'd left him asleep Mother came home for a few hours to see how we were faring, and it broke her heart to see the daffodils out all over the place—in the woods, under the trees, and along the sides of the avenue. There had never been so many, and she thought how awful it was that Father was missing them. "You sent up little bunches to him, you poor dears!" she said. "Sweet little bunches, too—squeezed tight as posies by your little fists! But stuffed into vases they couldn't really make up to him for not being able to see them growing!"

So on the way back to the hospital she stopped her car and pulled a great bunch—the full of her arms. "They took up the whole back seat," she said, "and I was so excited at the thought of walking into his room and dumping them on his bed—you know—just plomping them down so he could smell them, and feel them, and look and look! I didn't mean them to be put in vases, or anything ridiculous like that—it would have taken a rainwater barrel to hold them. Why, I could hardly see over them as I came up the steps; I kept tripping. But when I came into the hall, that nun—I told you about her—that nun came up to me, sprang out of nowhere it seemed, although I know now that she was waiting for me, knowing that somebody had to bring me to my senses. But the way she did it! Reached out and grabbed the flowers, letting lots of them fall—I remember them getting stood on. 'Where are you going with those foolish flowers, you foolish woman?' she said. 'Don't you know your husband is dying? Your prayers are all you can give him now!'

"She was right. I *was* foolish. But I wasn't cured. Afterwards, it was nothing but foolishness the way I dragged you children after me all over Europe. As if any one place was going to be different from another, any better, any less desolate. But there was great satisfaction in bringing you places your father and I had planned to bring you—although in fairness to him I must say that he would not perhaps have brought you so young. And he would not have had an ulterior motive. But above all, he would not have attempted those trips in such a dilapidated car."

Oh, that car! It was a battered and dilapidated red sports car, so depleted of accessories that when, eventually, we got a new car Mother still stuck out her hand on bends, and in wet weather jumped out to wipe the windscreen with her sleeve. And if fussed, she'd let down the window and shout at people, forgetting she now had a horn. How we had ever fitted into it with all our luggage was a miracle.

"You were never lumpish—any of you!" Mother said proudly. "But you were very healthy and very strong." She turned to me. "Think of how you got that car up the hill in Switzerland!"

"The Alps are not hills, Mother!" I pointed out coldly, as I had done at the time, when, as actually happened, the car failed to make it on one of the inclines. Mother let it run back until it wedged against the rock face, and I had to get out and push till she got going again in first gear. But when it got started it couldn't be stopped to pick me up until it got to the top, where they had to wait for me, and for a very long time.

"Ah, well," she said, sighing wistfully at the thought of those trips. "You got something out of them, I hope. All that travelling must have helped you with your geography and your history."

We looked at each other and smiled, and then Mother herself laughed. "Remember the time," she said, "when we were in Italy, and it was Easter, and all the shops were chock-full of food? The butchers' shops had poultry and game hanging up outside the doors, fully feathered, and with their poor heads dripping blood, and in the windows they had poor little lambs and suckling pigs and young goats, all skinned and hanging by their hind feet." Mother shuddered. "They think so much about food. I found it revolting. I had to hurry past. But Linda, who must have been only four then, dragged at me and stared and stared. You know how children are at that age; they have a morbid fascination for what is cruel and bloody. Her face was flushed and her eyes were wide. I hurried her back to the hotel.

But next morning she crept into my room. She crept up to me and pressed against me. 'Can't we go back, just once, and look again at that shop?' she whispered. 'The shop where they have the little children hanging up for Easter!' It was the young goats, of course, but I'd said 'kids,' I suppose. How we laughed." But her face was grave. "You were *so* good on those trips, all of you," she said. "You were really very good children in general. Otherwise I would never have put so much effort into rearing you, because I wasn't a bit maternal. You brought out the best in me! I put an unnatural effort into you, of course, because I was taking my standards from your father, forgetting that his might not have remained so inflexible if he had lived to middle age and was beset by life, like other parents."

"Well, the job is nearly over now, Vera," said Father Hugh. "And you didn't do so badly."

"That's right, Hugh," said Mother, and she straightened up, and put her hand to her back the way she sometimes did in the garden when she got up from her knees after weeding. "I didn't go over to the enemy anyway! We survived!" Then a flash of defiance came into her eyes. "And we were happy. That's the main thing!"

Father Hugh frowned. "There you go again!" he said.

Mother turned on him. "I don't think you realize the onslaughts that were made upon our happiness! The minute Robert died, they came down on me—cohorts of relatives, friends, even strangers, all draped in black, opening their arms like bats to let me pass into their company. 'Life is a vale of tears,' they said. 'You are privileged to find it out so young!' Ugh! After I staggered onto my feet and began to take hold of life once more, they fell back defeated. And the first day I gave a laugh—pouff, they were blown out like candles. They weren't living in a real world at all; they belonged to a ghostly world where life was easy: all one had to do was sit and weep. It takes effort to push back the stone from the mouth of the tomb and walk out."

Effort. Effort. Ah, but that strange-sounding word could invoke little sympathy from those who had not learned yet what it meant. Life must have been hardest for Mother in those years when we older ones were at college—no longer children, and still dependent on her. Indeed, we made more demands on her than ever then, having moved into new areas of activity and emotion. And our friends! Our friends came and went as freely as we did ourselves, so that the house was often like a café—and one where pets were not prohibited but took their places on our chairs and beds, as regardless as the people. And anyway it was hard to have sympathy for someone who got things into such a state as Mother. All over the house there was clutter. Her study was like the returned-letter department of a post office, with stacks of paper everywhere, bills paid and unpaid, letters answered and unanswered, tax returns, pamphlets, leaflets. If by mistake we left the door open on a windy day, we came back to find papers flapping through the air like frightened birds. Efficient only in that she managed eventually to conclude every task she began, it never seemed possible to outsiders that by Mother's methods anything whatever could be accomplished. In an attempt to keep order elsewhere, she made her own room the clearinghouse into which the rest of us put everything: things to be given away, things to be mended, things to be stored, things to be treasured, things to be returned—even things to be thrown out! By the end of the year, the room resembled an obsolescence dump. And no one could help her; the chaos of her life was as personal as an act of creation—one might as well try to finish another person's poem.

As the years passed, Mother rushed around more hectically. And although Bea and I had married and were not at home anymore, except at holiday time and for occasional weekends, Linda was noisier than the two of us put together had been, and for every follower we had brought home she brought twenty. The house was never still. Now that we were reduced to being visitors, we watched Mother's tension mount to vertigo, knowing that, like a spinning top, she could not rest till she fell. But now at the smallest pretext Father Hugh would call in the doctor and Mother would be put on the mail boat and dispatched for London. For it was essential that she get far enough away to make phoning home every night prohibitively costly.

Unfortunately, the thought of departure often drove a spur into her and she redoubled her effort to achieve order in her affairs. She would be up until the early hours ransacking her desk. To her, as always, the shortest parting entailed a preparation as for death. And as if it were her end that was at hand, we would all be summoned, although she had no time to speak a word to us, because five minutes before departure she would still be attempting to reply to letters that were the acquisition of weeks and would have taken whole days to dispatch.

"Don't you know the taxi is at the door, Vera?" Father Hugh would say, running his hand through his grey hair and looking very dishevelled himself. She had him at times as distracted as herself. "You can't do any more. You'll have to leave the rest till you come back."

"I can't, I can't!" Mother would cry. "I'll have to cancel my plans."

One day, Father Hugh opened the lid of her case, which was strapped up in the hall, and with a swipe of his arm he cleared all the papers on the top of the desk pell-mell into the suitcase. "You can sort them on the boat," he said, "or the train to London!"

Thereafter, Mother's luggage always included an empty case to hold the unfinished papers on her desk. And years afterwards a steward on the Irish Mail told us she was a familiar figure, working away at letters and bills nearly all the way from Holyhead to Euston. "She gave it up about Rugby or Crewe," he said. "She'd get talking to someone in the compartment." He smiled. "There was one time coming down the train I was just in time to see her close up the window with a guilty look. I didn't say anything, but I think she'd emptied those papers of hers out the window!"

Quite likely. When we were children, even a few hours away from us gave her composure. And in two weeks or less, when she'd come home, the well of her spirit would be freshened. We'd hardly know her—her step so light, her eye so bright, and her love and patience once more freely flowing. But in no time at all the house would fill up once more with the noise and confusion of too many people and too many animals, and again we'd be fighting our corner with cats and dogs, bats, mice, bees, and even wasps. "Don't kill it!" Mother would cry if we raised a hand to an angry wasp. "Just catch it, dear, and put it outside. Open the window and let it fly away!" But even this treatment could at times be deemed too harsh. "Wait a minute. Close the window!" she'd cry. "It's too cold outside. It will die. That's why it came in, I suppose! Oh dear, what will we do?" Life would be going full blast again.

There was only one place Mother found rest. When she was at breaking point and fit to fall, she'd go out into the garden— not to sit or stroll around but to dig, to drag up weeds, to move great clumps of corms or rhizomes, or indeed quite frequently to haul huge rocks from one place to another. She was always laying down a path, building a dry wall, or making compost heaps as high as hills. However jaded she might be going out, when dark forced her in at last her step had the spring of a daisy. So if she did not succeed in defining happiness to our understanding, we could see that whatever it was, she possessed it to the full when she was in her garden.

One of us said as much one Sunday when Bea and I had dropped round for the afternoon. Father Hugh was with us again. "It's an unthinking happiness, though," he cavilled. We were standing at the drawing-room window, looking out to where in the fading light we could see Mother on her knees weeding, in the long border that stretched from the house right down to the woods. "I wonder how she'd take it if she were stricken down and had to give up that heavy work!" he said. Was he perhaps a little jealous of how she could stoop and bend? He himself had begun to use a stick. I was often a little jealous of her myself, because although I was married and had children of my own, I had married young and felt the weight of living as heavy as a weight of years. "She doesn't take enough care of herself," Father Hugh said sadly. "Look at her out there with nothing under her knees to protect her from the damp ground." It was almost too dim for us to see her, but even in the drawing room it was chilly. "She should not be let stay out there after the sun goes down."

"Just you try to get her in then!" said Linda, who had come into the room in time to hear him. "Don't you know by now anyway that what would kill another person only seems to make Mother thrive?"

Father Hugh shook his head again. "You seem to forget it's not younger she's getting!" He fidgeted and fussed, and several times went to the window to stare out apprehensively. He was really getting quite elderly.

"Come and sit down, Father Hugh," Bea said, and to take his mind off Mother she turned on the light and blotted out the garden. Instead of seeing through the window, we saw into it as into a mirror, and there between the flower-laden tables and the lamps it was ourselves we saw moving vaguely. Like Father Hugh, we, too, were waiting for her to come in before we called an end to the day.

"Oh, this is ridiculous!" Father Hugh cried at last. "She'll have to listen to reason." And going back to the window he threw it open. "Vera!" he called. "Vera!"—sternly, so sternly that, more intimate than an endearment, his tone shocked us. "She didn't hear me," he said, turning back blinking at us in the lighted room. "I'm going out to get her." And in a minute he was gone from the room. As he ran down the garden path, we stared at each other, astonished; his step, like his voice, was the step of a lover. "I'm coming, Vera!" he cried.

Although she was never stubborn except in things that mattered, Mother had not moved. In the wholehearted way she did everything, she was bent down close to the ground. It wasn't the light only that was dimming; her eyesight also was failing, I thought, as instinctively I followed Father Hugh.

But halfway down the path I stopped. I had seen something he had not: Mother's hand that appeared to support itself in a forked branch of an old tree peony she had planted as a bride was not in fact gripping it but impaled upon it. And the hand that appeared to be grubbing in the clay in fact was sunk into the soft mould. "Mother!" I screamed, and I ran forward, but when I reached her I covered my face with my hands. "Oh Father Hugh!" I cried. "Is she dead?"

It was Bea who answered, hysterical. "She is! She is!" she cried, and she began to pound Father Hugh on the back with her fists, as if his pessimistic words had made this happen.

But Mother was not dead. And at first the doctor even offered hope of her pulling through. But from the moment Father Hugh lifted her up to carry her into the house we ourselves had no hope, seeing how effortlessly he, who was not strong, could carry her. When he put her down on her bed, her head hardly creased the pillow. Mother lived for four more hours.

Like the days of her life, those four hours that Mother lived were packed tight with concern and anxiety. Partly conscious, partly delirious, she seemed to think the counterpane was her desk, and she scrabbled her fingers upon it as if trying to sort out a muddle of bills and correspondence. No longer indifferent now, we listened, anguished, to the distracted cries that had for all our lifetime been so familiar to us. "Oh, where is it? Where is it? I had it a minute ago! Where on earth did I put it?"

"Vera, Vera, stop worrying," Father Hugh pleaded, but she waved him away and went on sifting through the sheets as if they were sheets of paper. "Oh, Vera!" he begged. "Listen to me. Do you not know—"

Bea pushed between them. "You're not to tell her!" she commanded. "Why frighten her?"

"But it ought not to frighten her," said Father Hugh. "This is what I was always afraid would happen—that she'd be frightened when it came to the end."

At that moment, as if to vindicate him, Mother's hands fell idle on the coverlet, palm upward and empty. And turning her head she stared at each of us in turn, beseechingly. "I cannot face it," she whispered. "I can't! I can't! I can't!"

"Oh, my God!" Bea said, and she started to cry.

"Vera. For God's sake listen to me," Father Hugh cried, and pressing his face to hers, as close as a kiss, he kept whispering to her, trying to cast into the dark tunnel before her the light of his own faith.

But it seemed to us that Mother must already be looking into God's exigent eyes. "I can't!" she cried. "I can't!"

Then her mind came back from the stark world of the spirit to the world where her body was still detained, but even that world was now a whirling kaleidoscope of things which only she could see. Suddenly her eyes focussed, and, catching at Father Hugh, she pulled herself up a little and pointed to something we could not see. "What will be done with them?" Her voice was anxious. "They ought to be put in water anyway," she said, and leaning over the edge of the bed, she pointed to the floor. "Don't step on that one!" she said sharply. Then more sharply still, she addressed us all. "Have them sent to the public ward," she said peremptorily. "Don't let that nun take them; she'll only put them on the altar. And God doesn't want them! He made them for *us*—not for Himself!"

It was the familiar rhetoric that all her life had characterized her utterances. For a moment we were mystified. Then Bea gasped. "The daffodils!" she cried. "The day Father died!" And over her face came the light that had so often blazed over Mother's. Leaning across the bed, she pushed Father Hugh aside. And, putting out her hands, she held Mother's face between her palms as tenderly as if it were the face of a child. "It's all right,

Mother. You don't *have* to face it! It's over!" Then she who had so fiercely forbade Father Hugh to do so blurted out the truth. "You've finished with this world, Mother," she said, and, confident that her tidings were joyous, her voice was strong.

Mother made the last effort of her life and grasped at Bea's meaning. She let out a sigh, and, closing her eyes, she sank back, and this time her head sank so deep into the pillow that it would have been dented had it been a pillow of stone. ⌒

INTERPRETIVE QUESTIONS
FOR DISCUSSION

By talking so much about happiness, is Vera trying to teach her daughters how to be happy, or is she trying to convince herself that she is happy?

1. Why does Vera tell her daughters that happiness is something that must be "guarded"? (179)

2. Why doesn't Vera think that sorrow is the "exact opposite" of happiness? Why does she think that happiness must never be confused with pleasure? (179)

3. Does Vera use Father Hugh's friendship as a "*substitute* for happiness"? (179)

4. How is Vera's philosophy of life shaped by her own mother's "complicated mixture of valiance and defeat"? (184)

5. What does Vera mean when she says that Father Hugh has a "flair" for happiness but rejects it? (185)

6. Why does Vera believe that happiness—like snowdrops and daffodils—holds its value always? Why does she think that happiness would have no value "if it could be erased without trace"? (187)

7. Why does Vera believe that her happiness took effort and that her relatives and friends conspired to take it away from her? (190)

8. Why are Vera's daughters persuaded that their mother possesses happiness "to the full" when she is tending her garden? (193)

9. Why does Father Hugh call Vera's happiness "unthinking"? (193)

10. Why does Vera envision on her own deathbed the daffodils she brought to her dying husband? As she is dying, why does Vera say that God made the daffodils "for *us*—not for Himself!"? (196)

Suggested textual analyses

Page 179: from the beginning of the story to " 'I've known people to make sorrow a *substitute* for happiness,' Mother said."

Pages 181–182: beginning, "But thoughts of the world to come," and ending, "felt obliged to leave it to your grandmother?"

Why does Vera think that rearing her daughters "brought out the best" in her?

1. Why do Vera's children feel that when their mother talked about happiness, "the wells she drew upon were deep, deep, deep"? (179)

2. Why does Vera say that the kind of heaven she would choose would be on earth with her children? (181)

3. Why is Vera sure that happiness can coexist with "annoyance and fatigue, . . . and even illness and pain"? (181)

4. Why does Vera dream about being a great singer and swimming the Channel—things she cannot do? (184)

5. Why do Vera's daughters doubt her contention that "of happiness she had had a lion's share"? (185)

6. Why does the tenderhearted Vera—who doesn't even like to kill an angry wasp—believe that she wasn't the least maternal? (190, 193)

7. Why does Vera say that the effort she put into raising her daughters was "unnatural"? (190)

8. When talking to Father Hugh about rearing her children, why does Vera say, "I didn't go over to the enemy anyway!" and then defiantly proclaim that they all were happy? (190)

9. As Vera grows older and her children strike out on their own, why does her life become increasingly chaotic?

Suggested textual analysis
Pages 189–191: beginning, "We looked at each other and smiled," and ending, "one might as well try to finish another person's poem."

Why does Bea end up receiving the legacy of her mother's happiness?

1. Why is Bea the "oracle" of the three sisters? (180)

2. Why does Vera refuse to accept Bea's suggestion that happiness is "a sort of legacy" that a parent can pass on to a child? (182)

3. Why is Vera, like her father, unable to make Grandmother happy?

4. Why does Bea call Vera's claim of happiness a "sham"? (185)

5. Why does the narrator say, "What was it worth—a happiness bought that dearly," when describing Vera's anguished summer after the death of her husband? (187)

6. Why did Vera never succeed in defining happiness for her daughters? (193)

7. Why, despite all of her instructions on happiness, can't Vera teach the narrator how to be happy? (194)

8. Why does Bea refuse to let Father Hugh tell Vera the truth—that she is dying—and then do it herself? (196, 197)

9. Why does Bea tell Vera, "You don't *have* to face it! It's over!"? (197)

10. Why is Bea confident that the tidings of death she gives Vera are joyous? (197)

Suggested textual analysis
Pages 195–197: from "Like the days of her life," to the end of the story.

FOR FURTHER REFLECTION

1. Can one choose to be happy?

2. Do we learn how to be happy through the examples set by our families?

3. Is sorrow the opposite of happiness, or is it a *"necessary ingredient"* of it?

4. Can parents teach their children how to be happy?

5. Is it possible to place too much importance on being happy?

6. Would you be happy if you lived according to Vera's philosophy of life?

ENDLESS MOUNTAINS

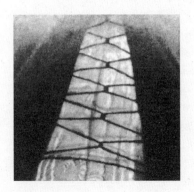

Reynolds Price

REYNOLDS PRICE (1933–) was born in Macon, North Carolina. He has published twelve novels and numerous volumes of short stories, poems, plays, essays, and biblical translations. After attending Oxford University as a Rhodes scholar, Price returned to his alma mater, Duke University, to teach literature and creative writing. He won the William Faulkner Foundation Award for his first novel, *A Long and Happy Life,* and the National Book Critics Circle Award for *Kate Vaiden;* both novels exemplify his gift for creating complex female characters. At the age of 51, Price was struck with cancer of the spinal cord, which left him paralyzed from the waist down. This catastrophic event eventually resulted in two memoirs, *Clear Pictures: First Loves, First Guides* and *A Whole New Life: An Illness and a Healing.* Price resides in North Carolina, where he continues to teach at Duke University as James B. Duke Professor of English.

T HE SHOT went through the white inside of my right thigh on Wednesday near noon. I lay in a little sweetgum thicket to the west of the battlefield the rest of that day and the sweltering night. Men worse off than me were dying all round me, telling their Jesus they could barely see him but were coming anyhow, or calling out long menus to the air for their mothers to cook, who were worlds away. I may have lain on, a very long time. Anyhow I remember the one night passed; and next it seemed like late afternoon with long light the color of brown clover-honey before the redhead scavenger found me, rummaged my pockets, read my papers, balled them up, and threw them aside, saying "Well now, Trump, it's your goddamned birthday."

Weak as I was, I said I could drink to the *goddamned* part.

But he just said "And it looks like your last, son"; then he bent towards me. That had to make it September fourteenth unless he was lying, which I doubt he was. Tall as I am, he picked me up like a back-broke doll, kissed my forehead, and strode on towards the bloody tent I'd nightmared about since the day I left home.

It must have been that night or the next, I managed to get upright on my feet. They held up under me long enough for my arms to feel out slow in the dark—empty around me. Had I dreamed there were other boys moaning near me, packed close as a flock of starlings in the snow? Maybe—I was dreaming from the morphia, steady. All my hands found now though was air, hot empty air; and both my legs still bore my weight. I reached down far enough to find my thigh and the crusty hole, size of an onion and hotter than all the rest of me; and then I thought I recalled a man's voice, maybe the surgeon's, saying I'd get two choices next dawn—I could give him that leg or take it to God myself by dark.

It was already dark. Was I already dead? If so, time had left me two long legs—one of them pierced deep (what I call *time,* most people call *God*). All right, I'd trust I was meant to use them. I took five short steps into the night, expecting something to stop me each instant; but no, and then my face seemed to cool—I was maybe outdoors again. The air was dry and a light breeze moved to call me on. For the first hundred yards, I barely hurt. Then a fire blazed up where my right leg hinged onto my body—the leg wouldn't take real steps from there on. Ten yards later the pain had plugged my head so full, I stopped and thought "Fall here in your tracks; and if you're still alive at dawn, let them cut you into however many pieces it takes to stop this pain." My eyes were likewise failing fast.

But something told me I had to go, I was meant to *leave* (not to save just a limb but the rest of my life); so my left leg took a long step on its own, dragging the right. Then it took three more—by now I could see the coals of small fires and occasional tents not twenty yards off—and I let it pull on down a slope till it dragged me into full dark again where I could smell what had to be water, the first clean water I'd smelled after drinking hot slop for days. Upright I groped before me with my hands, knowing that—close to water so clean—I might just slide into enemy

arms or hoist myself onto some warm bayonet waiting to end
me. *Christ, please let it.*

But no, I was next at what I could feel was the verge of the
stream. I wondered if I could manage to kneel—the pain by
then was like continuous lightning through me. It was more
like falling. Still I got to the ground; and when I'd scrabbled
forward on my fists, I found I could take one long reach down
into moving water, cold as the night (we were near the mountains). Just the feel of its kindness—unspoiled water, the fact
that it bore my touch without shrinking—gave my mind the
first firm thought I'd had since my wound. Deep in me, it said
They mean you to last. You find out how. It didn't tell me who
they was that meant my life to go on ahead, though I someway
knew it was not my people back at home, not the waiting
women; and it never said where it would lead nor when the
actual end would come.

But I chose to believe them, step by step, though next I slid
into thick black coma and lay there bathing that one hand till
a cloudless first-day cracked my eyes. I rushed to crawl
upright on my feet before some boy less mangled than me
could spot me and drill my head clean through or some of my
own boys could haul my ruins on back uphill and into that
reeking flyblown tent where I'd be stunned like a beef in the
stall, quartered with a blue-iron handforged cleaver, then
parceled out for all I knew to waiting cripples hungry as me. I
was dreaming half-awake by then—long scary visions of children that looked like offspring of mine, whom I'd never
known till now they were caught in an attic fire that would eat
everything they'd loved or trusted. They anyhow blanked the
actual pain of the world I was in.

I must have walked that whole bright day, using only my own
two legs and the dogwood stick I found by the path, a handy
crutch. I think I remember speaking to several women I passed

as they stood at stone gates holding their children or leading a horse no taller than me and scared nearly dead by the thunder beyond us—it was fresh killing surely but not for me, not now, no more. One of the young girls with no baby yet must have fed me something and found clean water that I could drink—I kept the strength to creep on forward—but who it was and what she might have asked from me, all that's gone completely now. What I remember is the ground beneath me. A whole lot smoother than I'd expected and always *up,* a gradual rise that even my bad leg managed to drag itself along.

It was night again with a hair of a moon—and the hole in my thigh scalded hotter than any outcry—when it dawned on me I was past all reach and truly alone. When that thought came down back of my eyes, I'd got to a ledge near the foot of what was all but a mountain. For a long time I'd strained not to rest, and I seldom stopped—rising and starting were still straight agony. But that new idea of being thoroughly on my own with nobody else in the whole world with me, that new idea sat me down hard on a cold flat rock; and it left me happy in tall waves of joy that rushed up through my legs and chest. It felt like I was the last live soul on a planet swept of the human race except for me, a lone man normal as milk in a bucket but the lord of all— nobody to owe, nobody to fail.

I may have sat there awake till day, a long time anyhow. And what I thought as the night died out was how the eyes I'd left might look if they were still living—my young wife and both our daughters, my pale strong mother and the brother I'd left to keep her alive through war and bone-deep deprivation (my father had been dead numerous years). Other eyes and faces flickered past me—some of them calling their full three names, some of them too far back to see or never glimpsed except in darkness and secret rooms—but of course my family's stayed with me longest. They were, every one of them, good to watch from this far off. They'd been good to know, give or take some hot silence and then cruel lies and the meanness they triggered (way over half the meanness was mine). But someway I knew my people were gone. And towards daybreak I knew their absence caused my joy—that sense I was *new* now, however near dead. Someway the entire Earth was mine to make from scratch in the time I had, which might be minutes.

At the first sight of the actual sun, I managed to stand and brace my knees. Right in the cold hard teeth of the light, I said my own name clear to the day and vowed my purpose. "Trump Ferrell," I said, "this time, get it true." Then by some means on a near-gone leg that steadily blanked my eyes in pain, I climbed on higher. Anybody could do it if the need arose as it had for me.

It was well past noon when I got to the ridge, and I'd lain down and dozed awhile in another bleak dream before I really looked at the place and saw it was more like an endless green table than a peak. I recalled several places I'd seen on maps that were called Table Mountain or maybe Flat Dome—western Virginia came to mind and down in the Smokies nearer my birthplace. But the fact was, I had no clear notion where I'd got to. I asked myself if I even cared whether this was ours or enemy country. Any cause for war I might have felt in my own mind—that had been fading for long months and seemed to have run out completely now right through my wound. So you might have guessed I'd be begging to die.

The cut of the light on these trees though and the dry ground deep in pinestraw beneath them—someway it threw me a thin thread of hope that I managed to catch. Holding just that much in my hand, I lay on through a chain of new dreams; and each dream had a lighted window in it—something to flee through to my new world or something to wait by till time showed a path. I thought I'd wait. I hadn't tried my leg again, and now I couldn't bear to see it. I stayed where I was in a pinestraw ditch in the ground in full glare and waited for what the sky intended.

The next I knew, and it may have been hours, I was moving steadily over ground—in the air, I mean, suspended someway. This time I truly took it for death and shut my eyes. The air felt cooler and smelled like far-off honeysuckle, and the pain was easing as I went. It seemed a long way. Then things got darker. Through my shut lids I understood the light was fading. It crossed my mind to wonder if my destination was up or down, Heaven or Hell, bright or black (I'm no churchgoer but no big fool; I believe in justice and I'd earned its toll). I even guessed that some tall man was bearing me in ample arms for his own purpose to a good dry place or a slaughter pen. But again slaughter seemed like a thing I'd gone through more than once and come out whole.

So I calmly figured that my fate anyhow was out of my hands. Whatever held me now would know wherever it needed to take my remains and how it would use me once we were there. The last clear thought I had for hours was *He knows it's me anyhow, knows it's Trump.* Some curious way I knew it was a *he* that bore me forward—likely because I'd been in the war and was just barely freed from its long mannish dream of glory, though I passed out again in the moving air and knew flat nothing for what turned out to be several more days.

Far as I know, the next human being that touched me was a woman. Whatever day of the year it was, it was late afternoon—the shine that fell in on me from a window was slanted and gold as a fall-in of old coins across my body. I seemed to be laid on my back on a table, long and narrow, with something comfortable under my head that felt like a folded sheet or sack. No fear, not even when my eyes first opened. The thing that said I was safe was the light, pure ripe late light. I'd slept a long time and was still myself, whatever good that was to the world. Next I felt down both my sides to see how much of my body was left. And that was when I heard the first certifiable voice I'd heard in what seemed weeks—a human voice, most likely a woman's.

It said from somewhere back of my head "Sir, you're in one piece anyhow. I can tell you that much, but this leg stinks and the other one's angry as any shot bull."

It had to be a woman, by the pitch and feel of how she cared. I shut my eyes in a flush of thanks.

And before I could speak or try to rise, she spoke again. "I'm praying you live though. Autry—he's gone now to make you the salve." I could almost hear her pointing towards Autry, marking the air where he'd last stood. She said "Old Autry's a healing soul. Hang on for him."

I understood her to mean my right leg was gangrened now and spreading to the other and death was close. By then it seemed just the next piece of news—the state of the weather, the casualty rate. My head must have nodded to urge her on.

But she said "*No,* you hang on here. Autry's planning to save you and he seldom fails."

I nodded again in courtesy.

Then I saw her face bend close—a pretty young face, sixteen or seventeen, perfectly heart-shaped with hazel eyes and chestnut hair. A face that in my former life I'd have risked at least one whole leg for. Her full lips were set in a hard line though; and while she tried to gentle her brow and steel my patience, she held up a stick of fresh fatwood and said "Chew down on this for the pain." She pulled my chin down and put in the stick.

I managed to say I wasn't in pain. I wasn't—it had gone past pain long since.

She said "You will be when I lance this pus."

I carefully spat the stick from my mouth. "You got any kind of license for this?" I had no idea what I meant.

But it set her back. She took a deep breath, then renewed her purpose. "I can't ask you to see this leg; but if you did, you'd know I'm bound by God to cut."

I raised my head and saw the bright razor she held like a torch. She brought it onward then—somewhere on the lower half of what had been my body for thirty-two years, the half that had given me plentiful fun far back as I knew, whoever it harmed or disobeyed.

With the use I'd made of women's bodies, I might have seen this as fair revenge. But weak as I was and addled with pain, I had one instant of seeing her hand as tame and welcome. All my grown life the sight of a woman's willing hand aimed towards that lower half of me had been the sight I'd struggled time and again to get, my permanent aim. And while I told myself as the razor met my skin, *This can't hurt worse than what I've known,* it hurt, Christ yes. A white-hot ramrod seared through my heart on into my mind, over and over for endless minutes. I'd long since gnawed the stick in two before the fire began to shrink, and then the girl was standing near me—younger still—laying a strong hand under my skull and lifting my head to help me drink from a shallow bowl. It was something cool, which was all I tasted; and in a few seconds I knew it had to be a powerful calmer.

Still I never felt a moment's fear, though I thought a drink as welcome as this might be merciful poison. And only when it had me addled and ready for sleep did I look round at the room I was in. A low small space walled with pine boards, no trace of whitewash; by the high rock fireplace, an eating table with two tin plates, a small stove, a clean wide bed, a pitcher and bowl with fuming water—all someway looking airless and untried as tombs in the hearts of granite hills waiting for God on Judgment Day with a firm chair ready to bear His weight and a cot for His rest.

The girl leaned on nearer down. "You got any message you want me to know?"

I tried to laugh but was too content. I said "No ma'm, I'm no kind of prophet."

She actually laughed then, clear as rung glass. It left her face as beautiful as any dawn I'd known (I'd risen at dawn since before the war). She said "I mean, you got any last instructions in case you pass on soon?"

I tried to tell her my wife's full name and where we'd lived. I know I managed my first daughter's name, which was Stella Dene.

The woman said "Look, I can't write a word; but I can remember—I've already memorized your keen eyes—so I'll tell Autry. He'll tell the world whatever you say, even if you pass before he's back. But you won't pass on from me, now will you?"

It felt like I was aimed right there, at restful death. Still I think I told her I'd enjoyed my stay, and I know that meant my entire life up till that time (give or take some hours when I got caught red-fisted in wrong). Anyhow by then it felt like I'd enjoyed every instant, though what I should have recollected was how much pain I'd leave behind in every head and heart that knew me, from my hard mother right on through every woman I'd touched and my smart daughters. But then I sank—no word, not a dream.

Then it was dark outside in the world; the windows and farthest walls of the room were nearly black. Around me though was a warm shine that clung tight to me, so close it was nearly hot to feel. I could smell lamp oil; but when I craned up to hunt for lamps or company near me, what I saw was the same sparse room surrendered to night. In my weak state and after so long with nothing to eat but that one drink, I took what came without strong question, not to speak of complaint. I even wondered calmly again if this didn't have to be the deep hereafter. If so, in my case it seemed to consist of lying still on a long pine table (I could smell it by now)—I'm more than six foot.

The next thing told me I was close to right. My hands went slowly down again and found I was naked below the waist, far as

I could reach at least. I hadn't thought of it when the girl worked on me, but now my warm hands found my privates all in place and safe to the touch like birds in a nest. Recalling how Jesus bore his wounds past resurrection, I didn't let myself hunt for mine—I someway trusted the girl had drained me and left my tenderest skin a lot cleaner. I still wore my old canvas shirt though.

Would saved souls lie around in Paradise hid to the waist but stark naked downward? Would that be all we learn in bliss—that, against our teaching, the belly and chest is our shameful half, where black hearts beat and the offal steams? Apparently I laughed at the thought—I heard a sound resembling a chuckle—and then my mind decided I was live. If this was late September though and I was in the lower mountains, why wasn't I cold?—I could just make out that the fireplace was dark too, no sign of a blaze. My mind made the words *Thank Christ I'm dead*. I'm nearly certain I didn't say them aloud in the room. But an answer came.

A low voice said "You feeling the chill?"

My head stayed down. "No sir, I'm not."

He said "You got to lie this way."

I knew I hadn't really tried to rise, not since I got here (and was he the one that brought me?); but I gave it my best and rose to my elbows. There was no big outcry from anywhere in me, no pain worse than before my leg putrefied. Still it wasn't my leg I tried to find. However strange I felt up here in this new world, what I yearned for was company; and it seemed a fair bet that this voice now belonged to a man, not a demon at least. My eyes settled on him, and I asked for his name.

He took a long wait and then didn't speak; and he wasn't a man—a boy maybe fifteen, to tell by his eyes, but taller than me. In the light that cupped us, he had black eyes set slant in his head like a wild bobcat's that met me, not shying. His hair was nearly the girl's fine color, darkest auburn (the warm light came from a glass lamp beside him on the lid of a keg—no razor, no knife, no bandage in view). His eyes were mainly what told me that he and the girl were closer kin than married.

Brother or sister, father and child. No, they had to be too young for that—even too young to marry anywhere but back in these hills, lawless and hid.

I asked him if his name wasn't Autry.

His white face made a try to smile, but his heart wasn't in it. "She tells people that."

"Told me, for one."

By then my eyes had opened enough to see he was dressed in parts of my uniform—the black wool pants that were clean of my blood and what was left of a black hunter's coat I'd brought from home. In the dark they blanked out his whole body but the burning face.

That was set on me, not wild-eyed but earnest. And then his hands moved into the shine. They were brown from work with fingers long as bamboo canes, knobbed at the knuckles from toil or age. *But he looked so young just now, just a boy.* He finally said "I got to ask you to lie back down and trust my work."

I recalled the salve the girl had mentioned—if this boy had any salve or balm, it was not in sight. And then I took the first look at my leg. It had not been washed since three hot days before the wound when I dipped up water from a muddy spring at the edge of a burnt-out wheelwright's shop and washed myself the best I could. Where the girl had cut across my wound, a thin pale track of the razor showed (was it already healed?). Round the bullet hole my skin was flooded with vicious blood and puckered to a near-black purple. Worse still, red streaks ran up past my crotch and belly—the poison reaching towards my heart. And across my privates the same thick color was spreading over to my left leg. I've seldom been a praying man, not for my lone self; but at that sight I said what must have sounded like prayer—*God spare me* or something equally weak.

Whatever the words, they made the boy smile, full at last on firm white teeth, and it left him looking like a son any father would gladly welcome (I had no sons and had given up hoping). He said "I'm not nobody's God, Captain; but if you trust me, I'll do my best."

I was nobody's captain either, never would be; and I figured he was either ignorant or crazy. But I was in no state of mind to shy from help, even here at the hands of a boy who—if he was truly a human and not some useless child of my fever—could scarcely do more than wash me clean and lay me into a deep enough grave by dawn or whenever the sure end came. I lay back flat and waited through what felt like a year, lifting my head by two or three inches every week or so to test his progress. It felt that slow.

To strain for memory, I figure his hands stayed on me, holding, till towards daybreak—well over an hour—him still as a shaft of upright rock with his old-man fingers round my ankles and sometimes sliding as high as my knees but, far as I know, never touching the wound, pressing hard but always steady. So I never felt he'd slacked or was gone. It seemed he was certain that honest pressure by one careful soul could turn death back from another live body far gone as me and friendless to boot. His eyes stayed shut a good part of the time, though his dry lips moved every now and then in what I tried to read as words, whole sentences—were they prayers or spells? But I never recognized one whole syllable and never felt like I was in danger or even in the wasteful hands of a fool.

I just stayed wide awake every minute and again took the chance to bring up the eyes I'd known and left—the usual family members, my girls, my staunch friend Ray that fell beside me (drilled through the eye) the day before I took my bullet and a few of the bodies I'd loved in darkness, moaning my name. All moved past me, bright as I'd ever seen them in life or dark and twisting; and they all nearly smiled. Still for the first time since I left, not one of them spoke to call me back. They each looked satisfied where they were and gave no sign of needing or hoping to see me again.

And when the first sun made its slow cold way through the window and reached us both, I felt so free from my old moorings that again I thought I was borne through the air well off the ground and onward through the mountain dawn like some kind of messenger skimming the Earth to do good will for no other master than God on high. That finally tired me; and the last I saw before my eyes shut down on the light was Autry easing up on my legs, then laying a heavy quilt across me and slowly moving away with his lamp. And what I figured I knew was a sentence that ran, like a big child's alphabet, behind my eyes—*These people are saving your flesh to eat.* Wild as it sounds, that dawn it left me calmer yet and eased me into a sleep so deep that all I knew for days to come was fitful dreams of war and blood, real as my life but harmless to watch.

Turned out the girl and boy had failed. Her lancing razor and the drink she gave me, his praying hands—they'd poured right into my sucking wound, a precious food it brewed and spread like perfect poison through my body. I was scarcely a rack of skin-tarred bones that were hot enough to cauterize a field hospital of bleeding men, but I stank with maggoty meat and the readable news of death. By the time I plunged to the pit of those fears in shuddering fever, I couldn't have kept but a slim two-thirds of my old size (which was near two hundred). All I took for nourishment was warm and cold drinks brought by the girl and, night after night, the boy's close hands and his dry lips moving through whatever code he used to whatever god.

I lay on, locked in further hard visions far past the point either one of my keepers thought I'd draw the next safe breath. They told me later they gave me up more times than one. And in every vision, staring again, stood a person I'd failed in the world—the old place everybody said was peaceful before the war but still the world I made my mess in, my sins of faithless greed I forced on any woman that would grin my way and let my starving mind inside her final secret to gorge itself.

It would be long months before I was safe enough to know how far into death I went, and then I only knew what they told me. They claimed I'd sleep through stretches of days, then wake up clawing at whatever came near. They said I'd make them promise me death with the white-hot blade (they swore I always called it that) or how other times I'd beg them to put their promise in writing and sign it plain before my eyes—that they'd keep me the rest of my days and alter my story so no one from my old life could find me.

And nobody found me; but down I went on rushing towards death till one cold midnight I howled for the boy to take some gouge—one big enough to serve—and dig my stinking leg off at last at the deep hip socket and burn it before it killed us all. By then I knew it had poisoned the air. I have a memory I think I can trust of howling the dreadful words in his face and then of seeing him go for a cleaver and bring it right to the edge of my side (I'd long since lain in an ample bed, the clean bed I'd noticed at first). I didn't feel a trace of fear; and I know my actual voice calmed down to confident peace as I said "Come *on.* Oh Autry, *help* me or fry in Hell."

He thought that through for a stunned minute, and I saw his eyes go darker still as the plan came on him like a dense bright veil that would have scalded any soul not chosen to do time's will. He gave one nod, accepting his duty. Then he laid the cleaver flat by his feet and quickly shucked his entire clothes, every layer of his and mine that had hid him. He stood there naked a long minute more, then turned the single quilt back off me and laid his clean length down my bones and the thin dry flesh that clung to me yet.

At first touch I thought he was on some private errand of his own that I couldn't help; but as he began to move and work, I guessed it might be purely a last hope of saving me. Far gone as I was, I saw the picture in my mother's Bible—Jacob wrestling a whole black night with the Angel of God and winning at daybreak.

And however long he truly stayed stretched on me there, however gone and weak I was, it felt till the end like a desperate fight between at least one human creature and something else like the will of God or even the evil face that lurks in the heart of a world run by any two sets of men as bent on havoc as the men I'd fought with, likewise the man I'd been till now. Wildest of all, at no one moment did I ever think it was strange or killing—what we did. It always felt like a *deed* we were doing. It felt like something planned for us (whoever he was) since time got started, and I always bet I'd end alive.

So in memory I guess there was new light near us, to show me we were still indoors with a roof above and a live world beyond us. The light could have come from the oil lamp or, Christ knows, maybe some shine from our struggle. It had the nature of fire in water, from old sea timbers, or far in the woods from slow decay. It played along my arms, his sides, his vise-grip legs, my straddled bones, his arms that were strong as any blacksmith's, and what rode hot from the pit of his belly—his tall man's root that seemed as much a part of his work, whatever he meant, as the toiling face and open eyes that moved above me, dark and near, and never left my own dazed sight. I recall I only thought two words that I kept silent—*Hurry, son,* by which I meant I guessed he was killing or healing or maybe just hoping to warm my chill; so end it fast—I sure-God felt he was using me up, though all he said was (time and again) "Captain, Captain, this is nothing but *help.*"

I knew if he worked on many more minutes, he'd be alone in the bed by day—there'd be no sign of me left but the stain of my last sweat, and that would be mist on the chill of morning. It must have been then I faded again for God knows how long—a long fit of dreams or actual life too strange to recall. It did seem though that Autry—or whatever Autry turned into—was back on me for a black string of nights and that I never doubted, every time we struggled, how he was bent on curing me finally just with the force of his own body, on driving death back with nothing but skin and the hot intention of a boy as fevered as I'd ever been (and far more desperate, for his own reasons and the orders he'd got from whatever power).

So time and again I still believe he lay down on me, burning to pass his young health to me or—failing that—to grind my pitiful scraps of bone to an ashy powder he could strow to the wind and then move on with his warm girl to a life they'd won through kindness to me. Over and over anyhow I'd sleep through baking fits of heat where dreams were nothing but coals banked on me, and then I'd wake soaked through to the bone with cold salt sweat from broken fever—proof his help was somehow working.

Her name was Ruth and when I finally swam towards light, it was her again that met me first—her face above me backed by a flood of shine from the window. She said "It's snowing. You ever seen snow?"

Close as my family lived to the coast, there'd only been one snow that lasted long enough to mark my mind. I'd been a young boy myself, sixteen; and the night before the weather turned, I'd joined another human body for the first full time, close and deep into joy. It had been with the girl I later married, made two daughters on, and left in tears. She was a younger distant cousin who came to us when her own people died of the red consumption that awful year when so many fell right where they stood—in fields, on horseback—foaming blood at their smiling lips (they mostly died smiling, strangest of all).

Anyhow when she'd been living with us for three long months—my distant cousin—she came to the loft where I slept one March night and dredged me up from a happy dream and asked without a single word for whatever comfort I could give her loss. Being my age then all I could think was to roll down on her and raise her shift the gentlest I could and visit her deep in the quick of her sorrow.

It did seem to help—her sleeping face was all but smiling when daylight woke me, blazing white at the frozen pane. At first I thought it was Judgment Day from the strength of the glare; still that didn't scare me or turn me against what she and I'd done. I calmly shook her arm to wake her and said "Something's new; look out here with me."

Together we crawled on our knees to the window; and all downhill from my old home, the better part of a mile towards the road, was untouched snow as pure as the hope we shared by then. I said to her "See, I knew we did right."

But bathed in the shine, she couldn't do more than say "Please, please." I understood she'd either spoken to the snow or me. She was telling the splendid sight to let up, it was too fine to watch; or she might have said it mainly to me, "Please keep me near you for good, here on."

I never could ask her to say more though, in explanation; and when she told me four months later she was toting my child in painful secret, I hitched a pony to Mother's green cart and drove us hard to a Baptist church six miles from home and married her legal, young as we were. Snow had done that to us, I always knew—the glare and the sheen like fire off the seraphim as they meet you, bent on either declaring pardon or haling your soul to postponed justice.

It was that bright anyhow when I came to with young Ruth near me in that same room I'd suffered in. So I managed to tell her that yes I'd seen one genuine snow.

She said "You feel like sitting up then? If you do I'll call him."

Him? By then I barely recalled my strong night visitor's name, but I said "Where is he?"

She pointed to the window. "Out melting snow. See, our spring's nearly two miles off; but Autry's out there now with a big fire, melting enough snow to warm you in if you mean to bathe."

If Ruth had said they were souls of the damned sent here to scorch me back to my home, I couldn't have felt any stranger than now. It was strangeness too that made me lie. I said "My name is Cullen, Cullen Duffy" (I'd someway remembered the redhaired man on the battlefield taking my papers; I'd come here nameless).

She was over by the fireplace poking logs. She said "I was hoping you'd live to tell us," and she threw a broad smile that reached me clear as the window shine.

I said "So I lived?"

"Sit up, man, and *look*." She came halfway back towards me on the bed.

I told myself not to reach down and feel, just try to get to my elbows and see what was left of my body. Weak as a drowned cat, I managed it slowly. The same quilt was on me, dark green and red; and beneath it there seemed to be two legs and feet. Then I noticed I was in a thick nightshirt, coarse as linen and clean as a shroud; and when I smelled my hands, they were sweet with maybe pine tar.

Ruth came the rest of the distance towards me and reached for the quilt. "You're way too feeble but let me show you."

The quilt spread back on her full arms, and there still on me were both my legs. The left leg was cloudy still near the thigh but normal size for a man that had starved through maybe long months. The right leg had shrunk to the size of an arm, and the wound hole was ugly but plainly closing with tender flesh. I knew I ought to be relieved; I figured I ought to burst into praise and gratitude. But what I found the strength to say was more a question than anything else, "This means I'm alive?"

She said "Either that or I'm in Heaven."

I mean to tell, I studied her slow and careful then. She looked as good as what I still guess Heaven contains if it's there at all. So I reached my right hand out and found her—just her wrist that was small but wiry as cable. I said "Sweet child, accept my thanks."

It seemed to shock her. She took a step back and looked behind as if for help or a quick retreat. Then she said "Oh we do." A frown crossed her brow, and it finally made her change her meaning. "It was Autry that saved you, Captain. Thank Autry."

I said "Your brother?" and when she looked puzzled, I mentioned how much they favored each other.

That nearly helped her to smile—not quite.

So I went further. "You might be twins."

She said "No, sir. We're not no kin on Earth to my knowledge."

"Husband and wife?"

Her whole face colored and again she looked towards the brilliant window. We could hear somebody outside chopping wood, and her eyes got urgent as she pointed that way. "We're trash. Just orphans scared of the killing."

By now I'd got enough strength back to prop myself on the high headboard. The room looked bigger than I recalled, still as clean as any picked bone, with no real signs of habitation but the coals of fire and her and my breathing eight feet apart. It was someway the emptiest place I'd been—there might not have been a roof and walls; the air was that vacant.

She caught my train of thought. "We don't stay here—" Her hand waved round; she meant the room.

"Who does?"

"Just you since the day Autry found you."

"But this is your home—"

"Oh no indeed. We stumbled on it when we'd been running so long we had to stop or die."

I said "You're saying you don't live here?" I meant I'd never seen them sleeping or eating in here, just working on me.

"No sir, when Autry found your body, we moved out yonder to give you air." She pointed again.

"But near, close by?"

She finally smiled and nodded behind her out the window. "In sound of your voice. Autry would hear you howling at night and run to help you."

Before I could say my thanks for that, the single door swung open on us; and there stood Autry taller maybe than I recalled but in my black clothes and finer across the brow and eyes than any son I'd dreamed of spawning and teaching the little I'd learned and could give. In his arms he strained to hold a copper tub that smoked like a cooking pit; but he stalled in place—facing me, not speaking.

I said "Son, if that's warm water bring it on."

Not looking at the girl, he said "It is" and brought it towards me, three feet from the bed. Then still watching me, he called her on—"Ruth, step here and help me show this man we saved his hide."

She said "I told him."

But he said "Step here."

As Ruth moved forward I thought better of it and said "Son, maybe I'm too weak for this."

Then he smiled too; his teeth were strong and white as a bear's. "If I'm your son, like you keep saying, then I'm the one you got to trust. Do what I tell you."

What could I do in painful joy but let those two afflicted souls wash my new body in clean hot snow?

That was in December—I'd crazed around and rested that long. And I stayed feeble the better part of three weeks, mostly up and dressed in my old clothes (that Autry surrendered without my asking). But I stayed low beside the fire, thinking of what time planned for me next. Or I'd lie hours across the bed, hoping to see some sign of a life to live in whatever world I joined if I left here. I already knew the war still lasted; the sky would light up most every night with phosphorus bombs from ten miles off and the burning spirits of men hurt worse than me or dead like mist down near the ground. I knew I was spending too much time alone for the good of my mind. My strength was coming back enough to start me thinking of things my fingers hadn't touched or my lips brushed for way too long (any number of which were in reach anytime Ruth was near me). I fought the hungers but they kept rising, and many times I begged young Autry to move himself and the girl back with me—I'd sleep on the hearth.

They'd nod and refuse and go on bringing me nourishment— dove, rabbit, squirrel, and various colors of rank hot tea they'd brew from roots. Sparse as the fare was, Ruth cooked it tasty; it filled my shrunk belly day by day till slowly I got back faith enough in both my legs to offer to work. I'd once been a hunter, so I offered to hunt the table meat. Autry could spend more time cutting firewood for my room and theirs as winter bore down.

They lived in a shed at the edge of the clearing. I'd never gone in, never been asked (the whole place, Autry claimed one evening, had stood here empty the day they came, worn from fleeing their own burned home—mother killed, father lost somewhere at war: I doubted his word after what Ruth had said). From the hour I got here, I'd never so much as shared a meal with them nor had any human conversation beyond the barest needs of life. And while I was bad off, the silence sufficed. But once I was stronger and played a useful part by luring and trapping the game (we had no rifles)—I figured I'd try to feed my hunger for simple company as the nights still came down early and freezing.

On what I'd almost surely figured was New Year's Eve, I went to Autry where he was chopping and said I thought it might be the New Year—did he know for sure, and couldn't we cook whatever I'd caught and mark the evening with food at least?

He shook his head—"That's some days from now"—but he stopped his work.

I said "In that case let's say it is—New Year's Eve—in case our luck runs out and they find us between now and then."

Autry looked like he'd never heard years could start or that luck was invented.

So I said "My family cooked a big spread for New Year's Eve—ham, chicken, and duck."

He barely faced me. "You got any people left down there?" When he gave a point behind to the valley, I recalled he'd never yet asked one fact about me or what I'd been before I was shot.

And what I told him was less than the truth. "My mother passed on some months back; my only brother's working the farm—he lacks one eye and can't fight a flea."

"You think I'm a coward?" It came out of Autry so low and fast, it tore his face. He might have been watching a wolf in the woods, blood on its teeth, not pale weak me.

I had to say "No and I didn't say you were."

He nodded. "I am."

So I said "Son, you rescued me when I was dead. And however dazed and childish I've been, I understand it was you that cured me." I'd told myself I understood it, which God knew I didn't—and don't today—but deep as my heart went, I knew this lanky boy had saved me by whatever means of skin or prayer, body or soul. And in my eyes that made him stronger than any six generals.

He leaned his axe against the block and finally met my face straight on. "I loved you," he said. "You were all we had."

If, that instant, killing light had poured from his eyes and blinded me, I couldn't have been any more amazed or scared any colder. I'd never leaned on the word *love* till now, not to stand for devotion of his size and kind. So I'd barely said it to my own kin, though I'd whispered it some to very-near strangers; and I hadn't heard the word used in the war, not in a decent way you could honor. I felt my tight chest wanting to laugh, in pure surprise and maybe true pleasure of a brand I'd lacked since my boyhood alone in trees with eagles at hand. But Autry's eyes were solemn still, waiting for me to take or turn back whatever offer he thought he'd made.

I said "I love *you*," having no real idea what I meant but someway knowing it ought to be true. Then I said the word *Thanks*—"I can thank you both." And when he nodded a calm acceptance—he knew what I owed, and he saw I'd paid—I rushed on further than I planned to go. "I can stay and help you two dig in. There's deep winter yet to come up here." I was thinking how much I'd need clean time and a big lost place to heal my mind and choose the path I'd take downhill.

He said "I mean you to stay for good."

I heard no threatful edge in his voice, and more than ever he looked like a son I'd have changed my life for. But now I knew not to make a binding promise. I just said what felt true again—they'd saved my life, especially him in his wild way, a way I still wasn't sure I'd fathom this side of the grave.

Autry took up his axe and said "You're welcome the rest of your life."

Four other people had offered as much to me in my time—my mother, my wife, and both my daughters whenever they laughed—and I'd refused them, needing more of the world than they could give (or so I believed). Now I stood my ground in the cold and said "All right." Since he'd called me Captain more than once, I saluted him fully; I could feel I was smiling.

And Autry joined me the nearest he could; I'd never seen his lips grin wider. And as I stepped on towards the woods to check my rabbit gum, he said "You trust me now with your name?" His grin spread wider—he knew I'd lied to Ruth awhile back.

I gave a dry laugh and asked if I could hold off a week. I told myself I was waiting in secret for time's new plan (I craved a plan). I thought it was nonsense, to cover my shame.

Autry said "Take the time you want. But it's Trump something, ain't it?"

That not only stunned me like his claim of love; it proved he had the magic of that contending angel I'd dreamt he was and may have been.

But he said "You kept calling *Trump* in your fever. I figured it was pity for yourself or your son."

I nodded. "It's me—Trump Ferrell. I lied to Ruth."

"How come?"

"I was scared."

"What of?"

"Both of you—I was crazy with fever."

He said "From all you raved about, I estimate you were crazy for years." It seemed plain fact; he was sober-eyed.

I said "I had too much to give," then bit my tongue.

He nodded. "You were strong."

"Strong and bad."

"We tried to be good to you," he said.

It sounded pure as a child's first speech, but it felt as true as the Ten Commandments, and it broke the last weak dam in my heart. I said "I'm in a whole new life, son. Whether you meant to or not, you caused it. I can't go back and live where I did. I burnt that down with nothing but greed."

He waited, then looked to the ground between us. "We'll call you any name you want, long as you stay."

I'd meant to check my traps before dark, so I said "Call me Trap." It seemed like a name from *Pilgrim's Progress* or some boy's book, but I let it stand.

Autry said "Yes, Captain" and turned back to work. He could split heartwood the width of my waist with a single stroke like the firmest apple.

My lures turned out to be empty that evening; and though we had enough laid by to feed us for two days yet, Autry was nowhere in sight when I got back. A little baffled I went to my own place. It felt different now—soon I knew I was waiting for company, not hands necessarily on my hide but open faces that didn't need words or permanent pledges. No word came from Autry or Ruth though, not even the usual light at their window; so I ate cold squirrel and slept on the floor to brace myself for what I understood I must do. They'd welcomed me here but left me alone, a healed stranger they'd never take in to their hid core, whatever it was. My course was set then; it opened before me straight as rails when I offered my presence and met just silence and a black windowpane that shut me off from the last two humans I'd knowingly trusted with my bare skin and the quick of my life. Time spoke it out in the frozen room above my head, *Strike out of here. You've paid your due.* It was something I'd never paid elsewhere, so that much anyhow was new ground gained.

And new ground was what lay all before me, though surely the war still straddled most paths I'd take out of here. I couldn't risk seeing another dead boy, the mouth of a gun, or a mad-eyed horse (not to speak of how they'd treat a deserter with two fit legs). I'd doze a few hours on the hard floor then and strike on inward—higher and deeper—before first day.

But whatever hand was moving me, sank me in a sleep so thick and dreamless that I didn't crack my eyelids once till warm sun slatted across my hands and took my face. It was well into morning; I'd missed one chance. All right, catch Autry and Ruth some game and leave tonight. *It's part of your plan.* I rose and broke the ice in my bowl to wash myself, then entered the clearing.

The usual thin smoke came from the stovepipe in their roof, and I walked on round the shed past the woodpile to check my traps. No sign of Autry chopping kindling, which he did most mornings—no fresh foot track. In a war most men lose half their hearing; mine someway improved. I stood in place in the empty clearing in full sunshine and listened hard—that way I could generally catch Ruth clinking a pan indoors or Autry yawning. Silence deep as any gorge. To my knowledge I'd never heard pure silence from them. If one of them went to the woods for something, the other one stayed in sight at least. Something hard in me said *They're gone; they've run again and it's from you, Trump.*

It actually shocked me and I felt a loss I'd never have guessed. *All right. It's yours. Leave clean or stay.* I stood a long moment, listening still. There was nothing for a while and then a high breath like the end of a laugh or a pitiful sigh. I went to the door and knocked one time. No answer. I tried it, a rusty latch but it opened.

It was one cold room that felt as low and round as a bowl tipped over and dark with just the square shaft of light from the window on a handsized piece of the swept dirt floor. A table made from the sawed-off stump of a sizable oak, a single white plate, two battered cups; then back in the shadows, a narrow pallet made out of croker sacks, a bolster stuffed with clean wood chips that spilled at one end—could it sleep two people? By now my eyes had widened to the dimness. Pegs on the walls bore a set and a half of faded clothes—two dresses, a man's shirt, a pair of trousers bigger than Autry and me together, remnants they'd snatched on their run or found here.

On the east wall alone hung one small picture, a tintype boxed in a walnut frame carved by hand with flat round roses. Before I got to it, the face burned towards me as strong as a thrust—a beautiful woman not twenty years old with dark hair glossy as horsetail pinned down tight at her ears and topped with a comb. Her eyes were plainly kin to Autry's and maybe Ruth's. Someway I knew I should make peace with her, the whole still presence of a woman clearly long-since dead; I took the last steps and kissed the glass lightly at her forehead.

Then the high breath sounded again from behind me, the sigh I'd heard in the clearing through walls. It froze me where I stood in midair bent towards the picture. I didn't look round but my empty hands rose up beside me to show I was harmless.

Nobody spoke though, no other noise.

And slowly my fright thawed sufficiently to turn me. At first my eyes saw nothing new. But just in the minutes I'd been indoors, the patch of light had moved towards the west wall another two inches and set up an odd white glow in that corner, a gentle shine like the memory of your best deed or dusk on the summer river, floating slow. Another pallet lay there, narrow; another pile of sacks for cover and one old quilt. Had they kept a dog or a pet wild creature that I'd never seen and was gone with them now? Or was it some secret final protection they'd kept and abandoned? For no sane cause I thought of great snakes I'd seen in books, Tasmanian Devils, and wolverines, and I actually laughed.

A child sat up from under the quilt. No nightmare jackal would have shied me worse. I lurched well back, both hands at my face, before my mind could recognize the gold brown hair and gray-green eyes, the skin so young you could read the blood that ran beneath like a confident promise of life to come with fair rewards. A girl all but surely, startled from sleep and unafraid. Maybe six years old with a tall clear forehead, the sign of calm.

I said "I'm Trump—you heard of me?" Something about her had kept me from lying.

Her lips stayed shut but she nearly nodded.

"I work for your folks—I catch the game."

She was in a tan nightshirt square as a box, and she didn't look cold.

"Let me build you a better fire." The low tin stove was barely warm though wood lay beside it.

All the child did was take both hands and work at her hair, laying it straight. The more she smoothed it, the grander she looked. Then while I worked she stayed there kneeling but looked round the room as slowly as if for the world's last crumb.

It made me think *They've left this child someway for good. She's mine to tend.* With my history of shirking plain duties, any such fact should have scared me worse than leaving for the world and its various wars; but for all the next long minutes we spent in silence together, it made me feel entirely in place for the first time in years—maybe since that snowy morning far back, my first day's love. And once the stove was cracking with heat, I rummaged in the corners further and turned up more things than I'd have dreamed after our recent fare. A big tin box with two pounds of raisins dry as stones but sweet to suck, a small keg of meal that the mice hadn't breeched, three jars of honey, and a glass quart of figs in clear syrup.

The child by now, when I looked again, seemed older still—maybe seven or eight. Surely she couldn't be Ruth and Autry's—weren't they too young? But with that hair like the tintype lady's, she could be their sister—their cousin or something they snatched from the house fire and brought here to leave. *They've gone and she's mine.* Now it made me happy to think so or warm at least. I said it out loud, "It may just be you and me here, darling. So tell me your name."

Her lips moved open and she raised a finger into the light, but where I expected words it was singing—some old-time tune I'd heard as a boy, too sad to carry onward through life. Just the first ten notes; then her hand came down. Silent again her eyes stayed on me.

So I went towards her.

And she never flinched. Whoever she was, wherever she belonged, you could tell nobody had treated her bad. Her spirit was in one close strong piece.

I stopped a yard this side of her pallet and went to my knees. I wanted her to see my face and eyes—the best parts of me, on the old Earth anyhow, that people thought they could trust right off.

She studied my eyes; then rummaged behind her deep in the sacks and held out her hand. A fancy comb carved in amber with mother of pearl inlay at the edge. It had been on the crown of the tintype lady's abundant hair, and now this child had clung to it through whatever she'd suffered. When I didn't move, she held it farther towards me.

One long moment later I was combing her hair, and she was accepting me naturally as kin or a friend. By the time I had it parted straight and was sorting the tangles, I felt the weight of this plain occasion. I'd touched no female creature in care for more than a year, and my hands trembled some at the pleasure. Whole tracts of my skin that hadn't known they were famished till now were all but weeping in silent thanks. I told myself *Trump, here's your chance—hell, you're in the midst of recompensing every woman you've harmed. Go gentle and use every-*

thing you've learned in waste and shame. So when my temples threatened to split, I spoke again. I leaned back on my haunches to see her. "If you don't have a name you remember, let me call you Joyce." It had been the name of the bravest girl I ever knew, that I'd seen once in my early manhood and then she'd died with her eyes full on me (one girl at least I'd honored and spared).

I thought the child was on the verge of gladly agreeing—her mouth came open—but from well behind me, a voice said "No, she's Margaret Jane."

It stalled me again but when I looked, it was Autry filling the whole door frame. From his right hand the axe hung ready.

Ruth was behind him with an armload of holly, long thick branches of spiky leaves and plentiful berries.

I said "I heard somebody, see—breathing through the walls— and I knew you were gone; so I came in thinking it might be a stranger."

Autry stood on silent.

But Ruth said "We've known her long years."

Then Autry reached back and, out of Ruth's hands, took a whole branch of holly which he held towards the child. He said "Look, Margaret. This here's your New Year."

The child didn't speak but nobody's eyes—no bride's or mother's—were ever so bright.

It made me nearly that glad to see her, knowing well I hadn't scared or harmed her. It also let me know again, and in far harder terms than before, that my path surely led out of here— soon, soon—and might never end.

Turned out, none of us really knew if this was New Year's Eve or not; we'd lost any count of actual time. But that didn't hinder the bountiful goodness that flowed from then till late in the night. Neither Ruth nor Autry asked any more about why I was in their curious room; and I didn't so much as glance at the fact of the beautiful child—her sudden mystery here among us, hid so close. It had come over me that they hadn't found this place on the run—they'd been here all their lives at least, and the three of them someway constituted a merciful clan hid back up here to serve the world if more of the desperate world than me should ever need drastic help again.

This child was the visible guarantee, not just that I'd live to finish my time but that life in the vicious world would eventually settle and tame. If not in my day surely in hers. For all we said about Margaret's breathing presence though—a natural-acting child whose beauty was marked by silence—she might have been a soul from bliss that nobody saw but me, Trump Ferrell, saved from death by the strength pumped out of this room through Ruth and Autry's hearts and skin, from Margaret's soul and into me.

For the present anyhow we stood together in the warming shed and acted as if we'd known each other most of our days and trusted our backs to each other's mercy. Nothing more was said about New Year; but once the child and Ruth had hung big clumps of holly along the walls, I thought again of how I'd failed to bring in food for the past two days. I stood in place a last still instant tasting my luck, and then I said I'd better get going and hunt us a meal.

Autry said they'd be much obliged.

I spent the better part of the day back deep in the woods, calming my thoughts and studying various ways downhill. There was one real trail, nearly vertical and edged with boulders, and several rough scrambles through sharper flint and huge evergreens. I even showed myself to the sky at two or three points overlooking the valley, trying to see where troops were camped or the smoke of a skirmish. But what was there that one cold noon was nothing but a million trees (stripped for winter to their firm bones) and what must have been the stream I drank from the night I ran—not a human house or a creature in motion. Still every nerve in my new skin said *Don't go back there. Push on up;* and when I looked behind me, the line of the ridge ran steep and naked, blue slate and granite on into the mist that shielded the sun. I'd climb farther on then when my time came, though I had to guess that meant a whole world empty of all but me and my dreams.

The time wasn't yet. I felt I had new debts to pay at the clearing to my benefactors, however they'd saved me. I didn't want to see them too soon and be tempted to mention my aim to leave. So I found a bright cove beside three hemlocks and lay down there to rest awhile (by then my body was so hardened to cold, I could sleep on ice). I managed it easy and when I woke in the low slant light, I jumped up strong and went to my traps. They'd had good luck. I'd caught a fat rabbit and a covey of bobwhites tame as pups nested down beneath an old crate I'd baited with corn and propped on a twig.

When Autry and I had cleaned the game, Ruth came outside and cooked it right on the coals we'd nurtured. I went on back to my place to wait; but when I looked out the window towards dusk, I saw that Margaret had come outdoors and stood by the fire, still not speaking but looking glad. Her skin in the late sun was whiter still; but it didn't look sick, only fine-grained and sheltered. I'd pretty well answered the questions about her to my satisfaction—at the least she was near kin to Autry and Ruth. For their own reasons which may have been wise they'd kept her hid; yet once I found her, they hadn't blamed me but told me her name and borne our nearness a few calm minutes. Who was I with my blotched record to dig on deeper and meaner than that into whatever mysteries these three held among them here? They'd saved my skin and maybe my soul— if I had one, which remained to be seen.

By then anyhow I'd searched my room for any small thing I'd left on the shelves and wanted to keep for my departure—the tailfeather fan of a grouse cock, the single picture I owned from my past life—a round tintype of my first daughter in her young mother's arms. I pocketed a blood-red rock I'd found in the woods that might be a ruby; and I kept the Indian black axehead I'd carried with me since I left home right through my battles (small but deadly, I'd yet to use it). My daughter's picture I slid between the head of the bed and its side rails. I'd remember their faces long as I needed; and I'd thank them this far by leaving their likeness here on the spot where death and I struggled—or I and an angel or just a kind boy, desperate as I. It was after all where I learned I must free my kin for better lives without my greed to drain their strength and harrow their peace.

Then a knock at my door, the first I'd heard (before now Autry and Ruth just walked in, sure I was ready for company). It scared me, knowing somebody stood there with a long-due bill for all my forfeits—a kinsman, my colonel, any one of the women I'd tried to use up. I couldn't answer.

Autry's voice spoke through the wood, "Trump, I told you it's New Year's Eve. Eat beside us."

Skittish as my old loyalty was, I'd always liked big family feasts. So this new invitation from Autry ought to have shook my heart in its moorings—I owed him that much; they were still good to watch. But still I was balked.

So he tried the door. It opened on me, upright square in the midst of the room. He studied my eyes in lantern shine. Then he said "She wants you to follow me."

I told him to thank Ruth and say I was tired.

"It ain't Ruth, Captain; it's Margaret Jane."

No coffin hinge was ever colder than I that instant—the old world of people was swarming back: kin, friends, children, mates of my body, every one of them empty-handed and staring at me like the fountain of grace. But then my mind someway heard a sentence; a silent voice said *Do this last thing. We'll set you loose.* I still couldn't talk but I nodded to Autry.

He led me onward.

∞

It was no big feast, but it filled our craws. We sat on the floor around the small table and just had the meat and a mush Ruth made from cornmeal and dried corn, the last they'd have till way into summer. I'd already forgot the things I saw in the corners that morning; and it came as a sweet surprise when Ruth and Margaret Jane slid back into darkness, laughing, and then returned with a jar of honey and the quart of figs. Each one of us ate with fingers scrubbed on a clean rag first—Ruth was clean as a bird. I'd eaten three figs and thought I was done when Margaret came forward to me with the honey. I thanked her and said I was way past full.

But she said "No"—I heard it clearly—and a smile spread on her to pick any lock on Heaven's gate.

The smile was so welcome, I barely noticed she'd said the first word, not to mention it was *No;* and all I wanted was to keep her talking. It seemed like something fairly enormous depended on that—her life or mine, the real world's future. I said "You'll have to say my name."

She held her ground, stone-silent again, with the honey held out.

Autry said "Captain, she's deaf and dumb."

I knew for a fact I'd heard her *No;* so my hand went out in the air towards her, clenched like a claw that could tear her skin. I think I was trying to tear something off her, some throttling fist that choked her throat or a plugged obstruction in her mind. I thought if a strange man scared her some she might break free (I'd thought that way too many times and trapped too many kindly girls).

It didn't faze Margaret. Or she didn't show it. Her right hand reached inside the jar, her white forefinger scooped down deep and brought up honey in neat cells of wax, then she brought it to me like gold I'd earned.

I knelt to meet her hand straight on and ate the warm wild sweetness off her that smelled like summer before the war, red clover and big old drowsy bees.

Next—swear to Christ—she said "Now rest." I'd never heard a child say *rest*.

I looked to Autry to see if he heard, but he'd moved away to the dark far corner. I could just make out that Ruth had already stretched out there on one of the pallets; it looked like Autry was ready to join her. And when I turned to Margaret again, she'd stepped back—still facing me—to her old quilt and was nesting there. I knew I hadn't obeyed a child since that first dawn I saw real snow, but I felt like pleasing this girl now. I said to the room "Would anybody care if I rest awhile?"

Nobody spoke, though the tin stove creaked on under our silence.

So I laid myself back full on the ground—the packed cold floor—as near to the midst of the room as I could.

Then we all rested, in proper places. Whoever Autry and Ruth might be to one another, they were fast asleep in a very few minutes with their work clothes on, ready to run or face daybreak. Margaret stayed busy a short while moving her hands in cold starlight to make horse heads on the wall beside her— mule heads, rabbits, and almost surely a unicorn, though how she made it with just ten fingers I couldn't see. It felt like I was wide awake; and likely I was more than blessed to be lying here in the core of something that, far as I knew, was entirely well-meant.

I thought I might be able to whisper and someway coax the child to talk. Maybe she had fresh orders for me, some sure destination entrusted to her in her barred throat but meant for me who'd got words from her when no one had. I know I whispered my love her way and felt I meant it.

But by the time those few words left me, her breath had slowed to a rate I heard as tranquil sleep, the daily trip of a simple human child into worlds beyond her power to change or fight.

I tried to recall some fitting single verse from the past—a psalm of praise requesting strength—but my mind lay as blank as the snow I'd likely find when I left this warmth. And then I fell into my trance too. If any dream walked through those hours, it left no fear or further instructions; and if any sleeping heart ever longed to stay where it was and grow tap roots forever more, it was mine right then—that near the midst of one world that plainly worked for its creatures.

Whatever woke me came as a word, but in my head, not the freezing room. I swam up knowing I'd heard a voice addressed to me and saying one word. Quick as it came it woke me fully, and I lay on long enough for the message. Nothing more sounded anywhere near me except the living trust and calm of the same three souls I'd lain down with, their healthy sighs on the ocean floor of brief blind safety. At last I told myself it was *Now;* the word that woke me had to be *Now.* I checked the window—no trace of light but the last of the moon that silvered my hands which I held up before me. Dim as it was I could see they were clean, not just of the honest dirt of hunting but all my past.

Strike out of here now before they rise and hold or win you. I tried to think if I'd left anything in my old cabin. No, not a crumb. All I needed was on me—all and more. I put my silent hand down slowly into my pocket and found the rock that might be a ruby, that red anyhow and clear at the heart. My arm went out towards where it felt the force of Margaret's perfect eyes and mind, and I set the redness down where she'd see it as first-day woke her.

Then limber as any recent ghost, I stood to my feet. My shot leg tried to buckle once, but next it held and promised to bear me. I moved in uncanny quiet to the door, spread it open by quiet inches, slid my frame through, and shut it behind me. Outside was barely colder than in, so my old summer coat would likely serve till sunup; I bound it round me and took a calm pause to listen again—nothing, just evergreens shifting in darkness, leading their ample harmless lives in one right place. Leftward the pitch of the sky burst open with white bomb light but still no sound.

So I turned right and crossed the clearing. In one more minute my feet were muffled in thick pinestraw; my legs could feel I was bound uphill and inward on these unplumbed mountains, aimed away from home and help except what my two hands could give. Endless mountains, utter freedom, lasting peace—a healed strong man now, done with war. ∾

Interpretive Questions
for Discussion

Why is Autry's desperate fight to save the dying Trump portrayed as both homoerotic and spiritual?

1. Why does Autry cure Trump by climbing naked on top of the dying man's bones and withered flesh? (218–220) Why is it only at night that Autry comes to lie down on Trump?

2. Why does Trump emphasize that Autry's "tall man's root" seemed as much a part of his work as his "toiling face and open eyes" that never left Trump's dazed sight? (219)

3. Why does Trump never doubt, every time he and Autry struggled, that the fevered and desperate boy was bent on curing him? (219) Why does Trump think that their struggle gives off a shine that has the "nature of fire in water, from old sea timbers, or far in the woods from slow decay"? (219)

4. Why does the author repeatedly associate radiance and light with both Ruth, who holds her razor like a "torch," and Autry, described as having a "burning face"? (210, 212, 215, 219, 220)

5. Why are we told that Trump considers Autry to be "finer across the brow and eyes than any son" he'd dreamed of spawning and teaching the little he knew? (224; cf. 227)

6. Why do Autry's words, "If I'm your son, like you keep saying, then I'm the one you got to trust," cause Trump to submit in "painful joy" to the bath that Autry has prepared for him? (224)

7. Why doesn't Trump believe in God? Why does he make a point of saying that what he calls *"time,* most people call *God"*? (206)

8. Why are we told that Trump feels most guilty about the pain he has caused the women he has known and touched? (213)

9. Thinking that it would only be just revenge for his selfish use of women's bodies if Ruth castrated him, why doesn't Trump experience even "a moment's fear" when she lances the wound in his groin? (212)

10. Are we meant to agree with Trump who believes that the primary source of his sins has been his greedy pursuit of sexual pleasure? What does Trump mean when he refers to his "starving mind" gorging itself inside the "final secret" of any woman who would grin his way? (217)

11. Why does Trump's belief that his family is dead give him joy— the sense that he "was *new* now, however near dead"? (208–209) Why does knowing that there is "nobody to owe, nobody to fail" make him feel like "the lord of all"? (208)

12. Why does Trump ask himself whether, contrary to what he's been taught, it's not the lower half of the human body that is shameful, but rather "the belly and chest . . . where black hearts beat and the offal steams"? (214)

Suggested textual analyses
Pages 210–213: beginning, "Far as I know," and ending, "But then I sank—no word, not a dream."

Pages 218–220: beginning, "And nobody found me," and ending, "proof his help was somehow working."

Is Trump, who admits to having been evil-hearted, transformed by his suffering?

1. Why does Trump's vow to "this time, get it true" give him the strength to creep up the mountain on his near-gone leg? What is it that Trump intends to "get true"? (209)

2. Why do Autry's "praying hands" on Trump's legs leave the wounded man feeling so free from his old moorings that he imagines himself "some kind of messenger skimming the Earth to do good will for no other master than God on high"? (216–217)

3. Why do Autry and Ruth's calming ministrations trigger in Trump the thought, *"These people are saving your flesh to eat"*—an idea that eases him into a deep sleep? (217)

4. Are we meant to think that Trump is unchanged—that his soul still harbors "faithless greed"—when he takes hold of Ruth's wrist and says, "Sweet child, accept my thanks"? (217, 223) Why does Trump's gesture seem to shock Ruth, so that she takes a step back and looks behind her "as if for help or a quick retreat"? (223)

5. Why does Trump think of Autry and Ruth as "those two afflicted souls" when they bathe him? Why does Trump emphasize that his "new body" is being washed in "clean hot snow"? (224)

6. Why do Autry and Ruth refuse to move back into the cabin with Trump when he begs them to? (225) Why don't they ever invite the lonely man to share a meal, or even converse with him "beyond the barest needs of life"? (225)

7. What does Trump mean when he tells Autry that he had been crazy for years because he had "too much to give"? (228) Why does Trump bite his tongue after saying this?

8. Why does Trump's discovery of Margaret, and his decision to take care of her, leave him feeling "entirely in place for the first

time in years"—perhaps since that snowy morning far back, his "first day's love"? (231; cf. 221)

9. If we are meant to think that Trump's desire to "tend" Margaret is a sign of his transformation—his newfound capacity for unselfish love—why does the author twice have Trump refer to Margaret as "mine"? (231, 232)

10. Are we meant to think that there is something illicit about Trump trembling at the sensual pleasure of combing Margaret's hair, even though he believes himself *"in the midst of recompensing every woman"* he's harmed? (232)

11. Why does the author emphasize that Trump no longer holds any illusions about war, that "long mannish dream of glory"? (210)

12. Is Trump right to view himself at the end of the story as "a healed strong man now"? (240) Are we meant to agree with Trump when he declares his hands clean, not just of the honest dirt of hunting, but of all his past? (239)

Suggested textual analyses

Pages 221–225: beginning, "It was that bright anyhow," and ending, "I figured I'd try to feed my hunger for simple company as the nights still came down early and freezing."

Pages 230–233: beginning, "And slowly my fright thawed sufficiently to turn me," and ending, "my path surely led out of here—soon, soon—and might never end."

Why does Trump decide to leave Autry, Ruth, and Margaret, concluding that it is the solitude of the "endless mountains" that will give him "lasting peace" and "utter freedom"?

1. Why does Trump's sense that he's in a whole new life mean that he can't go back and live where he did? Why does he say that he "burnt that down with nothing but greed"? (228)

2. When Autry tells Trump that he's welcome to stay the rest of his life, why does Trump tell the boy, "All right," if he can't even trust the boy with his real name? (227)

3. Why is Trump not just amazed but scared cold by Autry's declaration of love and need for him? (226)

4. Is Trump correct when he concludes that Autry and Ruth would never take him in to their "hid core"? (229)

5. Finding Autry and Ruth's cabin silent, why does Trump assume that the two young people have run from him, even though the "usual thin smoke came from the stovepipe in their roof"? (229) Why does Trump jump to the conclusion that the child, Margaret, has been abandoned by the nurturing Autry and Ruth? (231)

6. Even though Trump is planning on leaving, why doesn't he feel the loss of Autry and Ruth—a loss he'd "never have guessed"— until he thinks that *they* have left *him*? (229)

7. Why does Trump try to assuage his feelings of loss and shock by telling himself that the cabin and clearing are his, and that he is free either to leave or to stay? (229)

8. Why is it the knowledge that he hadn't harmed or scared Margaret that tells Trump he must leave Autry, Ruth, and the child? (233)

9. Does Trump's desire to put the "old world of people" behind him spring from a genuine desire to free those he loves from his greed, or is he simply rationalizing a wish to be free of the demands of all human connection? (236)

10. Why are we told that when Margaret's request to share a New Year's meal turns Trump as cold as a coffin hinge, a "silent voice" tells him, "*Do this last thing. We'll set you loose*"? Who is the "we" of the silent voice that speaks to Trump? (236)

11. Why does Trump leave the blood-red rock for Margaret, of the "perfect eyes and mind," rather than for Autry or Ruth, who "saved his hide"? (224, 239)

12. Considering how deeply Trump longs for permanent acceptance into Autry, Ruth, and Margaret's peaceful world, why does a voice in his head tell him, "*strike out of here now before they rise and hold or win you*"? (239)

Suggested textual analyses

Pages 226–230: beginning, "He barely faced me," and ending, "I tried it, a rusty latch but it opened."

Pages 238–240: from "Then we all rested," to the end of the story.

FOR FURTHER REFLECTION

1. Does happiness lie in the pursuit of one's individual identity or in the idea that family is paramount? Can the two be reconciled?

2. Why do particular places have the power to heal?

3. Is greed the greatest threat to human happiness?

4. When is illness, or physical suffering, a help rather than a hindrance to spiritual growth?

5. Does achieving inner peace automatically result in a person's happiness? Are peace and happiness the same thing?

6. Reynolds Price has said that "All narrative artists are very much involved in telling the only story we really want to hear, which is: 'History is the will of a just God who knows me.'" Do you agree?

AS YOU LIKE IT

William Shakespeare

WILLIAM SHAKESPEARE (1564–1616) was
born in Stratford-upon-Avon, England.
Although many details of Shakespeare's life
are unknown or contested, we know that
his father was a shopkeeper, glover, and
prominent local citizen who served as alderman
and bailiff for Stratford. William Shakespeare
was educated only at the local grammar school,
where he studied Latin and most likely read
the plays of Terence and Plautus. It is unclear
when and how Shakespeare went to London
and began working in the theater, but by 1594
he had joined the Lord Chamberlain's Men
acting company as an actor, playwright,
and shareholder. *As You Like It* was first
performed in 1599 or 1600. Shakespeare's plays
were published during his lifetime, but none
with his approval. He enjoyed some degree of
prosperity, purchasing one of the largest houses
in Stratford in 1597. Shakespeare retired to
Stratford sometime in 1611 or 1612 and lived
there until his death.

CHARACTERS

DUKE SENIOR	living in banishment
DUKE FREDERICK	his brother, and usurper of his dominions
AMIENS JAQUES	} lords attending on the banished Duke
LE BEAU	a courtier attending upon Frederick
CHARLES	wrestler to Frederick
OLIVER JAQUES ORLANDO	} sons of Sir Rowland de Boys
ADAM DENNIS	} servants to Oliver
TOUCHSTONE	a clown
SIR OLIVER MARTEXT	a vicar
CORIN SILVIUS	} shepherds
WILLIAM	a country fellow, in love with Audrey
HYMEN	god of marriage

ROSALIND	daughter to the banished Duke
CELIA	daughter to Frederick
PHEBE	a shepherdess
AUDREY	a country wench

LORDS, PAGES, and
ATTENDANTS, etc.

[SCENE: *Oliver's house; Duke Frederick's court;
and the Forest of Arden.*]

ACT I

[SCENE I: *The garden of Oliver's estate.*]

Enter ORLANDO *and* ADAM.

ORLANDO: As I remember, Adam, it was upon this fashion bequeath'd me by will but poor[1] a thousand crowns, and, as thou say'st, charg'd my brother, on his blessing, to breed me well; and there begins my sadness. My brother Jaques he keeps at school, and report speaks goldenly of his profit.[2] For my part, he keeps me rustically at home, or, to speak more properly, stays me here at home unkept; for call you that keeping for a gentleman of my birth, that differs not from the stalling of an ox? His horses are bred better; for, besides that they are fair with their feeding, they are taught their manage,[3] and to that end riders dearly hir'd. But I, his brother, gain nothing under him but growth, for the which his animals on his dunghills are as much bound to him as I. Besides this nothing that he so plentifully gives me, the something that nature gave me his countenance seems to take from me. He lets me feed with his hinds,[4] bars me the place of a brother, and as much as in him lies, mines[5] my gentility with my education. This is it, Adam, that grieves me; and the spirit of my father, which I think is within me, begins to mutiny against this servitude. I will no longer endure it, though yet I know no wise remedy how to avoid it.

Enter OLIVER.

---

1. [*but poor:* only.]   4. [*hinds:* farm hands.]

2. [*profit:* progress.]   5. [*mines:* undermines.]

3. [*manage:* paces.]

ADAM: Yonder comes my master, your brother.

ORLANDO: Go apart, Adam, and thou shalt hear how he will shake me up.

[ADAM *stands aside.*]

OLIVER: Now, sir, what make you here?

ORLANDO: Nothing. I am not taught to make anything.

OLIVER: What mar you then, sir?

ORLANDO: Marry, sir, I am helping you to mar that which God made, a poor unworthy brother of yours, with idleness.

OLIVER: Marry, sir, be better employ'd, and be naught awhile.[6]

ORLANDO: Shall I keep your hogs and eat husks with them? What prodigal portion have I spent, that I should come to such penury?

OLIVER: Know you where you are, sir?

ORLANDO: O, sir, very well; here in your orchard.

OLIVER: Know you before whom, sir?

ORLANDO: Ay, better than him I am before knows me. I know you are my eldest brother; and, in the gentle condition of blood, you should so know me. The courtesy of nations allows you my better, in that you are the first-born; but the same tradition takes not away my blood, were there twenty brothers betwixt us. I have as much of my father in me as you, albeit I confess your coming before me is nearer to his reverence.

OLIVER: What, boy!

[*Strikes him.*]

---

6. [*be naught awhile:* be quiet or go away.]

ORLANDO: Come, come, elder brother, you are too young[7] in this.

[Seizes him.]

OLIVER: Wilt thou lay hands on me, villain?[8]

ORLANDO: I am no villain; I am the youngest son of Sir Rowland de Boys. He was my father, and he is thrice a villain that says such a father begot villains. Wert thou not my brother, I would not take this hand from thy throat till this other had pull'd out thy tongue for saying so. Thou hast rail'd on thyself.

ADAM: Sweet masters, be patient! For your father's remembrance, be at accord.

OLIVER: Let me go, I say.

ORLANDO: I will not, till I please. You shall hear me. My father charg'd you in his will to give me good education. You have train'd me like a peasant, obscuring and hiding from me all gentleman-like qualities. The spirit of my father grows strong in me, and I will no longer endure it; therefore allow me such exercises as may become a gentleman, or give me the poor allottery my father left me by testament; with that I will go buy my fortunes.

[Releases him.]

OLIVER: And what wilt thou do? Beg, when that is spent? Well, sir, get you in. I will not long be troubled with you; you shall have some part of your will. I pray you, leave me.

ORLANDO: I will no further offend you than becomes me for my good.

OLIVER: Get you with him, you old dog.

---

7. [*young*: inexperienced (at wrestling).]

8. [*villain*: a scoundrel, but also a low-born person.]

ADAM: Is "old dog" my reward? Most true, I have lost my teeth in your service. God be with my old master! He would not have spoke such a word.

Exeunt ORLANDO [*and*] ADAM.

OLIVER: Is it even so? Begin you to grow upon me?[9] I will physic your rankness, and yet give no thousand crowns neither. Holla, Dennis!

Enter DENNIS.

DENNIS: Calls your worship?

OLIVER: Was not Charles, the Duke's wrestler, here to speak with me?

DENNIS: So please you, he is here at the door and importunes access to you.

OLIVER: Call him in. [DENNIS *goes to the door.*] 'Twill be a good way; and tomorrow the wrestling is.

Enter CHARLES.

CHARLES: Good morrow to your worship.

OLIVER: Good Monsieur Charles, what's the new news at the new court?

CHARLES: There's no news at the court, sir, but the old news: that is, the old Duke is banish'd by his younger brother the new Duke, and three or four loving lords have put themselves into voluntary exile with him, whose lands and revenues enrich the new Duke; therefore he gives them good leave to wander.

OLIVER: Can you tell if Rosalind, the Duke's daughter, be banish'd with her father?

---

9. [*grow upon me:* encroach on my place.]

CHARLES: O, no; for the Duke's daughter, her cousin, so loves her, being ever from their cradles bred together, that she would have follow'd her exile, or have died to stay behind her. She is at the court, and no less belov'd of her uncle than his own daughter, and never two ladies lov'd as they do.

OLIVER: Where will the old Duke live?

CHARLES: They say he is already in the forest of Arden, and a many merry men with him; and there they live like the old Robin Hood of England. They say many young gentlemen flock to him every day, and fleet the time carelessly, as they did in the golden world.

OLIVER: What, you wrestle tomorrow before the new Duke?

CHARLES: Marry, do I, sir; and I came to acquaint you with a matter. I am given, sir, secretly to understand that your younger brother Orlando hath a disposition to come in disguis'd against me to try a fall. Tomorrow, sir, I wrestle for my credit, and he that escapes me without some broken limb shall acquit him well. Your brother is but young and tender, and, for your love, I would be loath to foil him, as I must for my own honor if he come in. Therefore, out of my love to you, I came hither to acquaint you withal, that either you might stay him from his intendment, or brook such disgrace well as he shall run into, in that it is a thing of his own search and altogether against my will.

OLIVER: Charles, I thank thee for thy love to me, which thou shalt find I will most kindly requite. I had myself notice of my brother's purpose herein, and have by underhand means labor'd to dissuade him from it, but he is resolute. I'll tell thee, Charles, it is the stubbornest young fellow of France, full of ambition, an envious emulator of every man's good parts, a secret and villainous contriver against me his natural brother. Therefore use thy discretion. I had as lief thou didst break his neck as his finger. And thou wert best look to't; for if thou dost him any slight disgrace, or if he do not mightily grace himself on thee, he will practice against thee by poison, entrap thee by some treacherous device, and never leave thee till he hath ta'en thy life by some indirect means or other; for I assure thee, and almost with tears I speak it, there is not one so young and so villainous this day living. I speak but brotherly of him; but should I anatomize him to thee as he is, I must blush and weep, and thou must look pale and wonder.

CHARLES: I am heartily glad I came hither to you. If he come tomorrow, I'll give him his payment. If ever he go alone[10] again, I'll never wrestle for prize more. And so God keep your worship!

OLIVER: Farewell, good Charles.

Exit [CHARLES].

Now will I stir this gamester. I hope I shall see an end of him; for my soul, yet I know not why, hates nothing more than he. Yet he's gentle, never school'd and yet learned, full of noble device, of all sorts enchantingly belov'd, and indeed so much in the heart of the world, and especially of my own people, who best know him, that I am altogether mispris'd. But it shall not be so long; this wrestler shall clear all. Nothing remains but that I kindle[11] the boy thither, which now I'll go about.

Exit.

[SCENE II: *The grounds of Duke Frederick's palace.*]

Enter ROSALIND *and* CELIA.

CELIA: I pray thee, Rosalind, sweet my coz, be merry.

---

10. [*go alone*: walk without help.]
11. [*kindle*: urge.]

ROSALIND: Dear Celia, I show more mirth than I am mistress of; and would you yet I were merrier? Unless you could teach me to forget a banish'd father, you must not learn me how to remember any extraordinary pleasure.

CELIA: Herein I see thou lov'st me not with the full weight that I love thee. If my uncle, thy banish'd father, had banish'd thy uncle, the Duke my father, so thou hadst been still with me, I could have taught my love to take thy father for mine. So wouldst thou, if the truth of thy love to me were so righteously temper'd as mine is to thee.

ROSALIND: Well, I will forget the condition of my estate, to rejoice in yours.

CELIA: You know my father hath no child but I, nor none is like to have. And, truly, when he dies, thou shalt be his heir, for, what he hath taken away from thy father perforce, I will render thee again in affection. By mine honor, I will, and when I break that oath, let me turn monster. Therefore, my sweet Rose, my dear Rose, be merry.

ROSALIND: From henceforth I will, coz, and devise sports. Let me see; what think you of falling in love?

CELIA: Marry, I prithee, do, to make sport withal. But love no man in good earnest; nor no further in sport neither than with safety of a pure blush thou mayst in honor come off again.

ROSALIND: What shall be our sport, then?

CELIA: Let us sit and mock the good huswife Fortune from her wheel, that her gifts may henceforth be bestow'd equally.

ROSALIND: I would we could do so, for her benefits are mightily misplac'd, and the bountiful blind woman doth most mistake in her gifts to women.

CELIA: 'Tis true, for those that she makes fair she scarce makes honest,[12] and those that she makes honest she makes very ill-favoredly.

ROSALIND: Nay, now thou goest from Fortune's office to Nature's. Fortune reigns in gifts of the world, not in the lineaments of Nature.

Enter [TOUCHSTONE *the*] *Clown.*

CELIA: No; when Nature hath made a fair creature, may she not by Fortune fall into the fire? Though Nature hath given us wit to flout at Fortune, hath not Fortune sent in this fool to cut off the argument?

ROSALIND: Indeed, there is Fortune too hard for Nature, when Fortune makes Nature's natural[13] the cutter-off of Nature's wit.

CELIA: Peradventure this is not Fortune's work neither, but Nature's, who perceiveth our natural wits too dull to reason of such goddesses and hath sent this natural for our whetstone; for always the dullness of the fool is the whetstone of the wits. How now, wit, whither wander you?

TOUCHSTONE: Mistress, you must come away to your father.

CELIA: Were you made the messenger?

TOUCHSTONE: No, by mine honor, but I was bid to come for you.

ROSALIND: Where learn'd you that oath, fool?

TOUCHSTONE: Of a certain knight, that swore by his honor they were good pancakes and swore by his honor the mustard was naught. Now I'll stand to it, the pancakes were naught and the mustard was good, and yet was not the knight forsworn.

CELIA: How prove you that, in the great heap of your knowledge?

---

12. [*honest*: virtuous, chaste.]

13. [*natural*: simpleton, a born fool.]

ROSALIND: Ay, marry, now unmuzzle your wisdom.

TOUCHSTONE: Stand you both forth now. Stroke your chins, and swear by your beards that I am a knave.

CELIA: By our beards, if we had them, thou art.

TOUCHSTONE: By my knavery, if I had it, then I were; but if you swear by that that is not, you are not forsworn. No more was this knight, swearing by his honor, for he never had any; or if he had, he had sworn it away before ever he saw those pancakes or that mustard.

CELIA: Prithee, who is't that thou mean'st?

TOUCHSTONE: One that old Frederick, your father, loves.

CELIA: My father's love is enough to honor him enough. Speak no more of him; you'll be whipp'd for taxation[14] one of these days.

TOUCHSTONE: The more pity that fools may not speak wisely what wise men do foolishly.

CELIA: By my troth, thou sayest true; for since the little wit that fools have was silenc'd, the little foolery that wise men have makes a great show. Here comes Monsieur Le Beau.

Enter LE BEAU.

ROSALIND: With his mouth full of news.

CELIA: Which he will put on us, as pigeons feed their young.

ROSALIND: Then shall we be news-cramm'd.

CELIA: All the better; we shall be the more marketable. —*Bonjour,* Monsieur Le Beau. What's the news?

LE BEAU: Fair princess, you have lost much good sport.

CELIA: Sport? Of what color?

---

14. [*taxation:* wrongdoing (in this case, slander).]

Le Beau: What color, madam? How shall I answer you?

Rosalind: As wit and fortune will.

Touchstone: Or as the Destinies decree.

Celia: Well said; that was laid on with a trowel.

Touchstone: Nay, if I keep not my rank—

Rosalind: Thou losest thy old smell.

Le Beau: You amaze me, ladies. I would have told you of good wrestling, which you have lost the sight of.

Rosalind: Yet tell us the manner of the wrestling.

Le Beau: I will tell you the beginning; and, if it please your ladyships, you may see the end, for the best is yet to do; and here, where you are, they are coming to perform it.

Celia: Well, the beginning, that is dead and buried.

Le Beau: There comes an old man and his three sons—

Celia: I could match this beginning with an old tale.

Le Beau: Three proper young men, of excellent growth and presence.

Rosalind: With bills[15] on their necks, "Be it known unto all men by these presents."[16]

Le Beau: The eldest of the three wrestled with Charles, the Duke's wrestler; which Charles in a moment threw him and broke three of his ribs, that there is little hope of life in him. So he serv'd the second, and so the third. Yonder they lie, the poor old man, their father, making such pitiful dole over them that all the beholders take his part with weeping.

---

15. [*bills:* documents.]

16. [*by these presents:* by these present documents or words (with a pun on *presence*).]

ROSALIND: Alas!

TOUCHSTONE: But what is the sport, monsieur, that the ladies have lost?

LE BEAU: Why, this that I speak of.

TOUCHSTONE: Thus men may grow wiser every day. It is the first time that ever I heard breaking of ribs was sport for ladies.

CELIA: Or I, I promise thee.

ROSALIND: But is there any else longs to see this broken music in his sides? Is there yet another dotes upon rib-breaking? Shall we see this wrestling, cousin?

LE BEAU: You must, if you stay here; for here is the place appointed for the wrestling, and they are ready to perform it.

CELIA: Yonder, sure, they are coming. Let us now stay and see it.

Flourish. Enter DUKE [FREDERICK], LORDS, ORLANDO, CHARLES, *and* ATTENDANTS.

DUKE FREDERICK: Come on. Since the youth will not be entreated, his own peril on his forwardness.

ROSALIND: Is yonder the man?

LE BEAU: Even he, madam.

CELIA: Alas, he is too young! Yet he looks successfully.

DUKE FREDERICK: How now, daughter and cousin? Are you crept hither to see the wrestling?

ROSALIND: Ay, my liege, so please you give us leave.

DUKE FREDERICK: You will take little delight in it, I can tell you, there is such odds in the man.[17] In pity of the challenger's

---

17. [*there is such odds in the man*: i.e., Charles is so superior.]

youth I would fain dissuade him, but he will not be entreated. Speak to him, ladies; see if you can move him.

CELIA: Call him hither, good Monsieur Le Beau.

DUKE FREDERICK: Do so. I'll not be by.

[*Steps aside.*]

LE BEAU: Monsieur the challenger, the princess calls for you.

ORLANDO [*approaching the ladies*]: I attend them with all respect and duty.

ROSALIND: Young man, have you challeng'd Charles the wrestler?

ORLANDO: No, fair princess; he is the general challenger. I come but in, as others do, to try with him the strength of my youth.

CELIA: Young gentleman, your spirits are too bold for your years. You have seen cruel proof of this man's strength. If you saw yourself with your eyes or knew yourself with your judgment, the fear of your adventure would counsel you to a more equal enterprise. We pray you, for your own sake, to embrace your own safety and give over this attempt.

ROSALIND: Do, young sir. Your reputation shall not therefore be mispris'd. We will make it our suit to the Duke that the wrestling might not go forward.

ORLANDO: I beseech you, punish me not with your hard thoughts, wherein I confess me much guilty to deny so fair and excellent ladies anything. But let your fair eyes and gentle wishes go with me to my trial; wherein if I be foil'd, there is but one sham'd that was never gracious;[18] if kill'd, but one dead that is willing to be so. I shall do my friends no wrong, for I have none to lament me; the world no injury, for in it I have nothing. Only in the world I fill up a place, which may be better supplied when I have made it empty.

---

18. [*gracious:* graced, favored.]

ROSALIND: The little strength that I have, I would it were with you.

CELIA: And mine, to eke out hers.

ROSALIND: Fare you well. Pray heaven I be deceiv'd in you!

CELIA: Your heart's desires be with you!

CHARLES: Come, where is this young gallant that is so desirous to lie with his mother earth?

ORLANDO: Ready, sir, but his will hath in it a more modest working.

DUKE FREDERICK: You shall try but one fall.

CHARLES: No, I warrant your Grace, you shall not entreat him to a second, that have so mightily persuaded him from a first.

ORLANDO: You mean to mock me after; you should not have mock'd me before. But come your ways.

ROSALIND: Now Hercules be thy speed, young man!

CELIA: I would I were invisible, to catch the strong fellow by the leg.

[They] wrestle.

ROSALIND: O excellent young man!

CELIA: If I had a thunderbolt in mine eye, I can tell who should down.

Shout. [CHARLES *is thrown.*]

DUKE FREDERICK: No more, no more.

ORLANDO: Yes, I beseech your Grace. I am not yet well breath'd.

DUKE FREDERICK: How dost thou, Charles?

LE BEAU: He cannot speak, my lord.

DUKE FREDERICK: Bear him away. What is thy name, young man?

[CHARLES *is borne out.*]

ORLANDO: Orlando, my liege, the youngest son of Sir Rowland de Boys.

DUKE FREDERICK: I would thou hadst been son to some man else.
The world esteem'd thy father honorable,
But I did find him still mine enemy.
Thou shouldst have better pleas'd me with this deed
Hadst thou descended from another house.
But fare thee well; thou art a gallant youth.
I would thou hadst told me of another father.

Exit DUKE [*with train*].

CELIA: Were I my father, coz, would I do this?

ORLANDO: I am more proud to be Sir Rowland's son,
His youngest son, and would not change that calling
To be adopted heir to Frederick.

ROSALIND [*to* CELIA]: My father lov'd Sir Rowland as his soul,
And all the world was of my father's mind.
Had I before known this young man his son,
I should have given him tears unto entreaties,
Ere he should thus have ventur'd.

CELIA: Gentle cousin,
Let us go thank him and encourage him.
My father's rough and envious disposition
Sticks me at heart.—Sir, you have well deserv'd.
If you do keep your promises in love
But justly as you have exceeded all promise,
Your mistress shall be happy.

ROSALIND: Gentleman,

[*Giving him a chain from her neck.*]

Wear this for me, one out of suits with fortune,
That could give more, but that her hand lacks means.
Shall we go, coz?

CELIA: Ay. Fare you well, fair gentleman.

[They start to leave.]

ORLANDO: Can I not say, I thank you? My better parts
Are all thrown down, and that which here stands up
Is but a quintain,[19] a mere lifeless block.

ROSALIND: He calls us back. My pride fell with my fortunes;
I'll ask him what he would.—Did you call, sir?
Sir, you have wrestled well, and overthrown
More than your enemies.

CELIA: Will you go, coz?

ROSALIND: Have with you.—Fare you well.

Exit [with CELIA*].*

ORLANDO: What passion hangs these weights upon my tongue?
I cannot speak to her, yet she urg'd conference.
O poor Orlando, thou art overthrown!
Or Charles or something weaker masters thee.

Enter LE BEAU.

LE BEAU: Good sir, I do in friendship counsel you
To leave this place. Albeit you have deserv'd
High commendation, true applause, and love,
Yet such is now the Duke's condition
That he misconsters all that you have done.
The Duke is humorous.[20] What he is indeed
More suits you to conceive than I to speak of.

---

19. [*quintain:* a post used for tilting practice.]

20. [*humorous:* moody.]

ORLANDO: I thank you, sir. And, pray you, tell me this:
Which of the two was daughter of the Duke
That here was at the wrestling?

LE BEAU: Neither his daughter, if we judge by manners;
But yet indeed the taller[21] is his daughter.
The other is daughter to the banish'd Duke,
And here detain'd by her usurping uncle
To keep his daughter company, whose loves
Are dearer than the natural bond of sisters.
But I can tell you that of late this Duke
Hath ta'en displeasure 'gainst his gentle niece,
Grounded upon no other argument
But that the people praise her for her virtues
And pity her for her good father's sake;
And, on my life, his malice 'gainst the lady
Will suddenly break forth. Sir, fare you well.
Hereafter, in a better world than this,
I shall desire more love and knowledge of you.

ORLANDO: I rest much bounden to you. Fare you well.

[*Exit* LE BEAU.]

Thus must I from the smoke into the smother,
From tyrant Duke unto a tyrant brother.
But heavenly Rosalind!

Exit.

[SCENE III: *Duke Frederick's palace.*]

Enter CELIA *and* ROSALIND.

CELIA: Why, cousin, why, Rosalind! Cupid have mercy! Not a word?

ROSALIND: Not one to throw at a dog.

---

21. [*taller*: possibly a misprint for *smaller*. Rosalind is later shown to be taller than Celia.]

CELIA: No, thy words are too precious to be cast away upon curs; throw some of them at me. Come, lame me with reasons.

ROSALIND: Then there were two cousins laid up, when the one should be lam'd with reasons and the other mad without any.

CELIA: But is all this for your father?

ROSALIND: No, some of it is for my child's father. O, how full of briers is this working-day world!

CELIA: They are but burrs, cousin, thrown upon thee in holiday foolery; if we walk not in the trodden paths, our very petticoats will catch them.

ROSALIND: I could shake them off my coat; these burrs are in my heart.

CELIA: Hem[22] them away.

ROSALIND: I would try, if I could cry "hem" and have him.

CELIA: Come, come, wrestle with thy affections.

ROSALIND: O, they take the part of a better wrestler than myself!

CELIA: O, a good wish upon you! You will try in time, in despite of a fall. But, turning these jests out of service, let us talk in good earnest. Is it possible, on such a sudden, you should fall into so strong a liking with old Sir Rowland's youngest son?

ROSALIND: The Duke my father lov'd his father dearly.

CELIA: Doth it therefore ensue that you should love his son dearly? By this kind of chase, I should hate him, for my father hated his father dearly; yet I hate not Orlando.

ROSALIND: No, faith, hate him not, for my sake.

CELIA: Why should I not? Doth he not deserve well?

---

22. [*Hem*: cough or clear the throat.]

Enter DUKE [FREDERICK], *with* LORDS.

ROSALIND: Let me love him for that, and do you love him
  because I do. Look, here comes the Duke.

CELIA: With his eyes full of anger.

DUKE FREDERICK: Mistress, dispatch you with your safest haste
  And get you from our court.

ROSALIND: Me, uncle?

DUKE FREDERICK: You, cousin.
  Within these ten days if that thou beest found
  So near our public court as twenty miles,
  Thou diest for it.

ROSALIND: I do beseech your Grace
  Let me the knowledge of my fault bear with me.
  If with myself I hold intelligence
  Or have acquaintance with mine own desires,
  If that I do not dream or be not frantic—
  As I do trust I am not—then, dear uncle,
  Never so much as in a thought unborn
  Did I offend your Highness.

DUKE FREDERICK: Thus do all traitors.
  If their purgation did consist in words,
  They are as innocent as grace itself.
  Let it suffice thee that I trust thee not.

ROSALIND: Yet your mistrust cannot make me a traitor.
  Tell me whereon the likelihood depends.

DUKE FREDERICK: Thou art thy father's daughter, there's
  enough.

ROSALIND: So was I when your Highness took his dukedom;
  So was I when your Highness banish'd him.
  Treason is not inherited, my lord;
  Or, if we did derive it from our friends,

What's that to me? My father was no traitor.
Then, good my liege, mistake me not so much
To think my poverty is treacherous.

CELIA: Dear sovereign, hear me speak.

DUKE FREDERICK: Ay, Celia, we stay'd her for your sake,
Else had she with her father rang'd along.

CELIA: I did not then entreat to have her stay;
It was your pleasure and your own remorse.
I was too young that time to value her,
But now I know her. If she be a traitor,
Why so am I. We still have slept together,
Rose at an instant, learn'd, play'd, eat together,
And wheresoe'er we went, like Juno's swans,
Still we went coupled and inseparable.

DUKE FREDERICK: She is too subtle for thee; and her smoothness,
Her very silence and her patience
Speak to the people, and they pity her.
Thou art a fool. She robs thee of thy name,
And thou wilt show more bright and seem more virtuous
When she is gone. Then open not thy lips.
Firm and irrevocable is my doom
Which I have passed upon her; she is banish'd.

CELIA: Pronounce that sentence then on me, my liege!
I cannot live out of her company.

DUKE FREDERICK: You are a fool. You, niece, provide yourself.
If you outstay the time, upon mine honor,
And in the greatness of my word, you die.

Exit DUKE, *etc.*

CELIA: O my poor Rosalind, whither wilt thou go?
Wilt thou change fathers? I will give thee mine.
I charge thee, be not thou more griev'd than I am.

ROSALIND: I have more cause.

CELIA: Thou hast not, cousin.
Prithee, be cheerful. Know'st thou not the Duke
Hath banish'd me, his daughter?

ROSALIND: That he hath not.

CELIA: No, hath not? Rosalind lacks then the love
Which teacheth thee that thou and I am one.
Shall we be sund'red? Shall we part, sweet girl?
No, let my father seek another heir.
Therefore devise with me how we may fly,
Whither to go, and what to bear with us.
And do not seek to take your change upon you,
To bear your griefs yourself and leave me out;
For, by this heaven, now at our sorrows pale,
Say what thou canst, I'll go along with thee.

ROSALIND: Why, whither shall we go?

CELIA: To seek my uncle in the forest of Arden.

ROSALIND: Alas, what danger will it be to us,
Maids as we are, to travel forth so far!
Beauty provoketh thieves sooner than gold.

CELIA: I'll put myself in poor and mean attire
And with a kind of umber smirch my face;
The like do you. So shall we pass along
And never stir assailants.

ROSALIND: Were it not better,
Because that I am more than common tall,
That I did suit me all points like a man?
A gallant curtle-axe upon my thigh,
A boar-spear in my hand; and—in my heart
Lie there what hidden woman's fear there will—
We'll have a swashing and a martial outside,

As many other mannish cowards have
That do outface it with their semblances.

CELIA: What shall I call thee when thou art a man?

ROSALIND: I'll have no worse a name than Jove's own page,
And therefore look you call me Ganymede.
But what will you be call'd?

CELIA: Something that hath a reference to my state:
No longer Celia, but Aliena.

ROSALIND: But, cousin, what if we assay'd to steal
The clownish fool out of your father's court?
Would he not be a comfort to our travel?

CELIA: He'll go along o'er the wide world with me;
Leave me alone to woo him. Let's away,
And get our jewels and our wealth together,
Devise the fittest time and safest way
To hide us from pursuit that will be made
After my flight. Now go we in content
To liberty, and not to banishment.

Exeunt.

ACT II

[SCENE I: *The forest of Arden.*]

Enter DUKE SENIOR, AMIENS, *and two or three* LORDS, *like foresters.*

DUKE SENIOR: Now, my co-mates and brothers in exile,
Hath not old custom made this life more sweet
Than that of painted pomp? Are not these woods
More free from peril than the envious court?

Here feel we not[23] the penalty of Adam,
The seasons' difference, as the icy fang
And churlish chiding of the winter's wind,
Which, when it bites and blows upon my body,
Even till I shrink with cold, I smile and say
"This is no flattery; these are counselors
That feelingly persuade me what I am."
Sweet are the uses of adversity,
Which, like the toad, ugly and venomous,
Wears yet a precious jewel in his head;
And this our life, exempt from public haunt,
Finds tongues in trees, books in the running brooks,
Sermons in stones, and good in everything.

AMIENS: I would not change it. Happy is your Grace
That can translate the stubbornness of fortune
Into so quiet and so sweet a style.

DUKE SENIOR: Come, shall we go and kill us venison?
And yet it irks me the poor dappled fools,
Being native burghers of this desert city,
Should in their own confines with forked heads[24]
Have their round haunches gor'd.

FIRST LORD: Indeed, my lord,
The melancholy Jaques grieves at that,
And, in that kind, swears you do more usurp
Than doth your brother that hath banish'd you.
Today my Lord of Amiens and myself
Did steal behind him as he lay along
Under an oak whose antique root peeps out
Upon the brook that brawls along this wood,
To the which place a poor sequest'red stag,
That from the hunter's aim had ta'en a hurt,
Did come to languish; and indeed, my lord,

---

23. [*feel we not:* we do not mind.]
24. [*forked heads:* barbed arrows.]

The wretched animal heav'd forth such groans
That their discharge did stretch his leathern coat
Almost to bursting, and the big round tears
Cours'd one another down his innocent nose
In piteous chase; and thus the hairy fool,
Much marked of the melancholy Jaques,
Stood on th' extremest verge of the swift brook,
Augmenting it with tears.

DUKE SENIOR: But what said Jaques?
Did he not moralize this spectacle?

FIRST LORD: O, yes, into a thousand similes.
First, for his weeping into the needless²⁵ stream:
"Poor deer," quoth he, "thou mak'st a testament
As worldings do, giving thy sum of more
To that which had too much." Then, being there alone,
Left and abandoned of his velvet friends:
" 'Tis right," quoth he, "thus misery doth part
The flux of company." Anon a careless herd,
Full of the pasture, jumps along by him
And never stays to greet him. "Ay," quoth Jaques,
"Sweep on, you fat and greasy citizens;
'Tis just the fashion. Wherefore do you look
Upon that poor and broken bankrupt there?"
Thus most invectively he pierceth through
The body of the country, city, court,
Yea, and of this our life, swearing that we
Are mere usurpers, tyrants, and what's worse,
To fright the animals and to kill them up
In their assign'd and native dwelling place.

DUKE SENIOR: And did you leave him in this contemplation?

SECOND LORD: We did, my lord, weeping and commenting
Upon the sobbing deer.

---

25. [*needless:* not in need, already full.]

DUKE SENIOR: Show me the place.
I love to cope²⁶ him in these sullen fits,
For then he's full of matter.²⁷

FIRST LORD: I'll bring you to him straight.

Exeunt.

[SCENE II: *Duke Frederick's palace.*]

Enter DUKE [FREDERICK], *with* LORDS.

DUKE FREDERICK: Can it be possible that no man saw them?
It cannot be. Some villains of my court
Are of consent and sufferance in this.

FIRST LORD: I cannot hear of any that did see her.
The ladies, her attendants of her chamber,
Saw her a-bed, and in the morning early
They found the bed untreasur'd of their mistress.

SECOND LORD: My lord, the roynish²⁸ clown, at whom so oft
Your Grace was wont to laugh, is also missing.
Hisperia, the princess' gentlewoman,
Confesses that she secretly o'erheard
Your daughter and her cousin much commend
The parts and graces of the wrestler
That did but lately foil the sinewy Charles;
And she believes, wherever they are gone,
That youth is surely in their company.

DUKE FREDERICK: Send to his brother; fetch that gallant hither.
If he be absent, bring his brother to me;
I'll make him find him. Do this suddenly,

---

26. [*cope*: encounter.]

27. [*matter*: sense, substance.]

28. [*roynish*: coarse.]

And let not search and inquisition quail
To bring again these foolish runaways.

Exeunt.

[SCENE III: *Before Oliver's house.*]

Enter ORLANDO *and* ADAM, [*meeting*].

ORLANDO: Who's there?

ADAM: What, my young master? O my gentle master,
O my sweet master, O you memory
Of old Sir Rowland! Why, what make you here?
Why are you virtuous? Why do people love you?
And wherefore are you gentle, strong, and valiant?
Why would you be so fond to overcome
The bonny priser[29] of the humorous Duke?
Your praise is come too swiftly home before you.
Know you not, master, to some kind of men
Their graces serve them but as enemies?
No more do yours. Your virtues, gentle master,
Are sanctified and holy traitors to you.
O, what a world is this, when what is comely
Envenoms him that bears it!

ORLANDO: Why, what's the matter?

ADAM: O unhappy youth,
Come not within these doors! Within this roof
The enemy of all your graces lives.
Your brother—no, no brother; yet the son—
Yet not the son, I will not call him son
Of him I was about to call his father—
Hath heard your praises, and this night he means
To burn the lodging where you use to lie

---

29. [*bonny priser:* fine prizefighter.]

And you within it. If he fail of that,
He will have other means to cut you off.
I overheard him and his practices.
This is no place, this house is but a butchery;
Abhor it, fear it, do not enter it.

ORLANDO: Why, whither, Adam, wouldst thou have me go?

ADAM: No matter whither, so you come not here.

ORLANDO: What, wouldst thou have me go and beg my food?
Or with a base and boist'rous sword enforce
A thievish living on the common road?
This I must do, or know not what to do;
Yet this I will not do, do how I can.
I rather will subject me to the malice
Of a diverted blood and bloody brother.

ADAM: But do not so. I have five hundred crowns,
The thrifty hire I sav'd under your father,
Which I did store to be my foster-nurse
When service should in my old limbs lie lame,
And unregarded age in corners thrown.
Take that, and He that doth the ravens feed,
Yea, providently caters for the sparrow,
Be comfort to my age! Here is the gold;   [*Gives gold.*]
All this I give you. Let me be your servant.
Though I look old, yet I am strong and lusty,
For in my youth I never did apply
Hot and rebellious liquors in my blood,
Nor did not with unbashful forehead woo
The means of weakness and debility;
Therefore my age is as a lusty winter,
Frosty, but kindly. Let me go with you.
I'll do the service of a younger man
In all your business and necessities.

ORLANDO: O good old man, how well in thee appears
   The constant service of the antique world,
   When service sweat for duty, not for meed!
   Thou art not for the fashion of these times,
   Where none will sweat but for promotion,
   And having that do choke their service up
   Even with the having. It is not so with thee.
   But, poor old man, thou prun'st a rotten tree,
   That cannot so much as a blossom yield
   In lieu of[30] all thy pains and husbandry.
   But come thy ways; we'll go along together,
   And, ere we have thy youthful wages spent,
   We'll light upon some settled low content.

ADAM: Master, go on, and I will follow thee
   To the last gasp, with truth and loyalty.
   From seventeen years till now almost fourscore
   Here lived I, but now live here no more.
   At seventeen years many their fortunes seek,
   But at fourscore it is too late a week;
   Yet fortune cannot recompense me better
   Than to die well and not my master's debtor.

                             Exeunt.

[SCENE IV: *The forest of Arden.*]

Enter ROSALIND *for Ganymede,* CELIA *for Aliena, and Clown, alias* TOUCHSTONE.

ROSALIND: O Jupiter, how weary are my spirits!

TOUCHSTONE: I care not for my spirits, if my legs were not weary.

ROSALIND: I could find in my heart to disgrace my man's apparel and to cry like a woman; but I must comfort the weaker

---

30. [*In lieu of:* in return for.]

vessel, as doublet and hose ought to show itself courageous to petticoat. Therefore courage, good Aliena!

CELIA: I pray you, bear with me; I cannot go no further.

TOUCHSTONE: For my part, I had rather bear with you than bear you; yet I should bear no cross[31] if I did bear you, for I think you have no money in your purse.

ROSALIND: Well, this is the forest of Arden.

TOUCHSTONE: Ay, now am I in Arden, the more fool I. When I was at home, I was in a better place, but travelers must be content.

Enter CORIN *and* SILVIUS.

ROSALIND: Ay, be so, good Touchstone.—Look you who comes here, a young man and an old in solemn talk.

[They stand aside and listen.]

CORIN: That is the way to make her scorn you still.

SILVIUS: O Corin, that thou knew'st how I do love her!

CORIN: I partly guess, for I have lov'd ere now.

SILVIUS: No, Corin, being old, thou canst not guess,
Though in thy youth thou wast as true a lover
As ever sigh'd upon a midnight pillow.
But if thy love were ever like to mine—
As sure I think did never man love so—
How many actions most ridiculous
Hast thou been drawn to by thy fantasy?

CORIN: Into a thousand that I have forgotten.

SILVIUS: O, thou didst then never love so heartily!
If thou rememb'rest not the slightest folly

---

31. [*cross:* a burden, but also a coin having a cross stamped on it.]

That ever love did make thee run into,
Thou hast not lov'd.
Or if thou hast not sat as I do now,
Wearing thy hearer in thy mistress's praise,
Thou hast not lov'd.
Or if thou hast not broke from company
Abruptly, as my passion now makes me,
Thou has not lov'd.
O Phebe, Phebe, Phebe!   *Exit.*

ROSALIND: Alas, poor shepherd! Searching of thy wound,
I have by hard adventure found mine own.

TOUCHSTONE: And I mine. I remember, when I was in love I
broke my sword upon a stone and bid him take that for coming a-night to Jane Smile; and I remember the kissing of her
batler[32] and the cow's dugs that her pretty chopt[33] hands had
milk'd; and I remember the wooing of a peascod[34] instead of
her, from whom I took two cods and, giving her them again,
said with weeping tears, "Wear these for my sake." We that
are true lovers run into strange capers; but as all is mortal in
nature, so is all nature in love mortal in folly.

ROSALIND: Thou speak'st wiser than thou art ware of.

TOUCHSTONE: Nay, I shall ne'er be ware of mine own wit till I
break my shins against it.

ROSALIND: Jove, Jove! This shepherd's passion
Is much upon my fashion.

TOUCHSTONE: And mine; but it grows something stale with me.

CELIA: I pray you, one of you question yond man
If he for gold will give us any food.
I faint almost to death.

---

32. [*batler*: an implement used to beat wrinkles out of clothes.]

33. [*chopt*: chapped.]

34. [*peascod*: pea pod (a token of good luck).]

TOUCHSTONE: Holla, you clown!

ROSALIND: Peace, fool! He's not thy kinsman.

CORIN: Who calls?

TOUCHSTONE: Your betters, sir.

CORIN: Else are they very wretched.

ROSALIND: Peace, I say.—Good even to you, friend.

CORIN: And to you, gentle sir, and to you all.

ROSALIND: I prithee, shepherd, if that love or gold
    Can in this desert place buy entertainment,
    Bring us where we may rest ourselves and feed.
    Here's a young maid with travel much oppress'd,
    And faints for succor.

CORIN: Fair sir, I pity her
    And wish, for her sake more than for mine own,
    My fortunes were more able to relieve her;
    But I am shepherd to another man
    And do not shear the fleeces that I graze.
    My master is of churlish disposition,
    And little recks to find the way to heaven
    By doing deeds of hospitality.
    Besides, his cote,[35] his flocks, and bounds of feed
    Are now on sale, and at our sheepcote now,
    By reason of his absence, there is nothing
    That you will feed on. But what is, come see,
    And in my voice most welcome shall you be.

ROSALIND: What is he that shall buy his flock and pasture?

CORIN: That young swain that you saw here but erewhile,
    That little cares for buying any thing.

---

35. [*cote*: cottage.]

ROSALIND: I pray thee, if it stand with honesty,
    Buy thou the cottage, pasture, and the flock,
    And thou shalt have to pay for it of us.

CELIA: And we will mend thy wages. I like this place,
    And willingly could waste my time in it.

CORIN: Assuredly the thing is to be sold.
    Go with me. If you like upon report
    The soil, the profit, and this kind of life,
    I will your very faithful feeder be
    And buy it with your gold right suddenly.

Exeunt.

[SCENE V: *The forest.*]

Enter AMIENS, JAQUES, *and others.*

SONG

[AMIENS:]

        Under the greenwood tree
        Who loves to lie with me,
        And turn his merry note
        Unto the sweet bird's throat,
    Come hither, come hither, come hither.
            Here shall he see
            No enemy
    But winter and rough weather.

JAQUES: More, more, I prithee, more.

AMIENS: It will make you melancholy, Monsieur Jaques.

JAQUES: I thank it. More, I prithee, more. I can suck melancholy
    out of a song, as a weasel sucks eggs. More, I prithee, more.

AMIENS: My voice is ragged. I know I cannot please you.

JAQUES: I do not desire you to please me; I do desire you to sing. Come, more, another stanzo. Call you 'em stanzos?

AMIENS: What you will, Monsieur Jaques.

JAQUES: Nay, I care not for their names; they owe me nothing. Will you sing?

AMIENS: More at your request than to please myself.

JAQUES: Well then, if ever I thank any man, I'll thank you; but that they call compliment is like th' encounter of two dog-apes, and when a man thanks me heartily, methinks I have given him a penny and he renders me the beggarly thanks. Come, sing; and you that will not, hold your tongues.

AMIENS: Well, I'll end the song. Sirs, cover the while; the Duke will drink under this tree. He hath been all this day to look you.

[*They start to set out a light repast at a table.*]

JAQUES: And I have been all this day to avoid him. He is too disputable for my company. I think of as many matters as he, but I give heaven thanks and make no boast of them. Come, warble, come.

SONG

All together here.

    Who doth ambition shun
    And loves to live i' th' sun,
    Seeking the food he eats
    And pleas'd with what he gets,
Come hither, come hither, come hither.
      Here shall he see
      No enemy
But winter and rough weather.

JAQUES: I'll give you a verse to this note that I made yesterday in despite of my invention.

AMIENS: And I'll sing it. [*Takes verse.*] Thus it goes:

> If it do come to pass
> That any man turn ass,
> Leaving his wealth and ease,
> A stubborn will to please,
> Ducdame,[36] ducdame, ducdame.
>   Here shall he see
>   Gross fools as he,
> An if he will come to me.

What's that "ducdame"?

JAQUES: 'Tis a Greek invocation, to call fools into a circle. I'll go sleep, if I can; if I cannot, I'll rail against all the first-born of Egypt.

AMIENS: And I'll go seek the Duke. His banquet is prepar'd.

Exeunt [*severally*].

[SCENE VI: *The forest.*]

Enter ORLANDO *and* ADAM.

ADAM: Dear master, I can go no further. O, I die for food! Here lie I down, and measure out my grave. Farewell, kind master.

[*Lies down.*]

ORLANDO: Why, how now, Adam? No greater heart in thee? Live a little; comfort a little; cheer thyself a little. If this uncouth forest yield any thing savage, I will either be food for it or bring it for food to thee. Thy conceit[37] is nearer death than thy powers. For my sake be comfortable; hold death awhile at the arm's end. I will here be with thee presently, and if I bring thee

---

36. [*Ducdame*: origin uncertain; probably a version of "come hither."]
37. [*conceit*: thought.]

not something to eat, I will give thee leave to die; but if thou diest before I come, thou art a mocker of my labor. Well said! Thou look'st cheerly, and I'll be with thee quickly. Yet thou liest in the bleak air. Come, I will bear thee to some shelter; and thou shalt not die for lack of a dinner, if there live any thing in this desert. [*Picks up* ADAM.] Cheerly, good Adam!

Exeunt.

[SCENE VII: *The forest.*]

Enter DUKE SENIOR, *and* LORDS, *like outlaws.*

DUKE SENIOR: I think he be transform'd into a beast,
For I can nowhere find him like a man.

FIRST LORD: My lord, he is but even now gone hence.
Here was he merry, hearing of a song.

DUKE SENIOR: If he, compact of jars,[38] grow musical,
We shall have shortly discord in the spheres.
Go, seek him, tell him I would speak with him.

Enter JAQUES.

FIRST LORD: He saves my labor by his own approach.

DUKE SENIOR: Why, how now, monsieur, what a life is this,
That your poor friends must woo your company?
What, you look merrily!

JAQUES: A fool, a fool! I met a fool i' th' forest,
A motley fool. A miserable world!
As I do live by food, I met a fool,
Who laid him down and bask'd him in the sun,
And rail'd on Lady Fortune in good terms,
In good set terms, and yet a motley fool.
"Good morrow, fool," quoth I. "No, sir," quoth he,

---

38. [*compact of jars:* made up of discords.]

"Call me not fool till heaven hath sent me fortune."
And then he drew a dial from his poke,
And, looking on it with lack-luster eye,
Says very wisely, "It is ten o'clock.
Thus we may see," quoth he, "how the world wags.
'Tis but an hour ago since it was nine,
And after one hour more 'twill be eleven;
And so, from hour to hour, we ripe and ripe,
And then, from hour to hour, we rot and rot;
And thereby hangs a tale." When I did hear
The motley fool thus moral on the time,
My lungs began to crow like chanticleer,
That fools should be so deep-contemplative,
And I did laugh sans intermission
An hour by his dial. O noble fool!
A worthy fool! Motley's the only wear.

DUKE SENIOR: What fool is this?

JAQUES: O worthy fool! One that hath been a courtier,
And says, if ladies be but young and fair,
They have the gift to know it. And in his brain,
Which is as dry as the remainder biscuit
After a voyage, he hath strange places cramm'd
With observation, the which he vents
In mangled forms. O that I were a fool!
I am ambitious for a motley coat.

DUKE SENIOR: Thou shalt have one.

JAQUES: It is my only suit,
Provided that you weed your better judgments
Of all opinion that grows rank in them
That I am wise. I must have liberty
Withal, as large a charter as the wind,
To blow on whom I please, for so fools have.
And they that are most galled with my folly,
They most must laugh. And why, sir, must they so?

The "why" is plain as way to parish church:
He that a fool doth very wisely hit
Doth very foolishly, although he smart,
Not to seem senseless of the bob.³⁹ If not,
The wise man's folly is anatomiz'd
Even by the squand'ring glances⁴⁰ of the fool.
Invest me in my motley; give me leave
To speak my mind, and I will through and through
Cleanse the foul body of th' infected world,
If they will patiently receive my medicine.

DUKE SENIOR: Fie on thee! I can tell what thou wouldst do.

JAQUES: What, for a counter,⁴¹ would I do but good?

DUKE SENIOR: Most mischievous foul sin, in chiding sin.
For thou thyself hast been a libertine,
As sensual as the brutish sting itself;
And all th' embossed sores and headed evils,
That thou with license of free foot⁴² hast caught,
Wouldst thou disgorge into the general world.

JAQUES: Why, who cries out on pride⁴³
That can therein tax any private party?
Doth it not flow as hugely as the sea,
Till that the weary very means do ebb? ⁴⁴
What woman in the city do I name,
When that I say the city-woman bears
The cost of princes on unworthy shoulders?
Who can come in and say that I mean her,
When such a one as she, such is her neighbor?

---

39. [*bob*: jibe, taunt.]

40. [*squand'ring glances*: random jests or satirical hits.]

41. [*counter*: something of no value; may also suggest the idea of "on the contrary."]

42. [*with license of free foot*: with licentious freedom.]

43. [*pride*: ostentation, extravagance.]

44. [*Till that the weary very means do ebb*: until the money runs out.]

Or what is he of basest function
That says his bravery is not on my cost,[45]
Thinking that I mean him, but therein suits
His folly to the mettle of my speech?
There then; how then? What then? Let me see wherein
My tongue hath wrong'd him. If it do him right,
Then he hath wrong'd himself. If he be free,
Why then my taxing like a wild goose flies,
Unclaim'd of any man.—But who comes here?

Enter ORLANDO [*with his sword drawn*].

ORLANDO: Forbear, and eat no more.

JAQUES: Why, I have eat none yet.

ORLANDO: Nor shalt not, till necessity be serv'd.

JAQUES: Of what kind should this cock come of?

DUKE SENIOR: Art thou thus bolden'd, man, by thy distress,
  Or else a rude despiser of good manners,
  That in civility thou seem'st so empty?

ORLANDO: You touch'd my vein at first. The thorny point
  Of bare distress hath ta'en from me the show
  Of smooth civility; yet am I inland[46] bred,
  And know some nurture. But forbear, I say.
  He dies that touches any of this fruit
  Till I and my affairs are answered.

JAQUES: An you will not be answer'd with reason, I must die.

DUKE SENIOR: What would you have? Your gentleness shall force
  More than your force move us to gentleness.

ORLANDO: I almost die for food, and let me have it!

DUKE SENIOR: Sit down and feed, and welcome to our table.

---

45. [*his bravery is not on my cost*: his finery costs me nothing; i.e., it should not concern me.]

46. [*inland*: in a civilized part of the country.]

ORLANDO: Speak you so gently? Pardon me, I pray you.
  I thought that all things had been savage here,
  And therefore put I on the countenance
  Of stern commandment. But whate'er you are
  That in this desert inaccessible,
  Under the shade of melancholy boughs,
  Lose and neglect the creeping hours of time;
  If ever you have look'd on better days,
  If ever been where bells have knoll'd to church,
  If ever sat at any good man's feast,
  If ever from your eyelids wip'd a tear
  And know what 'tis to pity and be pitied,
  Let gentleness my strong enforcement be,
  In the which hope I blush, and hide my sword.

[Puts up his sword.]

DUKE SENIOR: True is it that we have seen better days,
  And have with holy bell been knoll'd to church,
  And sat at good men's feasts, and wip'd our eyes
  Of drops that sacred pity hath engend'red;
  And therefore sit you down in gentleness,
  And take upon command what help we have
  That to your wanting may be minist'red.

ORLANDO: Then but forbear your food a little while,
  Whiles, like a doe, I go to find my fawn
  And give it food. There is an old poor man,
  Who after me hath many a weary step
  Limp'd in pure love. Till he be first suffic'd,
  Oppress'd with two weak evils, age and hunger,
  I will not touch a bit.

DUKE SENIOR: Go find him out,
  And we will nothing waste till you return.

ORLANDO: I thank ye; and be blest for your good comfort!

[Exit.]

DUKE SENIOR: Thou seest we are not all alone unhappy.
This wide and universal theatre
Presents more woeful pageants than the scene
Wherein we play in.

JAQUES: All the world's a stage,
And all the men and women merely players.
They have their exits and their entrances,
And one man in his time plays many parts,
His acts being seven ages. At first the infant,
Mewling and puking in the nurse's arms.
Then the whining schoolboy, with his satchel
And shining morning face, creeping like snail
Unwillingly to school. And then the lover,
Sighing like furnace, with a woeful ballad
Made to his mistress's eyebrow. Then a soldier,
Full of strange oaths and bearded like the pard,[47]
Jealous in honor, sudden and quick in quarrel,
Seeking the bubble reputation
Even in the cannon's mouth. And then the justice,
In fair round belly with good capon lin'd,
With eyes severe and beard of formal cut,
Full of wise saws and modern instances;
And so he plays his part. The sixth age shifts
Into the lean and slipper'd pantaloon,[48]
With spectacles on nose and pouch on side,
His youthful hose, well sav'd, a world too wide
For his shrunk shank; and his big manly voice,
Turning again toward childish treble, pipes
And whistles in his sound. Last scene of all,
That ends this strange eventful history,
Is second childishness and mere oblivion,
Sans teeth, sans eyes, sans taste, sans everything.

Enter ORLANDO, *with* ADAM.

---

47. [*pard*: panther or leopard.]

48. [*pantaloon*: a foolish old man (a stock character in Italian comedy).]

DUKE SENIOR: Welcome. Set down your venerable burden
And let him feed.

ORLANDO: I thank you most for him.

[*Sets down* ADAM.]

ADAM: So had you need.
I scarce can speak to thank you for myself.

DUKE SENIOR: Welcome; fall to. I will not trouble you
As yet, to question you about your fortunes.
Give us some music; and, good cousin, sing.

[*They eat, while* ORLANDO *and* DUKE SENIOR
converse apart.]

SONG
[AMIENS:]

Blow, blow, thou winter wind,
Thou art not so unkind
    As man's ingratitude;
Thy tooth is not so keen,
Because thou art not seen,
    Although thy breath be rude.
Heigh-ho, sing, heigh-ho, unto the green holly.
Most friendship is feigning, most loving mere folly.
    Then, heigh-ho, the holly!
    This life is most jolly.

Freeze, freeze, thou bitter sky,
That dost not bite so nigh
    As benefits forgot;
Though thou the waters warp,
Thy sting is not so sharp
    As friend rememb'red not.
Heigh-ho, sing, etc.

DUKE SENIOR: If that you were the good Sir Rowland's son,
  As you have whisper'd faithfully you were,
  And as mine eye doth his effigies witness
  Most truly limn'd and living in your face,
  Be truly welcome hither. I am the Duke
  That lov'd your father. The residue of your fortune,
  Go to my cave and tell me. Good old man,
  Thou art right welcome as thy master is.
  Support him by the arm. Give me your hand,
  And let me all your fortunes understand.

                                        Exeunt.

ACT III

[SCENE I: *Duke Frederick's palace.*]

Enter DUKE [FREDERICK], LORDS, *and* OLIVER.

DUKE FREDERICK: Not see him since? Sir, sir, that cannot be.
  But were I not the better part made mercy,
  I should not seek an absent argument
  Of my revenge, thou present. But look to it:
  Find out thy brother, wheresoe'er he is;
  Seek him with candle; bring him dead or living
  Within this twelvemonth, or turn thou no more
  To seek a living in our territory.
  Thy lands and all things that thou dost call thine
  Worth seizure do we seize into our hands
  Till thou canst quit thee by thy brother's mouth
  Of what we think against thee.

OLIVER: O that your Highness knew my heart in this!
  I never lov'd my brother in my life.

DUKE FREDERICK: More villain thou. Well, push him out of
    doors,
And let my officers of such a nature
Make an extent upon[49] his house and lands.
Do this expediently and turn him going.

Exeunt.

[SCENE II: *The forest of Arden.*]

Enter ORLANDO [*with a paper*].

ORLANDO: Hang there, my verse, in witness of my love;
    And thou, thrice-crowned queen of night, survey
    With thy chaste eye, from thy pale sphere above,
    Thy huntress' name that my full life doth sway.
    O Rosalind! These trees shall be my books,
    And in their barks my thoughts I'll character,
    That every eye which in this forest looks
    Shall see thy virtue witness'd everywhere.
    Run, run, Orlando, carve on every tree
    The fair, the chaste, and unexpressive[50] she.

Exit.

Enter CORIN *and* [TOUCHSTONE *the*] *Clown.*

CORIN: And how like you this shepherd's life, Master
    Touchstone?

TOUCHSTONE: Truly, shepherd, in respect of itself, it is a good
    life; but in respect that it is a shepherd's life, it is naught. In
    respect that it is solitary, I like it very well; but in respect that
    it is private, it is a very vile life. Now, in respect it is in the
    fields, it pleaseth me well; but in respect it is not in the court,
    it is tedious. As it is a spare life, look you, it fits my humor

---

49. [*Make an extent upon:* seize legally.]

50. [*unexpressive:* inexpressible.]

well; but as there is no more plenty in it, it goes much against my stomach. Hast any philosophy in thee, shepherd?

CORIN: No more but that I know the more one sickens the worse at ease he is; and that he that wants money, means, and content is without three good friends; that the property of rain is to wet and fire to burn; that good pasture makes fat sheep, and that a great cause of the night is lack of the sun; that he that hath learn'd no wit by nature nor art may complain of good breeding, or comes of a very dull kindred.

TOUCHSTONE: Such a one is a natural philosopher. Wast ever in court, shepherd?

CORIN: No, truly.

TOUCHSTONE: Then thou art damn'd.

CORIN: Nay, I hope.

TOUCHSTONE: Truly, thou art damn'd, like an ill-roasted egg all on one side.

CORIN: For not being at court? Your reason.

TOUCHSTONE: Why, if thou never wast at court, thou never saw'st good manners; if thou never saw'st good manners, then thy manners must be wicked; and wickedness is sin, and sin is damnation. Thou art in a parlous state, shepherd.

CORIN: Not a whit, Touchstone. Those that are good manners at the court are as ridiculous in the country as the behavior of the country is most mockable at the court. You told me you salute not at the court but you kiss your hands; that courtesy would be uncleanly, if courtiers were shepherds.

TOUCHSTONE: Instance, briefly; come, instance.

CORIN: Why, we are still handling our ewes, and their fells,[51] you know, are greasy.

_____
51. [*fells*: fleeces.]

TOUCHSTONE: Why, do not your courtier's hands sweat? And is not the grease of a mutton as wholesome as the sweat of a man? Shallow, shallow. A better instance, I say; come.

CORIN: Besides, our hands are hard.

TOUCHSTONE: Your lips will feel them the sooner. Shallow again. A more sounder instance, come.

CORIN: And they are often tarr'd over with the surgery of our sheep; and would you have us kiss tar? The courtier's hands are perfum'd with civet.[52]

TOUCHSTONE: Most shallow man! Thou worms-meat, in respect of a good piece of flesh indeed! Learn of the wise, and perpend: civet is of a baser birth than tar, the very uncleanly flux of a cat. Mend the instance, shepherd.

CORIN: You have too courtly a wit for me. I'll rest.

TOUCHSTONE: Wilt thou rest damn'd? God help thee, shallow man! God make incision in thee! Thou art raw.

CORIN: Sir, I am a true laborer: I earn that I eat, get that I wear, owe no man hate, envy no man's happiness, glad of other men's good, content with my harm, and the greatest of my pride is to see my ewes graze and my lambs suck.

TOUCHSTONE: That is another simple sin in you, to bring the ewes and the rams together and to offer to get your living by the copulation of cattle; to be bawd to a bellwether, and to betray a she-lamb of a twelvemonth to a crooked-pated old cuckoldly[53] ram, out of all reasonable match. If thou beest not damn'd for this, the devil himself will have no shepherds; I cannot see else how thou shouldst scape.

CORIN: Here comes young Master Ganymede, my new mistress's brother.

---

52. [*civet*: a musky-smelling substance produced by the civet cat.]

53. [Horns were the symbol of the cuckold, hence the many jokes about horns in the play.]

Enter ROSALIND [*with a paper, reading*].

ROSALIND:
"From the east to western Ind,
No jewel is like Rosalind.
Her worth, being mounted on the wind,
Through all the world bears Rosalind.
All the pictures fairest lin'd
Are but black to Rosalind.
Let no face be kept in mind
But the fair of Rosalind."

TOUCHSTONE: I'll rhyme you so eight years together, dinners and suppers and sleeping hours excepted. It is the right butter-women's rank to market.[54]

ROSALIND: Out, fool!

TOUCHSTONE: For a taste:
If a hart do lack a hind,
Let him seek out Rosalind.
If the cat will after kind,
So be sure will Rosalind.
Wint'red garments must be lin'd,
So must slender Rosalind.
They that reap must sheaf and bind;
Then to cart[55] with Rosalind.
Sweetest nut hath sourest rind,
Such a nut is Rosalind.
He that sweetest rose will find
Must find love's prick and Rosalind.

This is the very false gallop of verses. Why do you infect yourself with them?

---

54. [*It is . . . market:* i.e., the rhymes are monotonous and plodding, like a line of farm women carrying butter to market.]

55. [*cart:* a farm cart, but also the cart used for public display and punishment of lewd women.]

ROSALIND: Peace, you dull fool! I found them on a tree.

TOUCHSTONE: Truly, the tree yields bad fruit.

ROSALIND: I'll graff it with you, and then I shall graff it with a medlar.[56] Then it will be the earliest fruit i' th' country; for you'll be rotten ere you be half ripe, and that's the right virtue of the medlar.

TOUCHSTONE: You have said; but whether wisely or no, let the forest judge.

Enter CELIA, *with a writing.*

ROSALIND: Peace! Here comes my sister, reading. Stand aside.

CELIA [*reads*]:
    "Why should this a desert be?
      For it is unpeopled? No;
    Tongues I'll hang on every tree,
      That shall civil sayings show:
    Some, how brief the life of man
      Runs his erring pilgrimage,
    That the stretching of a span
      Buckles in his sum of age;
    Some, of violated vows
      'Twixt the souls of friend and friend;
    But upon the fairest boughs,
      Or at every sentence end,
    Will I "Rosalinda" write,
      Teaching all that read to know
    The quintessence of every sprite
      Heaven would in little show.
    Therefore Heaven Nature charg'd
      That one body should be fill'd
    With all graces wide-enlarg'd.
      Nature presently distill'd

---

56. [*medlar*: a kind of fruit eaten after it starts to decay (with a pun on *meddler*).]

Helen's cheek, but not her heart,
  Cleopatra's majesty,
Atalanta's better part,[57]
  Sad Lucretia's modesty.
Thus Rosalind of many parts
  By heavenly synod was devis'd,
Of many faces, eyes, and hearts,
  To have the touches dearest priz'd.
Heaven would that she these gifts should have,
And I to live and die her slave."

ROSALIND: O most gentle Jupiter, what tedious homily of love have you wearied your parishioners withal, and never cried "Have patience, good people!"

CELIA: How now? Back, friends. Shepherd, go off a little. Go with him, sirrah.

TOUCHSTONE: Come, shepherd, let us make an honorable retreat; though not with bag and baggage, yet with scrip and scrippage.[58]

                           Exit [with CORIN].

CELIA: Didst thou hear these verses?

ROSALIND: O, yes, I heard them all, and more too; for some of them had in them more feet than the verses would bear.

CELIA: That's no matter. The feet might bear the verses.

ROSALIND: Ay, but the feet were lame and could not bear themselves without the verse, and therefore stood lamely in the verse.

CELIA: But didst thou hear without wondering how thy name should be hang'd and carv'd upon these trees?

---

57. [*Atalanta's better part*: i.e., her skill as a runner and huntress, not her haughtiness and greed.]

58. [*scrip and scrippage*: a small bag carried by a shepherd and its contents.]

ROSALIND: I was seven of the nine days out of the wonder before you came; for look here what I found on a palm tree. I was never so berhym'd since Pythagoras' time, that I was an Irish rat,[59] which I can hardly remember.

CELIA: Trow you who hath done this?

ROSALIND: Is it a man?

CELIA: And a chain, that you once wore, about his neck. Change you color?

ROSALIND: I prithee, who?

CELIA: O Lord, Lord, it is a hard matter for friends to meet; but mountains may be remov'd with earthquakes, and so encounter.

ROSALIND: Nay, but who is it?

CELIA: Is it possible?

ROSALIND: Nay, I prithee now with most petitionary vehemence, tell me who it is.

CELIA: O wonderful, wonderful, and most wonderful wonderful! And yet again wonderful, and after that, out of all hooping!

ROSALIND: Good my complexion! Dost thou think, though I am caparison'd like a man, I have a doublet and hose in my disposition? One inch of delay more is a South Sea of discovery. I prithee, tell me who is it quickly, and speak apace. I would thou couldst stammer, that thou mightst pour this conceal'd man out of thy mouth, as wine comes out of a narrow-mouth'd bottle, either too much at once, or none at all. I prithee, take the cork out of thy mouth that I may drink thy tidings.

---

59. [Pythagoras taught the doctrine of the transmigration of souls. It was believed that Irish magicians could kill rats and other animals with rhymed spells.]

CELIA: So you may put a man in your belly.

ROSALIND: Is he of God's making? What manner of man? Is his head worth a hat, or his chin worth a beard?

CELIA: Nay, he hath but a little beard.

ROSALIND: Why, God will send more, if the man will be thankful. Let me stay the growth of his beard, if thou delay me not the knowledge of his chin.

CELIA: It is young Orlando, that tripp'd up the wrestler's heels and your heart both in an instant.

ROSALIND: Nay, but the devil take mocking. Speak sad brow and true maid.

CELIA: I' faith, coz, 'tis he.

ROSALIND: Orlando?

CELIA: Orlando.

ROSALIND: Alas the day, what shall I do with my doublet and hose? What did he when thou saw'st him? What said he? How look'd he? Wherein went he? What makes he here? Did he ask for me? Where remains he? How parted he with thee? And when shalt thou see him again? Answer me in one word.

CELIA: You must borrow me Gargantua's mouth first; 'tis a word too great for any mouth of this age's size. To say ay and no to these particulars is more than to answer in a catechism.

ROSALIND: But doth he know that I am in this forest and in man's apparel? Looks he as freshly as he did the day he wrestled?

CELIA: It is as easy to count atomies⁶⁰ as to resolve the propositions of a lover. But take a taste of my finding him, and relish it with good observance. I found him under a tree, like a dropp'd acorn.

---

60. [*atomies*: atoms, motes.]

ROSALIND: It may well be call'd Jove's tree, when it drops forth such fruit.

CELIA: Give me audience, good madam.

ROSALIND: Proceed.

CELIA: There lay he, stretch'd along, like a wounded knight.

ROSALIND: Though it be pity to see such a sight, it well becomes the ground.

CELIA: Cry "holla" to thy tongue, I prithee; it curvets⁶¹ unseasonably. He was furnish'd like a hunter.

ROSALIND: O, ominous! He comes to kill my heart.

CELIA: I would sing my song without a burden. Thou bring'st me out of tune.

ROSALIND: Do you not know I am a woman? When I think, I must speak. Sweet, say on.

Enter ORLANDO *and* JAQUES.

CELIA: You bring me out.—Soft, comes he not here?

ROSALIND: 'Tis he. Slink by, and note him.

[They stand aside and listen.]

JAQUES: I thank you for your company; but, good faith, I had as lief have been myself alone.

ORLANDO: And so had I; but yet, for fashion sake, I thank you too for your society.

JAQUES: God buy you. Let's meet as little as we can.

ORLANDO: I do desire we may be better strangers.

---

61. [*curvets:* leaps about.]

JAQUES: I pray you, mar no more trees with writing love songs in their barks.

ORLANDO: I pray you, mar no moe of my verses with reading them ill-favoredly.

JAQUES: Rosalind is your love's name?

ORLANDO: Yes, just.

JAQUES: I do not like her name.

ORLANDO: There was no thought of pleasing you when she was christen'd.

JAQUES: What stature is she of?

ORLANDO: Just as high as my heart.

JAQUES: You are full of pretty answers. Have you not been acquainted with goldsmiths' wives, and conn'd them out of rings?[62]

ORLANDO: Not so; but I answer you right painted cloth, from whence you have studied your questions.

JAQUES: You have a nimble wit; I think 'twas made of Atalanta's heels. Will you sit down with me? And we two will rail against our mistress the world and all our misery.

ORLANDO: I will chide no breather in the world but myself, against whom I know most faults.

JAQUES: The worst fault you have is to be in love.

ORLANDO: 'Tis a fault I will not change for your best virtue. I am weary of you.

JAQUES: By my troth, I was seeking for a fool when I found you.

---

62. [*conn'd them out of rings:* learned the "pretty answers" from the mottoes inscribed inside rings.]

ORLANDO: He is drown'd in the brook. Look but in, and you shall see him.

JAQUES: There I shall see mine own figure.

ORLANDO: Which I take to be either a fool or a cipher.

JAQUES: I'll tarry no longer with you. Farewell, good Signior Love.

ORLANDO: I am glad of your departure. Adieu, good Monsieur Melancholy.

[*Exit* JAQUES.]

ROSALIND [*aside to* CELIA]: I will speak to him like a saucy lackey, and under that habit play the knave with him.—Do you hear, forester?

ORLANDO: Very well. What would you?

ROSALIND: I pray you, what is't o'clock?

ORLANDO: You should ask me what time o' day. There's no clock in the forest.

ROSALIND: Then there is no true lover in the forest, else sighing every minute and groaning every hour would detect the lazy foot of Time as well as a clock.

ORLANDO: And why not the swift foot of Time? Had not that been as proper?

ROSALIND: By no means, sir. Time travels in divers paces with divers persons. I'll tell you who Time ambles withal, who Time trots withal, who Time gallops withal, and who he stands still withal.

ORLANDO: I prithee, who doth he trot withal?

ROSALIND: Marry, he trots hard with a young maid between the contract of her marriage and the day it is solemniz'd. If the interim be but a se'nnight,[63] Time's pace is so hard that it seems the length of seven year.

ORLANDO: Who ambles Time withal?

ROSALIND: With a priest that lacks Latin and a rich man that hath not the gout, for the one sleeps easily because he cannot study and the other lives merrily because he feels no pain, the one lacking the burden of lean and wasteful learning, the other knowing no burden of heavy tedious penury. These Time ambles withal.

ORLANDO: Who doth he gallop withal?

ROSALIND: With a thief to the gallows, for though he go as softly as foot can fall, he thinks himself too soon there.

ORLANDO: Who stays it still withal?

ROSALIND: With lawyers in the vacation; for they sleep between term and term, and then they perceive not how Time moves.

ORLANDO: Where dwell you, pretty youth?

ROSALIND: With this shepherdess, my sister; here in the skirts of the forest, like fringe upon a petticoat.

ORLANDO: Are you native of this place?

ROSALIND: As the cony[64] that you see dwell where she is kindled.[65]

ORLANDO: Your accent is something finer than you could purchase in so remov'd a dwelling.

ROSALIND: I have been told so of many. But indeed an old religious uncle of mine taught me to speak, who was in his youth an inland man, one that knew courtship too well, for there he fell in love. I have heard him read many lectures against it,

---

63. [*se'nnight:* a week (seven nights).]

64. [*cony:* rabbit.]

65. [*kindled:* born.]

and I thank God I am not a woman, to be touch'd with so many giddy offences as he hath generally tax'd their whole sex withal.

ORLANDO: Can you remember any of the principal evils that he laid to the charge of women?

ROSALIND: There were none principal; they were all like one another as half-pence are, every one fault seeming monstrous till his fellow-fault came to match it.

ORLANDO: I prithee, recount some of them.

ROSALIND: No, I will not cast away my physic but on those that are sick. There is a man haunts the forest, that abuses our young plants with carving "Rosalind" on their barks, hangs odes upon hawthorns, and elegies on brambles, all, forsooth, deifying the name of Rosalind. If I could meet that fancy-monger, I would give him some good counsel, for he seems to have the quotidian[66] of love upon him.

ORLANDO: I am he that is so love-shak'd. I pray you, tell me your remedy.

ROSALIND: There is none of my uncle's marks upon you. He taught me how to know a man in love, in which cage of rushes I am sure you are not prisoner.

ORLANDO: What were his marks?

ROSALIND: A lean cheek, which you have not; a blue eye and sunken, which you have not; an unquestionable spirit, which you have not; a beard neglected, which you have not—but I pardon you for that, for simply your having in beard is a younger brother's revenue. Then your hose should be ungarter'd, your bonnet unbanded, your sleeve unbutton'd, your shoe untied, and everything about you demonstrating a careless desolation. But you are no such man; you are rather

---

66. [*quotidian*: a fever or an ague that recurs daily.]

point-device[67] in your accoutrements, as loving yourself, than seeming the lover of any other.

ORLANDO: Fair youth, I would I could make thee believe I love.

ROSALIND: Me believe it? You may as soon make her that you love believe it, which, I warrant, she is apter to do than to confess she does. That is one of the points in the which women still give the lie to their consciences. But, in good sooth, are you he that hangs the verses on the trees, wherein Rosalind is so admir'd?

ORLANDO: I swear to thee, youth, by the white hand of Rosalind, I am that he, that unfortunate he.

ROSALIND: But are you so much in love as your rhymes speak?

ORLANDO: Neither rhyme nor reason can express how much.

ROSALIND: Love is merely a madness, and, I tell you, deserves as well a dark house and a whip as madmen do; and the reason why they are not so punish'd and cur'd is, that the lunacy is so ordinary that the whippers are in love too. Yet I profess curing it by counsel.

ORLANDO: Did you ever cure any so?

ROSALIND: Yes, one, and in this manner. He was to imagine me his love, his mistress; and I set him every day to woo me. At which time would I, being but a moonish youth, grieve, be effeminate, changeable, longing and liking, proud, fantastical, apish, shallow, inconstant, full of tears, full of smiles; for every passion something and for no passion truly anything, as boys and women are for the most part cattle of this color; would now like him, now loathe him; then entertain him, then forswear him; now weep for him, then spit at him; that I drave my suitor from his mad humor of love to a living humor of madness, which was, to forswear the full stream of

_____
67. [*point-device*: meticulous.]

the world and to live in a nook merely monastic. And thus I cur'd him; and this way will I take upon me to wash your liver as clean as a sound sheep's heart, that there shall not be one spot of love in't.

ORLANDO: I would not be cur'd, youth.

ROSALIND: I would cure you, if you would but call me Rosalind and come every day to my cote and woo me.

ORLANDO: Now, by the faith of my love, I will. Tell me where it is.

ROSALIND: Go with me to it, and I'll show it you; and by the way you shall tell me where in the forest you live. Will you go?

ORLANDO: With all my heart, good youth.

ROSALIND: Nay, you must call me Rosalind. Come, sister, will you go?

Exeunt.

[SCENE III: *The forest.*]

Enter [TOUCHSTONE *the*] *Clown,* AUDREY; *and* JAQUES [*apart*].

TOUCHSTONE: Come apace, good Audrey. I will fetch up your goats, Audrey. And how, Audrey? Am I the man yet? Doth my simple feature content you?

AUDREY: Your features, Lord warrant us! What features?

TOUCHSTONE: I am here with thee and thy goats, as the most capricious poet, honest Ovid, was among the Goths.[68]

JAQUES [*aside*]: O knowledge ill-inhabited, worse than Jove in a thatch'd house!

---

68. [The sophisticated Roman poet Ovid lived in exile among the Goths, a Germanic tribe regarded as barbaric. Touchstone also puns on *goats* and *Goths*.]

TOUCHSTONE: When a man's verses cannot be understood, nor a man's good wit seconded with the forward child, understanding, it strikes a man more dead than a great reckoning in a little room. Truly, I would the gods had made thee poetical.

AUDREY: I do not know what "poetical" is. Is it honest in deed and word? Is it a true thing?

TOUCHSTONE: No, truly; for the truest poetry is the most feigning, and lovers are given to poetry, and what they swear in poetry may be said as lovers they do feign.

AUDREY: Do you wish then that the gods had made me poetical?

TOUCHSTONE: I do, truly; for thou swear'st to me thou art honest. Now, if thou wert a poet, I might have some hope thou didst feign.

AUDREY: Would you not have me honest?

TOUCHSTONE: No, truly, unless thou wert hard-favor'd; for honesty coupled to beauty is to have honey a sauce to sugar.

JAQUES [*aside*]: A material fool!

AUDREY: Well, I am not fair, and therefore I pray the gods make me honest.

TOUCHSTONE: Truly, and to cast away honesty upon a foul slut were to put good meat into an unclean dish.

AUDREY: I am not a slut, though I thank the gods I am foul.

TOUCHSTONE: Well, prais'd be the gods for thy foulness! Sluttishness may come hereafter. But be it as it may be, I will marry thee, and to that end I have been with Sir Oliver Martext, the vicar of the next village, who hath promis'd to meet me in this place of the forest and to couple us.

JAQUES [*aside*]: I would fain see this meeting.

AUDREY: Well, the gods give us joy!

TOUCHSTONE: Amen. A man may, if he were of a fearful heart, stagger in this attempt; for here we have no temple but the wood, no assembly but horn-beasts. But what though? Courage! As horns are odious, they are necessary. It is said, "Many a man knows no end of his goods." Right! Many a man has good horns, and knows end of them. Well, that is the dowry of his wife; 'tis none of his own getting. Horns? Even so. Poor men alone? No, no; the noblest deer hath them as huge as the rascal. Is the single man therefore bless'd? No; as a wall'd town is more worthier than a village, so is the forehead of a married man more honorable than the bare brow of a bachelor; and by how much defense is better than no skill, by so much is a horn more precious than to want.

Enter SIR OLIVER MARTEXT.

Here comes Sir Oliver. Sir Oliver Martext, you are well met. Will you dispatch us here under this tree, or shall we go with you to your chapel?

SIR OLIVER: Is there none here to give the woman?

TOUCHSTONE: I will not take her on gift of any man.

SIR OLIVER: Truly, she must be given, or the marriage is not lawful.

JAQUES [*advancing*]: Proceed, proceed. I'll give her.

TOUCHSTONE: Good even, good Master What-ye-call't. How do you, sir? You are very well met. God 'ild you for your last company. I am very glad to see you. Even a toy in hand here, sir. Nay, pray be cover'd.[69]

---

69. [*pray be cover'd*: put on your hat; i.e., there is no need to show respect.]

JAQUES: Will you be married, motley?

TOUCHSTONE: As the ox hath his bow, sir, the horse his curb, and the falcon her bells, so man hath his desires; and as pigeons bill, so wedlock would be nibbling.

JAQUES: And will you, being a man of your breeding, be married under a bush like a beggar? Get you to church, and have a good priest that can tell you what marriage is. This fellow will but join you together as they join wainscot; then one of you will prove a shrunk panel and, like green timber, warp, warp.

TOUCHSTONE [*aside*]: I am not in the mind but I were better to be married of him than of another, for he is not like to marry me well; and not being well married, it will be a good excuse for me hereafter to leave my wife.

JAQUES: Go thou with me, and let me counsel thee.

TOUCHSTONE: Come, sweet Audrey. We must be married, or we must live in bawdry. Farewell, good Master Oliver; not

"O sweet Oliver,
O brave Oliver,
Leave me not behind thee;"

but

"Wind away,
Begone, I say,
I will not to wedding with thee."

Exeunt [JAQUES, TOUCHSTONE, *and* AUDREY].

SIR OLIVER: 'Tis no matter. Ne'er a fantastical knave of them all shall flout me out of my calling.

[*Exit.*]

[SCENE IV: *The forest.*]

Enter ROSALIND *and* CELIA.

ROSALIND: Never talk to me; I will weep.

CELIA: Do, I prithee; but yet have the grace to consider that tears do not become a man.

ROSALIND: But have I not cause to weep?

CELIA: As good cause as one would desire; therefore weep.

ROSALIND: His very hair is of the dissembling color.

CELIA: Something browner than Judas's. Marry, his kisses are Judas's own children.

ROSALIND: I' faith, his hair is of a good color.

CELIA: An excellent color. Your chestnut was ever the only color.

ROSALIND: And his kissing is as full of sanctity as the touch of holy bread.

CELIA: He hath bought a pair of cast lips of Diana.[70] A nun of winter's sisterhood kisses not more religiously; the very ice of chastity is in them.

ROSALIND: But why did he swear he would come this morning, and comes not?

CELIA: Nay, certainly, there is no truth in him.

ROSALIND: Do you think so?

CELIA: Yes; I think he is not a pick-purse nor a horse-stealer, but for his verity in love, I do think him as concave as a cover'd goblet or a worm-eaten nut.

ROSALIND: Not true in love?

---

70. [The goddess of chastity.]

CELIA: Yes, when he is in; but I think he is not in.

ROSALIND: You have heard him swear downright he was.

CELIA: "Was" is not "is." Besides, the oath of a lover is no stronger than the word of a tapster;[71] they are both the confirmer of false reckonings. He attends here in the forest on the Duke your father.

ROSALIND: I met the Duke yesterday and had much question with him. He ask'd me of what parentage I was. I told him, of as good as he; so he laugh'd and let me go. But what talk we of fathers, when there is such a man as Orlando?

CELIA: O, that's a brave man! He writes brave verses, speaks brave words, swears brave oaths, and breaks them bravely, quite traverse, athwart the heart of his lover, as a puisny[72] tilter, that spurs his horse but on one side, breaks his staff like a noble goose. But all's brave that youth mounts and folly guides. Who comes here?

Enter CORIN.

CORIN: Mistress and master, you have oft inquir'd
After the shepherd that complain'd of love,
Who you saw sitting by me on the turf,
Praising the proud disdainful shepherdess
That was his mistress.

CELIA: Well, and what of him?

CORIN: If you will see a pageant truly play'd
Between the pale complexion of true love
And the red glow of scorn and proud disdain,
Go hence a little, and I shall conduct you,
If you will mark it.

---

71. [*tapster:* barkeeper.]

72. [*puisny:* puny, inferior.]

ROSALIND: O, come, let us remove!
   The sight of lovers feedeth those in love.
   Bring us to this sight, and you shall say
   I'll prove a busy actor in their play.

                                        Exeunt.

[SCENE V: *The forest.*]

Enter SILVIUS *and* PHEBE.

SILVIUS: Sweet Phebe, do not scorn me; do not, Phebe!
   Say that you love me not, but say not so
   In bitterness. The common executioner,
   Whose heart th' accustom'd sight of death makes hard,
   Falls not the axe upon the humbled neck
   But first begs pardon. Will you sterner be
   Than he that dies and lives by bloody drops?

              Enter ROSALIND, CELIA, *and* CORIN [*behind*].

PHEBE: I would not be thy executioner;
   I fly thee, for I would not injure thee.
   Thou tell'st me there is murder in mine eye.
   'Tis pretty, sure, and very probable,
   That eyes, that are the frail'st and softest things,
   Who shut their coward gates on atomies,
   Should be call'd tyrants, butchers, murderers!
   Now I do frown on thee with all my heart,
   And if mine eyes can wound, now let them kill thee.
   Now counterfeit to swoon; why, now fall down,
   Or if thou canst not, O, for shame, for shame,
   Lie not, to say mine eyes are murderers!
   Now show the wound mine eye hath made in thee.
   Scratch thee but with a pin, and there remains
   Some scar of it; lean but upon a rush,

The cicatrice[73] and capable impressure
Thy palm some moment keeps; but now mine eyes,
Which I have darted at thee, hurt thee not,
Nor, I am sure, there is no force in eyes
That can do hurt.

SILVIUS: O dear Phebe,
If ever—as that ever may be near—
You meet in some fresh cheek the power of fancy,
Then shall you know the wounds invisible
That love's keen arrows make.

PHEBE: But till that time
Come not thou near me; and when that time comes,
Afflict me with thy mocks, pity me not,
As till that time I shall not pity thee.

ROSALIND [*advancing*]: And why, I pray you? Who might be
     your mother,
That you insult, exult, and all at once,
Over the wretched? What though you have no beauty—
As, by faith, I see no more in you
Than without candle may go dark to bed—
Must you be therefore proud and pitiless?
Why, what means this? Why do you look on me?
I see no more in you than in the ordinary
Of nature's sale-work. 'Od's my little life,
I think she means to tangle my eyes too!
No, faith, proud mistress, hope not after it.
'Tis not your inky brows, your black silk hair,
Your bugle eyeballs, nor your cheek of cream
That can entame my spirits to your worship.
You foolish shepherd, wherefore do you follow her,
Like foggy south, puffing with wind and rain?
You are a thousand times a properer man
Than she a woman. 'Tis such fools as you

---

73. [*cicatrice*: scar.]

That makes the world full of ill-favor'd children.
'Tis not her glass, but you, that flatters her,
And out of you she sees herself more proper
Than any of her lineaments can show her.
But, mistress, know yourself. Down on your knees,
And thank heaven, fasting, for a good man's love;
For I must tell you friendly in your ear,
Sell when you can, you are not for all markets.
Cry the man mercy; love him, take his offer.
Foul is most foul, being foul to be a scoffer.
So take her to thee, shepherd. Fare you well.

PHEBE: Sweet youth, I pray you, chide a year together.
I had rather hear you chide than this man woo.

ROSALIND [*to* PHEBE]: He's fall'n in love with your foulness, [*to*
SILVIUS] and she'll fall in love with my anger. If it be so, as
fast as she answers thee with frowning looks, I'll sauce her
with bitter words.—Why look you so upon me?

PHEBE: For no ill will I bear you.

ROSALIND: I pray you, do not fall in love with me,
For I am falser than vows made in wine.
Besides, I like you not. If you will know my house,
'Tis at the tuft of olives here hard by.
Will you go, sister? Shepherd, ply her hard.
Come, sister. Shepherdess, look on him better,
And be not proud. Though all the world could see,
None could be so abus'd in sight as he.
Come, to our flock.

Exit [*with* CELIA *and* CORIN].

PHEBE: Dead shepherd,[74] now I find thy saw of might,
"Who ever lov'd that lov'd not at first sight?"

---

74. [*Dead shepherd:* i.e., the playwright and poet Christopher Marlowe, who died in 1593.
The line quoted is from *Hero and Leander.*]

SILVIUS: Sweet Phebe—

PHEBE: Ha, what say'st thou, Silvius?

SILVIUS: Sweet Phebe, pity me.

PHEBE: Why, I am sorry for thee, gentle Silvius.

SILVIUS: Wherever sorrow is, relief would be.
    If you do sorrow at my grief in love,
    By giving love, your sorrow and my grief
    Were both extermin'd.

PHEBE: Thou hast my love. Is not that neighborly?

SILVIUS: I would have you.

PHEBE: Why, that were covetousness.
    Silvius, the time was that I hated thee;
    And yet it is not that I bear thee love,
    But since that thou canst talk of love so well,
    Thy company, which erst was irksome to me,
    I will endure, and I'll employ thee too.
    But do not look for further recompense
    Than thine own gladness that thou art employ'd.

SILVIUS: So holy and so perfect is my love,
    And I in such a poverty of grace,
    That I shall think it a most plenteous crop
    To glean the broken ears after the man
    That the main harvest reaps. Loose now and then
    A scatt'red smile, and that I'll live upon.

PHEBE: Know'st thou the youth that spoke to me erewhile?

SILVIUS: Not very well, but I have met him oft;
    And he hath bought the cottage and the bounds
    That the old carlot[75] once was master of.

---

75. [*carlot*: peasant.]

PHEBE: Think not I love him, though I ask for him;
    'Tis but a peevish boy; yet he talks well.
    But what care I for words? Yet words do well
    When he that speaks them pleases those that hear.
    It is a pretty youth—not very pretty—
    But, sure, he's proud, and yet his pride becomes him.
    He'll make a proper man. The best thing in him
    Is his complexion; and, faster than his tongue
    Did make offense, his eye did heal it up.
    He is not very tall; yet for his years he's tall.
    His leg is but so so; and yet 'tis well.
    There was a pretty redness in his lip,
    A little riper and more lusty red
    Than that mix'd in his cheek; 'twas just the difference
    Betwixt the constant red and mingled damask.
    There be some women, Silvius, had they mark'd him
    In parcels[76] as I did, would have gone near
    To fall in love with him; but, for my part,
    I love him not nor hate him not; and yet
    I have more cause to hate him than to love him.
    For what had he to do to chide at me?
    He said mine eyes were black and my hair black;
    And, now I am rememb'red, scorn'd at me.
    I marvel why I answer'd not again.
    But that's all one; omittance is no quittance.
    I'll write to him a very taunting letter,
    And thou shalt bear it. Wilt thou, Silvius?

SILVIUS: Phebe, with all my heart.

PHEBE: I'll write it straight;
    The matter's in my head and in my heart.
    I will be bitter with him and passing short.
    Go with me, Silvius.

                                             Exeunt.

---

76. [*In parcels:* piece by piece.]

ACT IV

[SCENE I: *The forest.*]

Enter ROSALIND *and* CELIA, *and* JAQUES.

JAQUES: I prithee, pretty youth, let me be better acquainted with thee.

ROSALIND: They say you are a melancholy fellow.

JAQUES: I am so; I do love it better than laughing.

ROSALIND: Those that are in extremity of either are abominable fellows, and betray themselves to every modern censure worse than drunkards.

JAQUES: Why, 'tis good to be sad and say nothing.

ROSALIND: Why then, 'tis good to be a post.

JAQUES: I have neither the scholar's melancholy, which is emulation, nor the musician's, which is fantastical, nor the courtier's, which is proud, nor the soldier's, which is ambitious, nor the lawyer's, which is politic, nor the lady's, which is nice, nor the lover's, which is all these; but it is a melancholy of mine own, compounded of many simples, extracted from many objects, and indeed the sundry contemplation of my travels, in which my often rumination wraps me in a most humorous sadness.

ROSALIND: A traveler! By my faith, you have great reason to be sad. I fear you have sold your own lands to see other men's. Then to have seen much and to have nothing is to have rich eyes and poor hands.

JAQUES: Yes, I have gain'd my experience.

Enter ORLANDO.

ROSALIND: And your experience makes you sad. I had rather have a fool to make me merry than experience to make me sad—and to travel for it too!

ORLANDO: Good day and happiness, dear Rosalind!

JAQUES: Nay, then, God buy you, an you talk in blank verse.

ROSALIND: Farewell, Monsieur Traveler. Look you lisp and wear strange suits, disable all the benefits of your own country, be out of love with your nativity, and almost chide God for making you that countenance you are, or I will scarce think you have swam in a gundello.[77]

[*Exit* JAQUES.]

Why, how now, Orlando, where have you been all this while? You a lover? An you serve me such another trick, never come in my sight more.

ORLANDO: My fair Rosalind, I come within an hour of my promise.

ROSALIND: Break an hour's promise in love? He that will divide a minute into a thousand parts and break but a part of the thousandth part of a minute in the affairs of love, it may be said of him that Cupid hath clapp'd him o' th' shoulder, but I'll warrant him heart-whole.

ORLANDO: Pardon me, dear Rosalind.

ROSALIND: Nay, an you be so tardy, come no more in my sight. I had as lief be woo'd of a snail.

ORLANDO: Of a snail?

ROSALIND: Ay, of a snail; for though he comes slowly, he carries his house on his head—a better jointure, I think, than you make a woman. Besides, he brings his destiny with him.

---

77. [*swam in a gundello*: ridden in a gondola (in Venice).]

ORLANDO: What's that?

ROSALIND: Why, horns, which such as you are fain to be behold-
ing to your wives for. But he comes arm'd in his fortune and
prevents[78] the slander of his wife.

ORLANDO: Virtue is no horn-maker, and my Rosalind is virtuous.

ROSALIND: And I am your Rosalind.

CELIA: It pleases him to call you so; but he hath a Rosalind of a
better leer[79] than you.

ROSALIND: Come, woo me, woo me, for now I am in a holiday
humor and like enough to consent. What would you say to
me now, an I were your very very Rosalind?

ORLANDO: I would kiss before I spoke.

ROSALIND: Nay, you were better speak first, and when you were
gravel'd[80] for lack of matter, you might take occasion to kiss.
Very good orators, when they are out, they will spit; and for
lovers lacking—God warn us!—matter, the cleanliest shift is
to kiss.

ORLANDO: How if the kiss be denied?

ROSALIND: Then she puts you to entreaty, and there begins new
matter.

ORLANDO: Who could be out,[81] being before his belov'd mistress?

ROSALIND: Marry, that should you, if I were your mistress, or I
should think my honesty ranker than my wit.

ORLANDO: What, of my suit?

---

78. [*prevents:* anticipates.]

79. [*leer:* appearance.]

80. [*gravel'd:* stuck.]

81. [*out:* i.e., out of ideas. Rosalind then puns on *out* and *suit* to mean undressed.]

ROSALIND: Not out of your apparel, and yet out of your suit. Am not I your Rosalind?

ORLANDO: I take some joy to say you are, because I would be talking of her.

ROSALIND: Well, in her person I say I will not have you.

ORLANDO: Then in mine own person I die.

ROSALIND: No, faith, die by attorney. The poor world is almost six thousand years old, and in all this time there was not any man died in his own person, videlicet,[82] in a love-cause. Troilus had his brains dash'd out with a Grecian club; yet he did what he could to die before, and he is one of the patterns of love. Leander, he would have liv'd many a fair year, though Hero had turn'd nun, if it had not been for a hot midsummer night; for, good youth, he went but forth to wash him in the Hellespont and being taken with the cramp was drown'd; and the foolish chroniclers of that age found it was "Hero of Sestos." But these are all lies. Men have died from time to time, and worms have eaten them, but not for love.

ORLANDO: I would not have my right Rosalind of this mind, for, I protest, her frown might kill me.

ROSALIND: By this hand, it will not kill a fly. But come, now I will be your Rosalind in a more coming-on disposition, and ask me what you will, I will grant it.

ORLANDO: Then love me, Rosalind.

ROSALIND: Yes, faith, will I, Fridays and Saturdays and all.

ORLANDO: And wilt thou have me?

ROSALIND: Ay, and twenty such.

ORLANDO: What sayest thou?

---

82. [*videlicet*: that is to say.]

ROSALIND: Are you not good?

ORLANDO: I hope so.

ROSALIND: Why then, can one desire too much of a good thing? Come, sister, you shall be the priest and marry us. Give me your hand, Orlando. What do you say, sister?

ORLANDO: Pray thee, marry us.

CELIA: I cannot say the words.

ROSALIND: You must begin, "Will you, Orlando"—

CELIA: Go to. Will you, Orlando, have to wife this Rosalind?

ORLANDO: I will.

ROSALIND: Ay, but when?

ORLANDO: Why now, as fast as she can marry us.

ROSALIND: Then you must say, "I take thee, Rosalind, for wife."

ORLANDO: I take thee, Rosalind, for wife.

ROSALIND: I might ask you for your commission; but I do take thee, Orlando, for my husband. There's a girl goes before the priest, and certainly a woman's thought runs before her actions.

ORLANDO: So do all thoughts; they are wing'd.

ROSALIND: Now tell me how long you would have her after you have possess'd her.

ORLANDO: For ever and a day.

ROSALIND: Say "a day," without the "ever." No, no, Orlando; men are April when they woo, December when they wed. Maids are May when they are maids, but the sky changes when they are wives. I will be more jealous of thee than a

Barbary cock-pigeon over his hen, more clamorous than a parrot against rain, more newfangled than an ape, more giddy in my desires than a monkey. I will weep for nothing, like Diana in the fountain, and I will do that when you are dispos'd to be merry; I will laugh like a hyen, and that when thou art inclin'd to sleep.

ORLANDO: But will my Rosalind do so?

ROSALIND: By my life, she will do as I do.

ORLANDO: O, but she is wise.

ROSALIND: Or else she could not have the wit to do this; the wiser, the waywarder. Make the doors upon a woman's wit, and it will out at the casement; shut that, and 'twill out at the keyhole; stop that, 'twill fly with the smoke out at the chimney.

ORLANDO: A man that had a wife with such a wit, he might say "Wit, whither wilt?"

ROSALIND: Nay, you might keep that check for it till you met your wife's wit going to your neighbor's bed.

ORLANDO: And what wit could wit have to excuse that?

ROSALIND: Marry, to say she came to seek you there. You shall never take her without her answer, unless you take her without her tongue. O, that woman that cannot make her fault her husband's occasion,[83] let her never nurse her child herself, for she will breed it like a fool!

ORLANDO: For these two hours, Rosalind, I will leave thee.

ROSALIND: Alas, dear love, I cannot lack thee two hours!

ORLANDO: I must attend the Duke at dinner. By two o'clock I will be with thee again.

---

83. [*her husband's occasion*: an opportunity for attacking her husband.]

ROSALIND: Ay, go your ways, go your ways; I knew what you would prove. My friends told me as much, and I thought no less. That flattering tongue of yours won me. 'Tis but one cast away, and so, come, death! Two o'clock is your hour?

ORLANDO: Ay, sweet Rosalind.

ROSALIND: By my troth, and in good earnest, and so God mend me, and by all pretty oaths that are not dangerous, if you break one jot of your promise or come one minute behind your hour, I will think you the most pathetical break-promise, and the most hollow lover, and the most unworthy of her you call Rosalind, that may be chosen out of the gross band of the unfaithful. Therefore beware my censure and keep your promise.

ORLANDO: With no less religion than if thou wert indeed my Rosalind. So adieu.

ROSALIND: Well, Time is the old justice that examines all such offenders, and let Time try. Adieu.

Exit [ORLANDO].

CELIA: You have simply misus'd our sex in your love prate. We must have your doublet and hose pluck'd over your head, and show the world what the bird hath done to her own nest.

ROSALIND: O coz, coz, coz, my pretty little coz, that thou didst know how many fathom deep I am in love! But it cannot be sounded; my affection hath an unknown bottom, like the bay of Portugal.

CELIA: Or rather, bottomless, that as fast as you pour affection in, it runs out.

ROSALIND: No, that same wicked bastard of Venus[84] that was begot of thought, conceiv'd of spleen, and born of madness, that blind rascally boy that abuses everyone's eyes because his

---

84. [*wicked bastard of Venus*: Cupid.]

own are out, let him be judge how deep I am in love. I'll tell thee, Aliena, I cannot be out of the sight of Orlando. I'll go find a shadow and sigh till he come.

CELIA: And I'll sleep.

Exeunt.

[SCENE II: *The forest.*]

Enter JAQUES, *and* LORDS [*as*] *foresters.*

JAQUES: Which is he that kill'd the deer?

FIRST LORD: Sir, it was I.

JAQUES: Let's present him to the Duke, like a Roman conqueror; and it would do well to set the deer's horns upon his head, for a branch of victory. Have you no song, forester, for this purpose?

SECOND LORD: Yes, sir.

JAQUES: Sing it. 'Tis no matter how it be in tune, so it make noise enough.   *Music.*

SONG
SECOND LORD:

What shall he have that kill'd the deer?
His leather skin and horns to wear.
  Then sing him home.
        (*The rest shall bear this burden.*)
Take thou no scorn to wear the horn;
It was a crest ere thou wast born.
  Thy father's father wore it,
  And thy father bore it.
The horn, the horn, the lusty horn
Is not a thing to laugh to scorn.

Exeunt.

[SCENE III: *The forest.*]

Enter ROSALIND *and* CELIA.

ROSALIND: How say you now? Is it not past two o'clock? And
here much Orlando!
CELIA: I warrant you, with pure love and troubled brain, he
hath ta'en his bow and arrows and is gone forth—to sleep.

Enter SILVIUS.

Look who comes here.

SILVIUS: My errand is to you, fair youth.
My gentle Phebe bid me give you this.

[*Gives a letter.*]

I know not the contents; but, as I guess
By the stern brow and waspish action
Which she did use as she was writing of it,
It bears an angry tenor. Pardon me,
I am but as a guiltless messenger.

ROSALIND [*examining the letter*]: Patience herself would startle
at this letter
And play the swaggerer. Bear this, bear all!
She says I am not fair, that I lack manners;
She calls me proud, and that she could not love me
Were man as rare as phoenix. 'Od's my will!
Her love is not the hare that I do hunt.
Why writes she so to me? Well, shepherd, well,
This is a letter of your own device.

SILVIUS: No, I protest, I know not the contents.
Phebe did write it.

ROSALIND: Come, come, you are a fool,
And turn'd into the extremity of love.
I saw her hand. She has a leathern hand

327

A freestone-colored[85] hand. I verily did think
That her old gloves were on, but 'twas her hands;
She has a huswife's hand—but that's no matter.
I say she never did invent this letter;
This is a man's invention and his hand.

SILVIUS: Sure, it is hers.

ROSALIND: Why, 'tis a boisterous and a cruel style,
A style for challengers. Why, she defies me,
Like Turk to Christian. Women's gentle brain
Could not drop forth such giant-rude invention,
Such Ethiop words, blacker in their effect
Than in their countenance. Will you hear the letter?

SILVIUS: So please you, for I never heard it yet;
Yet heard too much of Phebe's cruelty.

ROSALIND: She Phebes me. Mark how the tyrant writes. *Read.*
    "Art thou god to shepherd turn'd,
    That a maiden's heart hath burn'd?"

Can a woman rail thus?

SILVIUS: Call you this railing?

ROSALIND: *Read.*

    "Why, thy godhead laid apart,
    Warr'st thou with a woman's heart?"

Did you ever hear such railing?

    "Whiles the eye of man did woo me,
    That could do no vengeance to me."

Meaning me a beast.

    "If the scorn of your bright eyne
    Have power to raise such love in mine,

---

85. [*freestone-colored*: the color of sandstone.]

Alack, in me what strange effect
Would they work in mild aspect!
Whiles you chid me, I did love;
How then might your prayers move!
He that brings this love to thee
Little knows this love in me;
And by him seal up thy mind,[86]
Whether that thy youth and kind
Will the faithful offer take
Of me and all that I can make,
Or else by him my love deny,
And then I'll study how to die."

SILVIUS: Call you this chiding?

CELIA: Alas, poor shepherd!

ROSALIND: Do you pity him? No, he deserves no pity. Wilt thou love such a woman? What, to make thee an instrument and play false strains upon thee? Not to be endur'd! Well, go your way to her, for I see love hath made thee a tame snake, and say this to her: that if she love me, I charge her to love thee; if she will not, I will never have her unless thou entreat for her. If you be a true lover, hence, and not a word; for here comes more company.

Exit SILVIUS.

Enter OLIVER.

OLIVER: Good morrow, fair ones. Pray you, if you know,
Where in the purlieus of this forest stands
A sheep-cote fenc'd about with olive trees?

CELIA: West of this place, down in the neighbor bottom;
The rank of osiers[87] by the murmuring stream
Left on your right hand brings you to the place.

---

86. [*seal up thy mind*: send your thoughts in a sealed letter.]
87. [*rank of osiers*: row of willows.]

But at this hour the house doth keep itself;
There's none within.

OLIVER: If that an eye may profit by a tongue,
Then should I know you by description,
Such garments and such years: "The boy is fair,
Of female favor, and bestows himself
Like a ripe sister;[88] the woman low,
And browner than her brother." Are not you
The owner of the house I did inquire for?

CELIA: It is no boast, being ask'd, to say we are.

OLIVER: Orlando doth commend him to you both,
And to that youth he calls his Rosalind
He sends this bloody napkin. Are you he?

[*Produces a bloody handkerchief.*]

ROSALIND: I am. What must we understand by this?

OLIVER: Some of my shame, if you will know of me
What man I am, and how, and why, and where
This handkercher was stain'd.

CELIA: I pray you, tell it.

OLIVER: When last the young Orlando parted from you
He left a promise to return again
Within an hour, and, pacing through the forest,
Chewing the food of sweet and bitter fancy,
Lo, what befell! He threw his eye aside,
And mark what object did present itself
Under an old oak, whose boughs were moss'd with age
And high top bald with dry antiquity:
A wretched ragged man, o'ergrown with hair,
Lay sleeping on his back. About his neck
A green and gilded snake had wreath'd itself,

---

88. [*bestows himself / Like a ripe sister*: acts like an older sister.]

Who with her head nimble in threats approach'd
The opening of his mouth; but suddenly,
Seeing Orlando, it unlink'd itself,
And with indented glides did slip away
Into a bush, under which bush's shade
A lioness, with udders all drawn dry,
Lay couching, head on ground, with catlike watch,
When that the sleeping man should stir; for 'tis
The royal disposition of that beast
To prey on nothing that doth seem as dead.
This seen, Orlando did approach the man
And found it was his brother, his elder brother.

CELIA: O, I have heard him speak of that same brother,
And he did render him the most unnatural
That liv'd amongst men.

OLIVER: And well he might so do,
For well I know he was unnatural.

ROSALIND: But, to Orlando: did he leave him there,
Food to the suck'd and hungry lioness?

OLIVER: Twice did he turn his back and purpos'd so;
But kindness, nobler ever than revenge,
And nature, stronger than his just occasion,
Made him give battle to the lioness,
Who quickly fell before him; in which hurtling
From miserable slumber I awak'd.

CELIA: Are you his brother?

ROSALIND: Was't you he rescu'd?

CELIA: Was't you that did so oft contrive to kill him?

OLIVER: 'Twas I; but 'tis not I. I do not shame
To tell you what I was, since my conversion
So sweetly tastes, being the thing I am.

ROSALIND: But, for the bloody napkin?

OLIVER: By and by.
  When from the first to last betwixt us two
  Tears our recountments[89] had most kindly bath'd,
  As how I came into that desert place,
  In brief, he led me to the gentle Duke
  Who gave me fresh array and entertainment,
  Committing me unto my brother's love;
  Who led me instantly unto his cave,
  There stripp'd himself, and here upon his arm
  The lioness had torn some flesh away,
  Which all this while had bled; and now he fainted
  And cried, in fainting, upon Rosalind.
  Brief, I recover'd him, bound up his wound,
  And, after some small space, being strong at heart,
  He sent me hither, stranger as I am,
  To tell this story, that you might excuse
  His broken promise, and to give this napkin
  Dyed in his blood unto the shepherd youth
  That he in sport doth call his Rosalind.

                                    [ROSALIND *swoons*.]

CELIA: Why, how now, Ganymede, sweet Ganymede!

OLIVER: Many will swoon when they do look on blood.

CELIA: There is more in it. Cousin Ganymede!

OLIVER: Look, he recovers.

ROSALIND: I would I were at home.

CELIA: We'll lead you thither.
  I pray you, will you take him by the arm?

                                    [*They help* ROSALIND *up*.]

---

89. [*recountments*: stories.]

OLIVER: Be of good cheer, youth. You a man? You lack a man's heart.

ROSALIND: I do so, I confess it. Ah, sirrah, a body would think this was well counterfeited! I pray you, tell your brother how well I counterfeited. Heigh-ho!

OLIVER: This was not counterfeit. There is too great testimony in your complexion that it was a passion of earnest.

ROSALIND: Counterfeit, I assure you.

OLIVER: Well then, take a good heart and counterfeit to be a man.

ROSALIND: So I do; but, i' faith, I should have been a woman by right.

CELIA: Come, you look paler and paler. Pray you, draw homewards. Good sir, go with us.

OLIVER: That will I, for I must bear answer back
How you excuse my brother, Rosalind.

ROSALIND: I shall devise something. But, I pray you, commend my counterfeiting to him. Will you go?

Exeunt.

ACT V

[SCENE I: *The forest.*]

Enter [TOUCHSTONE *the*] *Clown and* AUDREY.

TOUCHSTONE: We shall find a time, Audrey. Patience, gentle Audrey.

AUDREY: Faith, the priest was good enough, for all the old gentleman's saying.

TOUCHSTONE: A most wicked Sir Oliver, Audrey, a most vile Martext. But, Audrey, there is a youth here in the forest lays claim to you.

AUDREY: Ay, I know who 'tis. He hath no interest in me in the world. Here comes the man you mean.

Enter WILLIAM.

TOUCHSTONE: It is meat and drink to me to see a clown.[90] By my troth, we that have good wits have much to answer for. We shall be flouting; we cannot hold.

WILLIAM: Good ev'n, Audrey.

AUDREY: God ye good ev'n, William.

WILLIAM: And good ev'n to you, sir.   [*Removes hat.*]

TOUCHSTONE: Good ev'n, gentle friend. Cover thy head, cover thy head; nay, prithee, be cover'd. How old are you, friend?

WILLIAM: Five and twenty, sir.

TOUCHSTONE: A ripe age. Is thy name William?

WILLIAM: William, sir.

TOUCHSTONE: A fair name. Wast born i' th' forest here?

WILLIAM: Ay, sir, I thank God.

TOUCHSTONE: "Thank God"—a good answer. Art rich?

WILLIAM: Faith, sir, so so.

TOUCHSTONE: "So so" is good, very good, very excellent good; and yet it is not, it is but so so. Art thou wise?

WILLIAM: Ay, sir, I have a pretty wit.

TOUCHSTONE: Why, thou say'st well. I do now remember a saying, "The fool doth think he is wise, but the wise man knows

---

90. [*clown:* peasant.]

himself to be a fool." The heathen philosopher, when he had a desire to eat a grape, would open his lips when he put it into his mouth, meaning thereby that grapes were made to eat and lips to open. You do love this maid?

WILLIAM: I do, sir.

TOUCHSTONE: Give me your hand. Art thou learned?

WILLIAM: No, sir.

TOUCHSTONE: Then learn this of me: to have, is to have; for it is a figure in rhetoric that drink being pour'd out of a cup into a glass, by filling the one doth empty the other; for all your writers do consent that *ipse*[91] is he. Now, you are not *ipse,* for I am he.

WILLIAM: Which he, sir?

TOUCHSTONE: He, sir, that must marry this woman. Therefore, you clown, abandon—which is in the vulgar leave—the society—which in the boorish is company—of this female—which in the common is woman; which together is, abandon the society of this female, or, clown, thou perishest; or, to thy better understanding, diest; or, to wit, I kill thee, make thee away, translate thy life into death, thy liberty into bondage. I will deal in poison with thee, or in bastinado,[92] or in steel; I will bandy with thee in faction; I will o'errun thee with policy; I will kill thee a hundred and fifty ways. Therefore tremble, and depart.

AUDREY: Do, good William.

WILLIAM: God rest you merry, sir.   *Exit.*

Enter CORIN.

CORIN: Our master and mistress seeks you. Come, away, away!

---

91. [*ipse:* Latin for "he himself."]

92. [*bastinado:* a stick or cudgel.]

TOUCHSTONE: Trip, Audrey, trip, Audrey! I attend, I attend.

Exeunt.

[SCENE II: *The forest.*]

Enter ORLANDO *and* OLIVER.

ORLANDO: Is't possible that on so little acquaintance you should like her? That but seeing, you should love her? And loving, woo? And, wooing, she should grant? And will you persevere to enjoy her?

OLIVER: Neither call the giddiness of it in question, the poverty of her, the small acquaintance, my sudden wooing, nor her sudden consenting; but say with me, I love Aliena; say with her that she loves me; consent with both that we may enjoy each other. It shall be to your good; for my father's house and all the revenue that was old Sir Rowland's will I estate upon you, and here live and die a shepherd.

Enter ROSALIND.

ORLANDO: You have my consent. Let your wedding be tomorrow. Thither will I invite the Duke and all 's contented followers. Go you and prepare Aliena; for look you, here comes my Rosalind.

ROSALIND: God save you, brother.

OLIVER: And you, fair sister.

[*Exit.*]

ROSALIND: O, my dear Orlando, how it grieves me to see thee wear thy heart in a scarf!

ORLANDO: It is my arm.

ROSALIND: I thought thy heart had been wounded with the claws of a lion.

ORLANDO: Wounded it is, but with the eyes of a lady.

ROSALIND: Did your brother tell you how I counterfeited to swoon when he show'd me your handkercher?

ORLANDO: Ay, and greater wonders than that.

ROSALIND: O, I know where you are. Nay, 'tis true. There was never anything so sudden but the fight of two rams and Caesar's thrasonical[93] brag of "I came, saw, and overcame." For your brother and my sister no sooner met but they look'd, no sooner look'd but they lov'd, no sooner lov'd but they sigh'd, no sooner sigh'd but they ask'd one another the reason, no sooner knew the reason but they sought the remedy; and in these degrees have they made a pair of stairs to marriage which they will climb incontinent, or else be incontinent before marriage. They are in the very wrath of love, and they will together. Clubs cannot part them.

ORLANDO: They shall be married tomorrow, and I will bid the Duke to the nuptial. But, O, how bitter a thing it is to look into happiness through another man's eyes! By so much the more shall I tomorrow be at the height of heart-heaviness, by how much I shall think my brother happy in having what he wishes for.

ROSALIND: Why then, tomorrow I cannot serve your turn for Rosalind?

ORLANDO: I can live no longer by thinking.

ROSALIND: I will weary you then no longer with idle talking. Know of me then, for now I speak to some purpose, that I know you are a gentleman of good conceit.[94] I speak not this that you should bear a good opinion of my knowledge, insomuch I say I know you are; neither do I labor for a greater

---

93. [*thrasonical*: boastful.]

94. [*conceit*: understanding.]

esteem than may in some little measure draw a belief from you, to do yourself good and not to grace me. Believe then, if you please, that I can do strange things. I have, since I was three years old, convers'd with a magician, most profound in his art and yet not damnable. If you do love Rosalind so near the heart as your gesture cries it out, when your brother marries Aliena, shall you marry her. I know into what straits of fortune she is driven; and it is not impossible to me, if it appear not inconvenient to you, to set her before your eyes tomorrow; human as she is, and without any danger.[95]

ORLANDO: Speak'st thou in sober meanings?

ROSALIND: By my life, I do; which I tender dearly, though I say I am a magician. Therefore, put you in your best array; bid your friends; for if you will be married tomorrow, you shall, and to Rosalind, if you will.

Enter SILVIUS *and* PHEBE.

Look, here comes a lover of mine and a lover of hers.

PHEBE: Youth, you have done me much ungentleness,
To show the letter that I writ to you.

ROSALIND: I care not if I have. It is my study
To seem despiteful and ungentle to you.
You are there followed by a faithful shepherd;
Look upon him, love him; he worships you.

PHEBE: Good shepherd, tell this youth what 'tis to love.

SILVIUS: It is to be all made of sighs and tears;
And so am I for Phebe.

PHEBE: And I for Ganymede.

ORLANDO: And I for Rosalind.

---

95. [*human . . . danger:* i.e., the real Rosalind, not an illusion or evil spirit conjured up by magic.]

ROSALIND: And I for no woman.

SILVIUS: It is to be all made of faith and service;
    And so am I for Phebe.

PHEBE: And I for Ganymede.

ORLANDO: And I for Rosalind.

ROSALIND: And I for no woman.

SILVIUS: It is to be all made of fantasy,
    All made of passion and all made of wishes,
    All adoration, duty, and observance,
    All humbleness, all patience, and impatience,
    All purity, all trial, all observance;
    And so am I for Phebe.

PHEBE: And so am I for Ganymede.

ORLANDO: And so am I for Rosalind.

ROSALIND: And so am I for no woman.

PHEBE [*to* ROSALIND]: If this be so, why blame you me to love
    you?

SILVIUS [*to* PHEBE]: If this be so, why blame you me to love
    you?

ORLANDO: If this be so, why blame you me to love you?

ROSALIND: Why do you speak too, "Why blame you me to love
    you?"

ORLANDO: To her that is not here, nor doth not hear.

ROSALIND: Pray you, no more of this; 'tis like the howling of
    Irish wolves against the moon. [*To* SILVIUS.] I will help you,
    if I can. [*To* PHEBE.] I would love you, if I could. Tomorrow
    meet me all together. [*To* PHEBE.] I will marry you, if ever I
    marry woman, and I'll be married tomorrow. [*To* ORLANDO.]

I will satisfy you, if ever I satisfied man, and you shall be married tomorrow. [*To* SILVIUS.] I will content you, if what pleases you contents you, and you shall be married tomorrow. [*To* ORLANDO.] As you love Rosalind, meet. [*To* SILVIUS.] As you love Phebe, meet. And as I love no woman, I'll meet. So fare you well. I have left you commands.

SILVIUS: I'll not fail, if I live.

PHEBE: Nor I.

ORLANDO: Nor I.

Exeunt.

[SCENE III: *The forest.*]

Enter [TOUCHSTONE *the*] *Clown and* AUDREY.

TOUCHSTONE: Tomorrow is the joyful day, Audrey; tomorrow will we be married.

AUDREY: I do desire it with all my heart; and I hope it is no dishonest desire to desire to be a woman of the world. Here come two of the banish'd Duke's pages.

Enter two PAGES.

FIRST PAGE: Well met, honest gentleman.

TOUCHSTONE: By my troth, well met. Come, sit, sit, and a song.

[*They sit.*]

SECOND PAGE: We are for you. Sit i' th' middle.

FIRST PAGE: Shall we clap into't roundly, without hawking or spitting or saying we are hoarse, which are the only prologues to a bad voice?

SECOND PAGE: I' faith, i' faith; and both in a tune, like two gipsies on a horse.

SONG

It was a lover and his lass,
　　With a hey, and a ho, and a hey nonino,
That o'er the green cornfield did pass
　　In spring time, the only pretty ring time,
When birds do sing, hey ding a ding, ding.
Sweet lovers love the spring.

Between the acres of the rye,
　　With a hey, and a ho, and a hey nonino,
These pretty country folks would lie
　　In spring time, etc.

This carol they began that hour,
　　With a hey, and a ho, and hey nonino,
How that a life was but a flower
　　In spring time, etc.

And therefore take the present time,
　　With a hey, and a ho, and a hey nonino,
For love is crowned with the prime
　　In spring time, etc.

TOUCHSTONE: Truly, young gentlemen, though there was no great matter in the ditty, yet the note was very untuneable.

FIRST PAGE: You are deceiv'd, sir. We kept time, we lost not our time.

TOUCHSTONE: By my troth, yes; I count it but time lost to hear such a foolish song. God buy you; and God mend your voices! Come, Audrey.

Exeunt.

[SCENE IV: *The forest.*]

Enter DUKE SENIOR, AMIENS, JAQUES, ORLANDO, OLIVER, [*and*] CELIA.

DUKE SENIOR: Dost thou believe, Orlando, that the boy
  Can do all this that he hath promised?

ORLANDO: I sometimes do believe, and sometimes do not,
  As those that fear they hope, and know they fear.

> *Enter* ROSALIND, SILVIUS, *and* PHEBE.

ROSALIND: Patience once more, whiles our compact is urg'd.
  You say, if I bring in your Rosalind,
  You will bestow her on Orlando here?

DUKE SENIOR: That would I, had I kingdoms to give with her.

ROSALIND: And you say you will have her, when I bring her?

ORLANDO: That would I, were I of all kingdoms king.

ROSALIND: You say, you'll marry me, if I be willing?

PHEBE: That will I, should I die the hour after.

ROSALIND: But if you do refuse to marry me,
  You'll give yourself to this most faithful shepherd?

PHEBE: So is the bargain.

ROSALIND: You say that you'll have Phebe, if she will?

SILVIUS: Though to have her and death were both one thing.

ROSALIND: I have promis'd to make all this matter even.
  Keep you your word, O Duke, to give your daughter;
  You yours, Orlando, to receive his daughter;
  Keep you your word, Phebe, that you'll marry me,
  Or else, refusing me, to wed this shepherd;
  Keep your word, Silvius, that you'll marry her
  If she refuse me; and from hence I go,
  To make these doubts all even.

> *Exeunt* ROSALIND *and* CELIA.

DUKE SENIOR: I do remember in this shepherd boy
Some lively touches of my daughter's favor.

ORLANDO: My lord, the first time that I ever saw him
Methought he was a brother to your daughter.
But, my good lord, this boy is forest-born,
And hath been tutor'd in the rudiments
Of many desperate studies by his uncle,
Whom he reports to be a great magician,
Obscured in the circle of this forest.

Enter [TOUCHSTONE *the*] *Clown and* AUDREY.

JAQUES: There is, sure, another flood toward, and these couples are coming to the ark. Here comes a pair of very strange beasts, which in all tongues are call'd fools.

TOUCHSTONE: Salutation and greeting to you all!

JAQUES: Good my lord, bid him welcome. This is the motley-minded gentleman that I have so often met in the forest. He hath been a courtier, he swears.

TOUCHSTONE: If any man doubt that, let him put me to my purgation. I have trod a measure; I have flatt'red a lady; I have been politic with my friend, smooth with mine enemy; I have undone[96] three tailors; I have had four quarrels, and like to have fought one.

JAQUES: And how was that ta'en up?

TOUCHSTONE: Faith, we met, and found the quarrel was upon the seventh cause.[97]

JAQUES: How seventh cause? Good my lord, like this fellow.

DUKE SENIOR: I like him very well.

---

96. [*undone*: ruined, bankrupted.]

97. [Here, and in following passages, Touchstone ridicules books on the etiquette of quarreling and dueling that were popular at the time.]

TOUCHSTONE: God 'ild you, sir; I desire you of the like. I press in here, sir, amongst the rest of the country copulatives, to swear and to forswear, according as marriage binds and blood breaks. A poor virgin, sir, an ill-favor'd thing, sir, but mine own; a poor humor of mine, sir, to take that that no man else will. Rich honesty dwells like a miser, sir, in a poor house, as your pearl in your foul oyster.

DUKE SENIOR: By my faith, he is very swift and sententious.

TOUCHSTONE: According to the fool's bolt,[98] sir, and such dulcet diseases.[99]

JAQUES: But, for the seventh cause. How did you find the quarrel on the seventh cause?

TOUCHSTONE: Upon a lie seven times remov'd—bear your body more seeming, Audrey—as thus, sir. I did dislike the cut of a certain courtier's beard. He sent me word, if I said his beard was not cut well, he was in the mind it was: this is call'd the Retort Courteous. If I sent him word again it was not well cut, he would send me word he cut it to please himself: this is call'd the Quip Modest. If again, it was not well cut, he disabled my judgment: this is call'd the Reply Churlish. If again, it was not well cut, he would answer I spake not true: this is call'd the Reproof Valiant. If again, it was not well cut, he would say I lie: this is call'd the Counter-check Quarrelsome. And so to the Lie Circumstantial and the Lie Direct.

JAQUES: And how oft did you say his beard was not well cut?

TOUCHSTONE: I durst go no further than the Lie Circumstantial, nor he durst not give me the Lie Direct; and so we measur'd swords and parted.

---

98. [*According to the fool's bolt*: in the manner of the proverb that says, "A fool's bolt [arrow] is soon shot."]

99. [*dulcet diseases*: pleasant afflictions.]

JAQUES: Can you nominate in order now the degrees of the lie?

TOUCHSTONE: O sir, we quarrel in print, by the book, as you have books for good manners. I will name you the degrees. The first, the Retort Courteous; the second, the Quip Modest; the third, the Reply Churlish; the fourth, the Reproof Valiant; the fifth, the Countercheck Quarrelsome; the sixth, the Lie with Circumstance; the seventh, the Lie Direct. All these you may avoid but the Lie Direct; and you may avoid that too, with an If. I knew when seven justices could not take up a quarrel, but when the parties were met themselves, one of them thought but of an If, as, "If you said so, then I said so"; and they shook hands and swore brothers. Your If is the only peacemaker; much virtue in If.

JAQUES: Is not this a rare fellow, my lord? He's as good at anything and yet a fool.

DUKE SENIOR: He uses his folly like a stalking-horse, and under the presentation of that he shoots his wit.

Enter HYMEN, ROSALIND, *and* CELIA. *Still Music.*

HYMEN:
    Then is there mirth in heaven,
    When earthly things made even
        Atone together.
    Good Duke, receive thy daughter;
    Hymen from heaven brought her,
        Yea, brought her hither,
    That thou mightst join her hand with his
    Whose heart within his bosom is.

ROSALIND [*to* DUKE]: To you I give myself, for I am yours.
[*To* ORLANDO.] To you I give myself, for I am yours.

DUKE SENIOR: If there be truth in sight, you are my daughter.

ORLANDO: If there be truth in sight, you are my Rosalind.

PHEBE: If sight and shape be true,
  Why then, my love adieu!

ROSALIND [*to* DUKE]: I'll have no father, if you be not he.
  [*To* ORLANDO.] I'll have no husband, if you be not he.
  [*To* PHEBE.] Nor ne'er wed woman, if you be not she.

HYMEN:
  Peace, ho! I bar confusion.
  'Tis I must make conclusion
    Of these most strange events.
  Here's eight that must take hands
  To join in Hymen's bands,
    If truth holds true contents.
  [*To* ORLANDO *and* ROSALIND.]
  You and you no cross shall part.
  [*To* OLIVER *and* CELIA.]
  You and you are heart in heart.
  [*To* PHEBE.]
  You to his love must accord,
  Or have a woman to your lord.
  [*To* TOUCHSTONE *and* AUDREY.]
  You and you are sure together,
  As the winter to foul weather.
  [*To all.*]
  Whiles a wedlock hymn we sing,
  Feed yourselves with questioning,
  That reason wonder may diminish,
  How thus we met, and these things finish.

SONG

  Wedding is great Juno's crown,
    O blessed bond of board and bed!
  'Tis Hymen peoples every town;
    High wedlock then be honored.
  Honor, high honor, and renown,
    To Hymen, god of every town!

DUKE SENIOR: O my dear niece, welcome thou art to me!
Even daughter, welcome, in no less degree.

PHEBE [*to* SILVIUS]: I will not eat my word, now thou art
    mine;
Thy faith my fancy to thee doth combine.

Enter Second Brother [JAQUES DE BOYS].

JAQUES DE BOYS: Let me have audience for a word or two.
I am the second son of old Sir Rowland,
That bring these tidings to this fair assembly.
Duke Frederick, hearing how that every day
Men of great worth resorted to this forest,
Address'd a mighty power, which were on foot
In his own conduct, purposely to take
His brother here and put him to the sword;
And to the skirts of this wild wood he came,
Where, meeting with an old religious man,
After some question with him, was converted
Both from his enterprise and from the world,
His crown bequeathing to his banish'd brother,
And all their lands restor'd to them again
That were with him exil'd. This to be true,
I do engage my life.

DUKE SENIOR: Welcome, young man.
Thou offer'st fairly to thy brothers' wedding:
To one his lands withheld, and to the other
A land itself at large, a potent dukedom.
First, in this forest let us do those ends
That here were well begun and well begot;
And after, every of this happy number
That have endur'd shrewd days and nights with us
Shall share the good of our returned fortune,
According to the measure of their states.
Meantime, forget this new-fall'n dignity

And fall into our rustic revelry.
Play, music! And you, brides and bridegrooms all,
With measure heap'd in joy, to th' measures fall.

JAQUES: Sir, by your patience. If I heard you rightly,
The Duke hath put on a religious life
And thrown into neglect the pompous court.

JAQUES DE BOYS: He hath.

JAQUES: To him will I. Out of these convertites
There is much matter to be heard and learn'd.
[*To* DUKE.] You to your former honor I bequeath;
Your patience and your virtue well deserves it.
[*To* ORLANDO.] You to a love that your true faith doth merit;
[*To* OLIVER.] You to your land and love and great allies;
[*To* SILVIUS.] You to a long and well-deserved bed;
[*To* TOUCHSTONE.] And you to wrangling, for thy loving voyage
Is but for two months victuall'd. So, to your pleasures.
I am for other than for dancing measures.

DUKE SENIOR: Stay, Jaques, stay.

JAQUES: To see no pastime I. What you would have
I'll stay to know at your abandon'd cave.

Exit.

DUKE SENIOR: Proceed, proceed. We'll begin these rites,
As we do trust they'll end, in true delights.

Exeunt [*in a dance*].

EPILOGUE

ROSALIND: It is not the fashion to see the lady the epilogue;
but it is no more unhandsome than to see the lord the pro-
logue. If it be true that good wine needs no bush,[100] 'tis true
that a good play needs no epilogue. Yet to good wine they do
use good bushes, and good plays prove the better by the help
of good epilogues. What a case am I in then, that am neither
a good epilogue nor cannot insinuate with you in the behalf
of a good play! I am not furnish'd like a beggar, therefore to
beg will not become me. My way is to conjure you, and I'll
begin with the women. I charge you, O women, for the love
you bear to men, to like as much of this play as please you;
and I charge you, O men, for the love you bear to women—
as I perceive by your simp'ring, none of you hates them—
that between you and the women the play may please. If I
were a woman I would kiss as many of you as had beards
that pleas'd me, complexions that lik'd[101] me, and breaths
that I defied not; and, I am sure, as many as have good
beards or good faces, or sweet breaths will, for my kind offer,
when I make curtsy, bid me farewell.

Exit. ∾

---

100. [A proverb meaning good wine doesn't need advertising.]
101. [*lik'd*: pleased.]

INTERPRETIVE QUESTIONS
FOR DISCUSSION

Why must the characters in the play go to the forest of Arden to find happiness?

1. Why do many young gentlemen and "men of great worth" flock to Duke Senior in the forest of Arden? (257, 347) Why are we told that the men are merry and live like "the old Robin Hood" or people in the "golden world"? (257)

2. Why does Duke Senior prefer the hardships of nature, which he says "persuade me what I am," to those inflicted by envious people? Why does Duke Senior call the uses of adversity "sweet"? (274)

3. Why does Orlando rebel against being kept "rustically at home" by his brother? (253) Why does Orlando attribute his rebellion against Oliver to the spirit of his father within him? (253, 255)

4. Why doesn't Oliver know why he hates nothing more than the noble and popular Orlando? (258) Why does Oliver first try to destroy Orlando by denying him a proper education?

5. Why does Celia think that Rosalind's love for her should outweigh her cousin's grief for a banished father? (258–259)

6. Why does Shakespeare have Celia say that Duke Frederick kept Rosalind at court for his own pleasure and remorse? (271)

7. Why does Celia prefer the hardships of banishment with Rosalind to being able to "show more bright and seem more virtuous" at court with Rosalind gone? (271) Why is it Celia who takes the initiative and suggests seeking Rosalind's father in the forest of Arden after her own father banishes Rosalind? (272)

8. Why does Duke Frederick, who has banished his own brother, call Oliver "a villain" for saying he has never loved his brother in his life? (293–294)

9. Why does the banished Rosalind continue to disguise herself as Ganymede even after she meets her father in the forest of Arden? (313)

10. Why does Shakespeare have both Oliver and Duke Frederick experience a sudden conversion in the forest of Arden? Why does the play end with Duke Frederick renouncing the world and Oliver marrying Celia?

11. Why does Shakespeare make the salvation and restoration of Duke Senior and his followers depend on Duke Frederick's unexpected meeting with an old religious man? (347)

12. Why do Duke Senior and "all 's contented followers" leave their happy life in the forest of Arden and return to the world of court and society at the end? (336, 347–348)

Suggested textual analyses
Pages 273–274: beginning, "Now, my co-mates and brothers in exile," and ending, "Into so quiet and so sweet a style."

Pages 347–348: beginning, "Let me have audience for a word or two," and ending, "With measure heap'd in joy, to th' measures fall."

Why does Rosalind, disguised as the boy Ganymede, propose to cure Orlando of love by having him woo her as Rosalind?

1. Why does Rosalind decide to "play the knave" with Orlando? (304)

2. Why does Rosalind tell Orlando that "love is merely a madness"? (307) Why does she tell him that the only other person she cured went from a "mad humor of love to a living humor of madness"—becoming a recluse? (307–308)

3. Why does Orlando first say he doesn't want to be cured of love, but then agree to Rosalind's proposal? (308)

4. Why does Rosalind expose women's faults and waywardness to Orlando? (305–306, 323–324) When Celia accuses Rosalind of having "misus'd our sex," why does Rosalind simply say how deeply in love she is? (325)

5. Why does Rosalind make Orlando enact a marriage ceremony with her? (323)

6. Why does Rosalind decide to be a "busy actor" in the "play" of Silvius and Phebe? (314) Why does Rosalind take Silvius' side and help him obtain Phebe even though he is a "tame snake" and not deserving of pity? (329)

7. Why does Shakespeare have Phebe fall in love with Rosalind as Ganymede? Why does Phebe prefer to hear Rosalind's chiding to Silvius' wooing? (316)

8. Why does Rosalind mock the idea of dying for love in much the same way that Phebe ridicules the idea to Silvius? (314–315, 322)

9. Why does Orlando keep up the "sport" of wooing Ganymede even when he has been wounded by a lion, but then say he can "live no longer by thinking" after his brother finds love with Celia? (332, 337)

10. Why does Rosalind insist that Oliver commend her "counterfeiting" of fainting to Orlando? (333)

11. Why, having stated that she will no longer engage in "idle talking," does Rosalind claim to be a magician? (337–338)

12. Why does Rosalind make Duke Senior, Orlando, Phebe, and Silvius agree to keep their word before she reveals herself? (342)

Suggested textual analyses

Pages 305–308: beginning, "I have been told so of many," and ending, "Come, sister, will you go?"

Pages 322–326: beginning, "Then in mine own person I die," and ending, "I'll go find a shadow and sigh till he come."

Why does the melancholy Jaques think that if he were a professional fool like Touchstone, he would be able to "cleanse the foul body of th' infected world"?

1. Why does Jaques love melancholy better than laughing? Why is Jaques proud that his melancholy is a "melancholy of mine own"? (319)

2. Why does Jaques say that, because they kill the deer in the forest of Arden, Duke Senior and his companions are worse usurpers than Duke Frederick? (274–275) Why does Shakespeare have Duke Senior express similar regrets about killing the deer? (274)

3. Why does Duke Senior enjoy encountering Jaques when Jaques is in one of his "sullen fits" and "full of matter"? (276) Why does Jaques say that Duke Senior is "too disputable" for his company? (284)

4. In the verse Jaques adds to the song about shunning ambition, why does he attribute leaving wealth and ease to a "stubborn will"? Why does Jaques imply that Duke Senior and his followers, including himself, are "gross fools"? (285)

5. Why is Jaques made uncharacteristically merry by his meeting with the fool Touchstone in the forest? (286–287)

6. Why does Duke Senior say that Jaques would do "most mischievous foul sin" in chiding sin? Why does Duke Senior accuse Jaques of having been a libertine himself? (288)

7. Why does Orlando's arrival at Duke Senior's dinner make Jaques elaborate on the idea that "all the world's a stage, / And all the men and women merely players"? Why does Jaques call every phase of human life, even infancy, a "part"? (291)

8. Why do Orlando and Jaques call each other a fool? Why is Orlando glad of Jaques' departure? (303–304)

9. Why does Rosalind enjoy Touchstone's company and take him with her to the forest of Arden, but mockingly dismiss Jaques? (273, 319–320) Why is Rosalind not impressed by Jaques' experienced melancholy?

10. Why does Jaques want Touchstone to be married properly—even offering to counsel him—but later predict that the marriage will not last more than two months? (311, 348)

11. Why does Shakespeare have Touchstone, who "hath been a courtier," win Audrey from the simple country fellow William? (343) Why does Touchstone refer to Audrey before the others as "an ill-favor'd thing, sir, but mine own"? (344)

12. Why does Jaques choose to learn "matter" from the converted Duke Frederick, rather than return to court with Duke Senior and his followers? Why does the cynical Jaques part by commending the virtue, patience, and faith of Duke Senior and Orlando? (348)

Suggested textual analyses
Pages 274–276: beginning, "Come, shall we go and kill us venison?" and ending, "For then he's full of matter."

Pages 286–291: beginning, "Why, how now, monsieur," and ending, "Sans teeth, sans eyes, sans taste, sans everything."

FOR FURTHER REFLECTION

1. Why do people often think that they would be happier and more content in a rural setting? Are such ideas realistic or are they a fantasy?

2. Is it contradictory to enjoy melancholy?

3. Does education make happiness harder to come by?

4. Is happiness different in each of the seven ages of man, or is it a constant throughout life?

5. Can one be happy in a world where the Olivers and Duke Fredericks do not convert?

6. Does one have a right to be happy?

7. Is happiness an attitude toward life that is largely independent of circumstance?

POETRY

Emily Dickinson

EMILY DICKINSON (1830–1886), one of the world's masters of the short lyric poem, was born in Amherst, Massachusetts, into a family well known for its involvement in education and politics. As a student at Mount Holyoke Female Seminary, Dickinson withstood the pressure to become a professing Christian, choosing instead to remain a skeptic all her life. Despite her skepticism, Dickinson continued to hold strong religious beliefs. This tension is evident in her writings—a total of 1,775 poems and nearly as many surviving letters. The tone of her poems is as complex as her unorthodox language is deceptively simple. Although she owed much to the meters of the English hymn writer Isaac Watts, and to Shakespeare and the King James version of the Bible, she was also experimental in prosody, breaking new ground, for example, in a wide use of off rhymes. Dickinson's contemporaries were not receptive to the oddities of her verse and consequently only seven of her poems were published in her lifetime, five of them in the *Springfield Republican*.

There's a Certain Slant of Light

THERE'S a certain Slant of light,
Winter Afternoons—
That oppresses, like the Heft
Of Cathedral Tunes—

Heavenly Hurt, it gives us—
We can find no scar,
But internal difference,
Where the Meanings, are—

None may teach it—Any—
'Tis the Seal Despair—
An imperial affliction
Sent us of the Air—

When it comes, the Landscape listens—
Shadows—hold their breath—
When it goes, 'tis like the Distance
On the look of Death—

Emily Dickinson

After Great Pain, a Formal Feeling Comes

AFTER great pain, a formal feeling comes—
The Nerves sit ceremonious, like Tombs—
The stiff Heart questions was it He, that bore,
And Yesterday, or Centuries before?

The Feet, mechanical, go round—
Of Ground, or Air, or Ought—
A Wooden way
Regardless grown,
A Quartz contentment, like a stone—

This is the Hour of Lead—
Remembered, if outlived,
As Freezing persons, recollect the Snow—
First—Chill—then Stupor—then the letting go—

Emily Dickinson

Because I Could Not Stop for Death

BECAUSE I could not stop for Death—
He kindly stopped for me—
The Carriage held but just Ourselves—
and Immortality.

We slowly drove—He knew no haste
And I had put away
My labor and my leisure too,
For His Civility—

We passed the School, where Children strove
At Recess—in the Ring—
We passed the Fields of Gazing Grain—
We passed the Setting Sun—

Or rather—He passed Us—
The Dews grew quivering and chill—
For only Gossamer, my Gown—
My Tippet—only Tulle—

We paused before a House that seemed
A Swelling of the Ground—
The Roof was scarcely visible—
The Cornice—in the Ground—

Since then—'tis Centuries—and yet
Feels shorter than the Day
I first surmised the Horses' Heads
Were toward Eternity—

Emily Dickinson

INTERPRETIVE QUESTIONS
FOR DISCUSSION

In "There's a Certain Slant of Light," does the poet's experience of the "Heavenly Hurt" leave her in a state of spiritual gain or loss?

1. Why does the poet associate her sensation of oppression with something as insubstantial and amorphous as light? Why does the poet specify that the light slants and comes on winter afternoons?

2. Why does the poet compare the oppression of the slant of light to that of cathedral tunes?

3. Why does the poet say that the oppressive light gives a "Heavenly Hurt"? Is the hurt strictly internal, or are we meant to think that the source of the poet's despair is divine—sent from a greater reality beyond the material world?

4. Why does the hurt leave no scar, but only "internal difference"? What kinds of "Meanings" does the poet have in mind when she says that none may teach the "Heavenly Hurt"?

5. When the poet says that the hurt is an "imperial affliction / Sent us of the Air," is she suggesting the possibility of Despair's reverse, that is, heavenly redemption sent to humankind?

6. Why are we told that the "Landscape listens" and "Shadows— hold their breath" when the slant of light comes?

7. What does the poet mean when she says that when the "certain Slant of light" goes it is "like the Distance/On the look of Death—"?

8. For the poet, is death more or less distant when the slant of light goes? Is this distance good or bad?

In "After Great Pain, a Formal Feeling Comes," is the "formal feeling" the speaker's defense against mental dissolution, or a barrier to the discharge of her grief or pain?

1. Why does the speaker describe the experience following great sorrow or mental pain as a "formal" feeling?

2. Why does the speaker say that "the Nerves sit ceremonious, like Tombs"? Why does the poet choose to imagine the nerves as *sitting* ceremoniously?

3. Why does the poet have the stiff heart ask, "was it He, that bore,/And Yesterday, or Centuries before"? Why does the speaker question the reality of her own pain?

4. Are we meant to think that the "He" to whom the speaker refers is an oblique reference to the suffering Christ?

5. What does the speaker mean when she says that her feet, going around mechanically, have become regardless of "Ground, or Air, or Ought"?

6. Why does the speaker identify this state of inanimate lifelessness as a "Quartz contentment"?

7. Does the poem's final stanza, which refers to the "Hour of Lead—/Remembered, if outlived," offer the possibility of recuperation? Why does the poet imply that few outlive the "Hour of Lead" to be able to recollect it for others?

8. Why does the poem conclude with the ambiguous image of "letting go"—the freezing person who no longer resists the cold and slips into oblivion? Are we meant to think that this freezing "Stupor" is of another, and far more dangerous, order than that suggested by the earlier images of tomb, wood, and stone?

9. Is the poet suggesting that spiritual or emotional regeneration can only come when self-preservation or "form" is relaxed?

In "Because I Could Not Stop for Death," is the speaker reconciled to the fact of death?

1. Why does the speaker personify Death as a gentleman caller, perhaps even a courtly lover?

2. Why does the speaker go willingly with Death, putting away her labor and her "leisure too, / For His Civility"?

3. Why does the speaker call Death kind for stopping for her? Is the poet being ironic?

4. Why does the speaker emphasize that the carriage holds Immortality as well as herself and Death?

5. Why does the poet specifically include in the speaker's journey these three scenes: the striving schoolchildren, the "Gazing Grain," and the "Setting Sun"? Why does the poet emphasize the speaker's separateness from these scenes by repeating the phrase "We passed"?

6. Why does the poet describe the grain as "Gazing" rather than as gazed upon? Why does the speaker correct herself, saying, "We passed the Setting Sun—/ Or rather—He passed Us—"?

7. Why does the speaker stress the reality of the coldness of the grave, recalling the chill of the dews and the thinness of her gossamer gown and tippet made of tulle?

8. Why are we told that the carriage "paused," rather than stopped, before the grave?

9. Why does the speaker say that although centuries have passed, it "Feels shorter than the Day" she "first surmised the Horses' Heads/Were toward Eternity—"?

10. Does Dickinson's poem suggest an effort to confront her fear of mortality, or a wish to be freed from consciousness and the inevitable losses that time brings?

FOR FURTHER REFLECTION

1. Is a happy life with an exquisite awareness of one's mortality an oxymoron?

2. Is it better to seek happiness in the moment or to hold to a belief in life after death?

3. Do you see Dickinson, who lived in quiet seclusion and almost entirely for her art, as a fulfilled human being?

4. Is the modern consciousness less disturbed by spiritual doubts than by more materialistic concerns?

Questions for

MIDDLEMARCH

George Eliot

GEORGE ELIOT (1819–1880) was the pen name of Marian Evans, born the daughter of an estate manager in the largely agricultural English Midlands. After an early, intense involvement with Evangelicalism, she lost her faith, but retained throughout life a humanistic philosophy deeply imbued with moral and ethical values. She read widely and translated scholarly works from the German. After the death of her father, she moved to London to become assistant editor of the progressive *Westminster Review*. She lived with the writer and intellectual George Henry Lewes, who was already married and unable to divorce, from 1854 until his death in 1878. With Lewes's encouragement, she turned to writing fiction, beginning with the stories which became *Scenes of Clerical Life*. The novels *Adam Bede, The Mill on the Floss,* and *Silas Marner* followed in rapid succession. *Middlemarch* was published in installments in 1871 and 1872.

NOTE: All page references are from the Penguin Classics edition of *Middlemarch* (first printing 1994); chapter numbers appear in **boldface**, with page numbers following. Because of the length of *Middlemarch,* groups might want to hold two discussions, breaking their reading at the end of Book Five. Questions about the remainder of the book, and about the novel as a whole, can then be discussed at a second meeting.

INTERPRETIVE QUESTIONS
FOR DISCUSSION

BOOKS I-V

Why do Dorothea and Lydgate—both intelligent, ardent, compassionate people—make marriages that have the potential to destroy their humanitarian goals and personal happiness?

1. Why does Dorothea have a childlike view of marriage and think that a husband should be like a father who "could teach you even Hebrew, if you wished it"? (**1: 10**) Why has Dorothea's wish in life always been "to help some one who did great works, so that his burthen might be lighter"? (**37: 363**)

2. Why does Lydgate think that Miss Brooke is not his style of woman, when in fact she seems to be exactly the kind of wife he needs? (**10, 11: 93–95**) Why have women like Dorothea "not entered into his traditions"? (**30: 289**)

3. Why does Lydgate become engaged to Rosamond with no promise of a dowry when he had been thoroughly determined to postpone marriage until he was established? (**11: 94, 31: 296–302, 36: 354–356**) Why is Lydgate's soul no longer his own after he becomes engaged? (**31: 302**)

4. Why is Lydgate a radical only in terms of medicine and science? (**36: 348**) Why does the author remark that Lydgate's personal pride and unreflecting egoism are manifestations of his "commonness"? (**36: 349; cf. 15: 150**)

5. Why does Dorothea feel anger, repulsion, and weariness when she discovers that Casaubon's mind is not as brilliant as she had thought? (**20**: 195–196) Why does Dorothea see clearly that no benefit will come from pursuing the Key to all Mythologies? (**48**: 478–479)

6. Are we meant to think that Lydgate's dream of discovering the primitive tissue of human anatomy is as elusive and misguided as Casaubon's search for the Key to all Mythologies? (**15**: 146–149, **21**: 208, **22**: 221–222, **45**: 455)

7. Why is Lydgate interested in the human "drama" suggested by Dorothea's anxiety for Casaubon's health? (**30**: 287) Why does Lydgate remember for years afterward Dorothea's plea to advise her about Casaubon—a "cry from soul to soul, without other consciousness than their moving with kindred natures in the same embroiled medium"? (**30**: 289–290; cf. **58**: 592–593)

8. Why does Dorothea lose her religious fervor after she marries Casaubon? Why does her religion turn into a "mysticism" that compels her to desire "what is perfectly good, even when we don't quite know what it is"? (**39**: 392)

9. Why are Dorothea and Lydgate the only people to feel pity for Casaubon? (**37**: 365, 367, **42**: 423)

10. Even though Casaubon has forced her to "shut her best soul in prison," why does Dorothea refuse to hate her husband, as most women would have done? (**42**: 426–427; cf. **10**: 91, **37**: 361, 375, **39**: 389) Why can't Dorothea break out of the "virtual tomb" of her marriage to live in the "world of warm activity and fellowship" that she so desires? (**48**: 475)

11. Why does Dorothea decide to promise Casaubon that she will carry out his wishes after his death, even though she believes that in doing so she will be saying " 'Yes' to her own doom"? (**48**: 481)

12. Why does Dorothea feel that she is undergoing a metamorphosis when she hears about the codicil to her husband's will? When she experiences a shock of repulsion against Casaubon, why does Dorothea feel as if she were committing a sin? (**50: 490**)

Suggested textual analyses
Pages 144–154 (from Chapter 15): from "We are not afraid," to the end of the chapter.

Pages 474–482 (Chapter 48)

Why does Casaubon write a codicil to his will saying that Dorothea must give up her inheritance if she marries Will Ladislaw?

1. Why does Casaubon's intellectual insecurity prevent him from finding happiness in marriage? (**29:** 279–280, **37:** 376–377; cf. **10:** 85–87, 90–91)

2. Why is Casaubon incapable of writing his Key to all Mythologies? Why is his life's work that of *preparing* to write the book and not the act of *creating* it? (**29:** 279–281)

3. Why is Dorothea the means of igniting both Casaubon's insecurity about himself and his hatred for Will? (**38:** 379–380) Why does Casaubon's dislike for Will increase once Will declines his help? (**37:** 360)

4. Why does society perceive Casaubon as having been "absorbed and dried" by his scholarly pursuits, when in truth he is a highly sensitive man whose intellectual ambition is deeply wounded by his sense of failure? (**20:** 200, **29:** 279, **42:** 418)

5. Why does Casaubon become convinced that Will "meant to defy and annoy him, meant to win Dorothea's confidence and sow her mind with disrespect, and perhaps aversion, towards her husband"? (**37:** 375) Why can Casaubon pick up subtle motives in Will but remain so insensitive to Dorothea's feelings? (**42:** 425)

6. Why does Casaubon shrink from being the object of pity?
   (**29:** 279, **42:** 417, 425)

7. Why does Casaubon feel more keenly the shame of not being
   respected by his colleagues than the shame of his inability to
   write the Key to all Mythologies? (**42:** 417)

8. Why does Casaubon distrust Dorothea's affection for him?
   (**44:** 441) Why does he perceive her as a "critical wife" and not
   as the tender, submissive, ministering helpmate that she becomes?
   (**42:** 418)

9. Why can't Casaubon—a clergyman—bear to think that persons
   whom he hates might enjoy "transient earthly bliss" after he has
   died and "entered into glory"? (**42:** 420)

10. Why does Casaubon want Dorothea not to use her own
    judgment, but to carry on the futile work of the Key to all
    Mythologies after his death? (**48:** 476–478)

11. Why does Casaubon's codicil shock and disgust all the
    gentlemen—"men of ordinary honour"? (**49:** 483–484, **50:** 493)
    Why is Casaubon, who cared so deeply about always acting with
    perfect propriety, blind to how the codicil would damage his own
    reputation and compromise Dorothea's? (**50:** 493; cf. **29:** 279)

12. Why does the author invite us to sympathize with Casaubon—
    a selfish, intellectually limited, jealous man? (**10:** 84,
    29: 278–281, **37:** 375)

Suggested textual analyses
Pages 278–285 (Chapter 29)

Pages 357–377 (Chapter 37)

Pages 417–427 (Chapter 42)

Why does Fred Vincy love the caustic "brown patch" Mary Garth?

1. Why is Mary the only one of Fred's friends and relations who understands that he should not be a clergyman? (**14:** 137, **52:** 516) Why does she think that "any hardship is better than pretending to do what one is paid for, and never really doing it"? (**14:** 137)

2. Why does Fred allow himself to get into debt and then compound his folly by having the Garths, who can least afford it, finance his extravagance?

3. Why are Fred and Rosamond Vincy not close, even though both are more refined than the other members of their family? (**11:** 98–103, **27:** 268)

4. Are we meant to think that Fred is made just as spoiled and ill-prepared for life by his Oxford education as Rosamond is by her studies at Mrs. Lemon's school for young ladies? (**11:** 96, **12:** 119, **13:** 128)

5. Why is Fred, who has pretensions of being a fine gentleman, attracted to the entire Garth family, who don't mind living "in a small way"? (**23:** 231, **24:** 251)

6. Why doesn't the otherwise superficial Fred care about physical beauty in a wife?

7. Why is Mary's father, Caleb, whose "prince of darkness was a slack workman," so fond of the idle young Fred? Why are we told that Caleb considers "business" the most noble human employment, more so than "politics, preaching, learning, and amusement"? (**24:** 251)

8. Why does Mary refuse to become engaged to Fred until he finds a meaningful vocation without her help? (**14:** 139–140, **25:** 257, **52:** 516)

9. Why does Mary believe that Fred will be better off without an inheritance from Peter Featherstone? (**35:** 340) Why does Mary nonetheless feel guilty about depriving Fred of the ten thousand pounds that Featherstone wished to bequeath him? (**40:** 406–407)

10. Why does Mary prefer the wayward Fred to the admirable Camden Farebrother? (**40:** 407–408)

11. Why does Fred use Farebrother as his emissary to Mary to find out whether she loves him and what she thinks he should do with his life? (**52:** 512–518) Why does Farebrother agree to fulfilling this "duty" when it is so painful to him? (**52:** 513, 518)

12. Why is Mary's love for Fred founded upon her gratitude to him for always loving her best? (**52:** 517)

Suggested textual analyses

Pages 252–258 (Chapter 25)

Pages 509–518 (Chapter 52)

BOOKS I–VIII

Are we meant to think that, by marrying Will Ladislaw and being "absorbed into" his life, Dorothea, like Lydgate, becomes a failure?

1. Why does Dorothea fall in love with and marry Will?

2. Why do people think it is a pity that "so substantive and rare a creature" as Dorothea should be known only as a wife and mother, but then have no ideas about what else she could have done? (**Finale:** 836)

3. Why does Celia see Dorothea's ideas not as noble principles but as "notions," perpetually leading her to make mistakes? (**4:** 36, **50:** 489) Are we meant to agree with Celia, who knows and loves Dorothea, but thinks she is "always" wrong? (**84:** 821)

4. Why does Will seem to Dorothea to be "so likely to understand everything"? (21: 210) Why does Dorothea admire Will's ability to enter into everyone's feelings and "take the pressure of their thought instead of urging his own with iron resistance"? (50: 496)

5. Why does Dorothea hate her wealth and constantly feel that it is a burden? (37: 372, 76: 767, 83: 811)

6. Why is Dorothea certain that Casaubon will see the justice of changing his will to provide money to Will? Why is Dorothea blind to the "obvious" misinterpretations a husband might place on her "pure purpose"? (37: 371–372)

7. Why is it only when she first finds Will with Rosamond that Dorothea begins to understand that Casaubon disliked Will's visits to her in his absence? Why does Dorothea feel a "vague discomfort" and decide that she may have been mistaken "in many things"? (43: 434)

8. Why does Dorothea feel a sudden yearning of heart toward Will, rather than shame or embarrassment, when she learns of the codicil excluding her from Casaubon's money if she marries Will? (50: 490)

9. Why does Will fall in love with Dorothea after only a few meetings with her in Rome? Why is he at first satisfied to idealize Dorothea—to make her an object of romantic contemplation—without entertaining any thought of being united with her? (22: 218, 47: 469–470)

10. Why does the author have Will's career as a public man begin simply as a desire to be near Dorothea and a lack of knowing what else to do? (46: 460–461)

11. After finding Will apparently making love to Rosamond, why does Dorothea feel that the lives of Rosamond, Will, and Lydgate lay an obligation on her "as if they had been suppliants bearing the sacred branch"? Why does she feel that they are "chosen for her" to rescue? (80: 788)

12. Why can't Dorothea ever carry out any of her plans for social improvement, even when she is independent and wealthy? Why does Dorothea place the fault in herself, feeling that she might have done more "if she had only been better and known better"? (**Finale:** 835)

Suggested textual analyses
Pages 626–636 (Chapter 62)

Pages 784–800 (Chapters 80 and 81)

Why does Rosamond ultimately prove stronger than Lydgate?

1. Why is Lydgate confident that he will be able to avoid becoming involved in Middlemarch politics? (**17:** 174–175) Why is the "petty medium" of Middlemarch too strong for Lydgate in the vote for the hospital chaplain? (**18:** 187)

2. Why doesn't Lydgate foresee that in a place like Middlemarch his progressive medical ideas, such as performing autopsies and refusing to dispense drugs, will offend both the medical profession and the laity and affect his success? (**45:** 444, 448, 454)

3. Why does Lydgate expect the perfect wife to worship his profession and ideals without in the least understanding them? (**27:** 268, **36:** 352, **58:** 586) Why is his ideal wife a kind of "accomplished mermaid"? (**58:** 583)

4. Why doesn't Lydgate's experience with Mme. Laure prevent him from spinning the web of romance with Rosamond? (**15:** 150–153, **36:** 346)

5. Why are we told that Rosamond acted her own character so well "that she did not know it to be precisely her own"? (**12:** 117)

6. As different as they are in many ways, why do Rosamond and Lydgate share similarly impractical notions of setting up a household in which everything is of the best quality? (**58:** 595)

7. Why doesn't even the loss of her baby make Rosamond question her assumption that whatever she likes to do is "the right thing"? (**58:** 585) Why does Rosamond, "who had never expressed herself unbecomingly," equate propriety and self-control with righteousness? (**58:** 597, **64:** 654, **65:** 665)

8. Why does Lydgate intensely desire that Rosamond's hold on his heart remain strong? Why is the certainty that Rosamond will never love him much easier to bear than the fear that he will stop loving her? (**64:** 652)

9. Why does Lydgate refuse Dorothea's offer to support his continuation at the hospital, but accept her money to repay Bulstrode? (**76:** 767, **81:** 791–792) Why is he surprised to find in Dorothea a woman with whom friendship is possible? (**76:** 768–769)

10. After Rosamond learns of the scandal, why does Lydgate miss the occasion, "which was not to be repeated," of opening himself to her? Why does he lack the strength "to be more because she was less" and possibly win her to a willing spirit? (**75:** 757–758)

11. Why does Rosamond convince herself that she is in love with Will, even though he is more rootless and poorer and of lesser rank than her husband? (**75:** 753)

12. Why are Will and Dorothea able to do what Lydgate cannot— turn Rosamond back to the "old despised shelter" of her husband? (**78:** 780, **81:** 797–800) Why, although grateful for Rosamond's little mark of interest in him, is Lydgate unable to imagine any better relationship than forever carrying her as a burden "pitifully"? (**81:** 800)

Suggested textual analyses

Pages 581–598 (Chapter 58)

Pages 752–769 (Chapters 75 and 76)

Why can neither Bulstrode's religious faith nor his need for "high consideration" save him from acting immorally?

1. Why does Bulstrode's "immense need of being something important and predominating" take the form of seeing himself as God's instrument? (**61:** 620) Why has Bulstrode been able to convince himself that all his actions, even his "secret misdeeds," are to further God's cause? (**53:** 525, **61:** 616–619)

2. Why does Bulstrode spearhead the establishment of the new fever hospital? Why does the self-righteous Bulstrode think he might begin to be a "better man" by sponsoring Lydgate, the stranger in town? (**13:** 124–125)

3. Why is public opinion so against Bulstrode that even his good works are rejected? (**44:** 439) Why does hardly anyone doubt that there is a scandalous secret behind Bulstrode's generosity to Lydgate? (**71:** 720)

4. Why in his confrontations with Mr. Vincy does Bulstrode not infrequently start by admonishing him, and end by seeing "a very unsatisfactory reflection of himself in the coarse unflattering mirror" of Mr. Vincy's mind? (**13:** 131)

5. Why, despite his other misdeeds, does Bulstrode shrink from direct falsehood? (**53:** 528, **68:** 686)

6. Why does his trouble with Raffles make Bulstrode behave more tenderly toward his wife? (**61:** 613)

7. Why would the loss of recognized supremacy be as the beginning of death to Bulstrode? (**61:** 614) Why does a man who cares so much about being a leading citizen of Middlemarch not care that he gets little love or respect?

8. Why does Bulstrode consider his youth as "Brother Bulstrode," a poor dissenting preacher, the happiest time of his life? Why does Bulstrode think that if he could return to that time of his life, he would choose to be a missionary? (**61:** 615, 617)

9. Why is Bulstrode able to tell himself that he did not contrive Raffles' death, but only accepted what Providence provided? (**70:** 709–710) Why does Bulstrode regard his later sins as "hypothetic" and pray hypothetically for their pardon? (**71:** 724)

10. Why does Mrs. Bulstrode remain loyal to her husband, even though she feels his life with her has been an odious deceit? (**74:** 749–750)

11. Why is it ultimately his wife who is the most daunting tribunal for Bulstrode? Why is he able to win "invisible pardon" for his acts by inwardly washing and diluting them, but still remain terrified of exposing them to his wife's judgment? (**85:** 824)

12. Does Bulstrode ever realize the extent of his guilt?

Suggested textual analyses

Pages 612–625 (Chapter 61)

Pages 703–714 (Chapter 70)

Pages 748–751 (from Chapter 74): from "She said good-bye with nervous haste," to the end of the chapter.

FOR FURTHER REFLECTION

1. If, like Dorothea, one seeks what is good—sometimes not quite knowing what it is—will one eventually find contentment?

2. Does one need both meaningful work and romantic love to have a fulfilling life?

3. Are some people naturally disposed to find happiness in their lives, and others to find unhappiness?

4. Why does wealth so often fail to ensure happiness?

5. Is "business" as Caleb Garth defines it the most noble of all human employments—more so than "politics, preaching, learning, and amusement"?

6. Do men still tend to be like Lydgate and Casaubon in wanting their wives merely to adore them uncritically? Do women generally want the same sort of adoration from their husbands?

7. Is duty as important as love in maintaining a happy marriage?

8. Does society's acceptance of divorce make obsolete those dilemmas Dorothea and Lydgate face in their unhappy marriages?

9. Are people generally good judges of what would make them happy, or do most of us have mistaken ideas about where our happiness lies?

10. Is it practical to attempt to model our lives on others who have found happiness—such as the Garth family? Can one learn how to be happy from observing others?

Questions for

AN IMAGINARY LIFE

David Malouf

DAVID MALOUF (1934–   ), born in Brisbane
of Lebanese and English parents, is an
Australian novelist, poet, short fiction writer,
librettist, and editor. Educated at the University
of Queensland, Malouf lived in Europe from
1959 to 1968 and worked as a teacher. He
taught English at the University of Sydney from
1968 to 1977, but now devotes himself full-
time to his writing, residing alternately in
Sydney, Australia, and in southern Tuscany.
Malouf has won numerous Australian prizes
for his novels, as well as two international
awards—the Commonwealth Prize and the
Prix Femina Etranger—for *The Great World.*
Other major works include *The Conversations
at Curlow Creek, Remembering Babylon,
Harland's Half-Acre,* and *Selected Poems.*
In 1987 Malouf was made an Officer of the
Order of Australia.

NOTE: All page references are from the
Vintage International edition of *An Imaginary Life*
(first printing 1996).

INTERPRETIVE QUESTIONS
FOR DISCUSSION

Why must Ovid be banished to Tomis and exiled from his native tongue before he can begin the process of becoming something new?

1. Why must Ovid enter the silence of his exiled state before he can find "release" from his own life? (32) What does Ovid mean when he says of himself, "You will be separated from yourself and yet be alive"? (33)

2. Why does naming the wildflower—saying the words "scarlet" and "poppy" over and over again—give Ovid the power of "making the spring" that he remembers from his childhood on the farm at Sulmo, with all its myriad flowers and colors? (31)

3. Why does Ovid say that the incident of the poppy "recovered the earth" for him? (32)

4. Why is Ovid convinced that the process of self-transformation— the quickening of the gods in us—begins with the process of naming? (32)

5. Why does Ovid's wild ride among the skeletons of the funerary mounds cause him to think, for perhaps the first time in thirty years, of the brother who died when Ovid was a young man, and whose place Ovid took as his father's heir? (45) Why does Ovid feel "free, at last," to prepare a death of his own? (47)

6. Why does Ovid's guilt at replacing his dead brother as heir to the farm cause him to deny his feelings of joy and connection to the earth during the Parilia ceremony? (88–89) What does Ovid mean when he says that he "killed something" in himself that night when, atoning for his "moment of belief," he strewed himself with earth? (88)

7. Why does the illiterate headman, whose stories suggest that he sees the world as "bare, cruel, terrible, comic," seem daily to Ovid "nobler and more gentle than any Roman"? (58)

8. Why does Ovid view the world differently once he learns to see it through the Getae's tongue, a language that the poet regards as presenting "the raw life and unity of things"? (65)

9. Why does Ovid feel himself "loosen and flow again, reflecting the world" once he is able to appreciate and enter into the physical beauty of the landscape of his exile? (65)

10. What does Ovid mean when he says that, having learned to accept creation, he understands that "we have some power in us that knows its own ends"—that "we have only to conceive of the possibility" of what we wish to become "and somehow the spirit works in us to make it actual"? (64)

Suggested textual analyses

Pages 30–33: beginning, "Out walking today in my old sandals and cloak," and ending, "Now I too must be transformed."

Pages 63–65: beginning, "It all happens as I knew it would," and ending, "That is what spring means."

Why does Ovid dream that a horde of gigantic, untamed centaurs comes thundering out of the sky toward him, uttering cries of mourning that seem to be asking the poet to believe in them?

1. Why does Ovid immediately recognize the dream creatures as gods and yet declare his lack of belief in them? (24)

2. Why must Ovid suffer the loss of his own language before he can begin to "listen for another meaning" in the warm breathing of the centaurs? (24)

3. What does Ovid mean when he says that something in him that was the centaur's reflection came up to meet the powerful creature when he put out his hand and touched it? (24–25)

4. Why does the word that Ovid utters when he awakens from his centaur dream, a word that is not in his own tongue, seem to him to hold the key to the meaning of what he has encountered? (25)

5. After the centaur dream, why is Ovid convinced that there is something out there in the vast landscape waiting to receive him? (25)

6. Why does Ovid insist that it is through imagination and creativity that the world has evolved, "as if each creature had the power to dream itself out of one existence into a new one, a step higher on the ladder of things"? (28–29)

7. Why has Ovid become convinced that "the spirits have to be recognized to become real"? (28)

8. What does Ovid mean when he says that the spirits are "not outside us, nor even entirely within, but flow back and forth between us and the objects we have made, the landscape we have shaped and move in"? (28)

9. Are we meant to take Ovid's words literally when he says that "it is our self we are making out there, and when the landscape is complete we shall have become the gods who are intended to fill it"? (28)

10. Why does Ovid compare the warring Dacian horsemen to the godlike creatures of his centaur dream, calling them "ghostly figures out of the north, out of my dream"? (55)

11. Why does Ovid's experience of being returned to the bleak beginnings of civilization awaken in him a renewed faith in the perfectibility of human life? (30)

12. Why does Ovid eventually come to see himself as being in exile not from Rome but from the universe? (98)

Suggested textual analysis
Pages 23–30: beginning, "I dreamt, one night lately," and ending, "and led on their long path to perfection."

Why is Ovid determined, despite the headman's fear and disapproval, to capture the wild Child and bring him back to Tomis?

1. Why does Ovid become convinced that the wild Child of the deer forest is the wild boy of his childhood who has come back to him? (54)

2. When Ovid returns to the deer forest for the third time, why does he dream that the whole group of hunters has become part of the woods—mushrooms and stones—and he himself, a pool of water? (61) In his dream, why is Ovid filled with tenderness for the deer that laps water from the pool that he has become? (62)

3. Why doesn't Ovid feel at all diminished when the deer takes part of him into itself? (62)

4. Imagining the possibility of a wolf consuming the whole pool of his being, why does Ovid tell himself, "That too is possible. . . . I prepare for it"? (62)

5. In his dream, when the Child scoops up a handful of water from the pool, why is Ovid's experience of being "broken again" described as both exquisitely pleasurable—with the Child's breath shivering his surface—and fearful, a "noisy crashing of waves against the edges" of him? (62)

6. What is it that Ovid believes has "passed between" the Child and himself during his third visit to the deer forest? What does he mean when he says that they have spoken in "a language beyond tongues"? (63)

7. Why does Ovid feel "an immense pity" for the Child and a need to lead the boy "into the society of his own kind," in contrast to the women, who harbor a suspicious fear of and hostility toward the Child? (77, 81–82)

8. Why does Ovid insist that speech is the essential aspect of identity, so that by learning to speak the language of humans the Child will be "making himself a man"? (92)

9. Why are we told that, just as Ovid teaches the Child to speak, the Child—by revealing his consciousness of the world as an extension of himself—becomes Ovid's teacher? Why is Ovid willing to try to think as the Child thinks, and in so doing risk losing himself in the multiplicity of things? (93–94, 96)

10. Empathizing with the Child in order to "lead him into his lost childhood," why does Ovid recover his own rejected or forgotten childhood, recalling in particular the female farm servants' world of joyful sensuality? (82–85)

11. Why is the story told so that the introduction of the Child into Ryzak's household overturns the headman's authority, allowing the old woman and her dark magic to rule in his place? (125–126)

12. Why is Ovid, who has been critical of the old woman's fear of demons and animal spirits, equally terrified of "the unknown monster . . . bringing itself to birth again" in the dying headman? (130–131)

Suggested textual analyses

Pages 61–63: beginning, "It is a clear still day," and ending, "and I must wait for another whole winter to pass."

Pages 90–96: beginning, "I am teaching the Child to speak," and ending, "We shall be whole."

Why is Ovid's final, dying thought "I am immeasurably, unbearably happy. . . . I am there"?

1. Why does Ovid say that the Ister is the final boundary of his life, the border he must cross in order to find his "true life," his "true death at last"? (136)

2. Why is it in the immense emptiness of the grasslands, a landscape with no landmark as far as the eye can see, that Ovid experiences a fulfillment of spirit? (141)

3. Why is it that when Ovid imagines seeing himself and the Child from "a great height, two tiny figures parting the grassland," he experiences a sense of his spirit expanding "to become the whole landscape . . . filling the whole land . . . and the whole arch of sky"? (142)

4. Are we meant to think that Ovid's reference to his expanded spirit as "myriad particles of light, each one a little center from which the whole can be grasped at a single glance" means that he has achieved the Child's vision of nature as ordered and whole? (142)

5. Why has Ovid's journey with the Child given Ovid a new sense of "a life that stretches beyond the limits of measureable time"? (144–145)

6. Why does Ovid no longer fear the earth and the interchange that will occur between his body and the black soil when he dies, but rather believe in their "common being"? (147)

7. Why does Ovid insist that driving out his old, separate self and letting the universe in is the way to wholeness, not just for himself but for the human race? (96)

8. Why does Ovid say that the language of silence that he has learned to speak with the Child—and which we must all rediscover—is "a language whose every syllable is a gesture of reconciliation"? (97–98)

9. Why does Ovid, while recognizing the Child's tender kinship with men, regard the boy as belonging to "a world that lies utterly beyond" Ovid himself and his "human imagining"? (149) Why does Ovid ask himself if it is the Child's "own nature as a god that his body is straining towards"? (150)

10. Why does the dying Ovid think to himself that the fullness of his final moment is in the Child's moving away from him, "in his stepping so lightly, so joyfully, naked, into his own distance at last" while fading in and out of the dazzle of light off the stream? (152)

11. Why does Ovid, at the moment of his death, envision the Child walking on the water's light, taking the "first step off it . . . above the earth, above the water, on air"? (152)

12. Are we meant to think that Ovid's final, transcendent vision offers the promise of life after death?

Suggested textual analyses

Pages 141–147: beginning, "No more dreams," and ending, "Between our bodies and the world there is unity and commerce."

Pages 150–152: from "And so we come to it, the place," to the end of the novel.

FOR FURTHER REFLECTION

1. Do you agree with the novel's emphasis on the role of imagination as "the first principle of creation" in the process of evolution?

2. Do you believe in the power of self-transformation—that "we have only to conceive of the possibility" of what we wish to become "and somehow the spirit works in us to make it actual"?

3. Is it possible to be happy without achieving spiritual fulfillment?

4. Why has language—what Ovid calls "the process of naming"—been both a positive and a negative force for human happiness?

5. In Malouf's view of the world, is human happiness dependent upon the reality of death? Are the creative forces that are responsible for wholeness and reconciliation possible without the powerful, dark forces that produce fear, discord, and disease?

6. Why is a sense of personal authenticity or wholeness a necessary prerequisite for a good death? Is a sense of unity or commonality with the natural world also necessary for a good death?

ACKNOWLEDGMENTS

All possible care has been taken to trace ownership and secure permission for each selection in this anthology. The Great Books Foundation wishes to thank the following authors, publishers, and representatives for permission to reprint copyrighted material.

The Highest Good, from NICOMACHEAN ETHICS, by Aristotle. Translated by Martin Ostwald. Copyright 1962. Reprinted by permission of Prentice-Hall, Inc.

A River Sutra, by Gita Mehta. Copyright 1993 by Gita Mehta. Reprinted by permission of Doubleday, a division of Bantam Doubleday Dell Publishing Group, Inc.

The Three Lives of Lucie Cabrol, from PIG EARTH, by John Berger. Copyright 1979 by John Berger. Reprinted by permission of Pantheon Books, a division of Random House, Inc.

Happiness, by Mary Lavin. Copyright 1969 by Mary Lavin. Reprinted by permission of the Wallace Literary Agency, Inc.

Endless Mountains, from THE COLLECTED STORIES, by Reynolds Price. Copyright 1993 by Reynolds Price. Reprinted by permission of Scribner, a division of Simon & Schuster.

There's a Certain Slant of Light; After Great Pain, a Formal Feeling Comes; and *Because I Could Not Stop for Death,* from THE COMPLETE POEMS OF EMILY DICKINSON, edited by Thomas H. Johnson. Copyright 1929, 1935 by Martha Dickinson Bianchi; renewed 1957, 1963 by Mary L. Hampson. Reprinted by permission of Little, Brown and Company.

Cover photography: Jay Corbett, New York

Cover and book design: William Seabright and Associates

Special thanks to Linda Rahm for helping with questions for *As You Like It* and *Middlemarch.*